WRITING BETTER LYRICS

SECOND EDITION

THE ESSENTIAL GUIDE TO ★★★★★★ POWERFUL SONGWRITING

PAT PATTISON

FOREWORD BY GILLIAN WELCH

Writer's Digest Books
An imprint of Penguin Random House LLC
penguinrandomhouse.com

Printed in the United States of America
29th Printing

ISBN 978-1-58297-577-1

Edited by Scott Francis
Designed by Claudean Wheeler

ABOUT THE AUTHOR

Pat Pattison is a professor at Berklee College of Music, where he teaches lyric writing and poetry. His books include *The Essential Guide to Lyric Form and Structure*, and *The Essential Guide to Rhyming*. In addition, Pat has developed three online lyric writing courses for Berklee's online school, and has written articles for a variety of industry publications. His internationally successful students include multiple Grammy winners John Mayer and Gillian Welch. Pat's website is: http://patpattison.com.

THANKS

To my students, especially those who have allowed me to include their work in this book. Their creativity and questions always challenge me, requiring me to look further to make sure I get it right.

To my fellow faculty at Berklee College of Music for trying out these ideas and making them work; for their support, suggestions, and insights.

To the writers and publishers who allowed me to include such excellent material, especially Gillian Welch, Beth Nielsen Chapman, and Janis Ian for their interest and encouragement.

To Mike Reid for his enthusiasm, and for diving into Object Writing with such passion.

To John Mayer, Gillian Welch, Melissa Ferrick, Greg Becker, Kami Lyle, Dave Rawlings, Andrea Stolpe, Scarlet Keys, Ben Romans, Jonelle Vette, Rob Giles, Emily Shackleton, Clare McLeod, and a host of other Berklee transplants to Nashville, New York, Los Angeles, and internationally for showing how well all this stuff can work.

To all the folks that keep showing up for my seminars, allowing me not only to travel the world, but to enlarge my vision in new and interesting ways.

To my son Jason and my daughter Holly Ann. To Mia and Olivia.

I especially want to thank Susan Benjamin for her encouragement, for editing the original articles, and for her comments, focus, and inspiration; in short, for making this book possible.

TABLE OF CONTENTS

FOREWORD

I will be brief and not delay with a long introduction, for there is too much good instruction ahead, and there are too many good songs to be written. I know of no other book like this one. One need only follow these tenets and discipline oneself to the task and the songs will come. It is a priceless map through the minefields of cliché, boredom, and laziness that often destroy even the best efforts. Sometimes, I think that *Writing Better Lyrics* is an unfair advantage, a secret weapon of sorts, and yet it is here for any and all who aspire to write and write better. I count myself lucky and proud to have studied with Mr. Pattison. I would not be the writer I am today without his teaching and his unique and comprehensive understanding of language, rhyme, rhythm, and structure. To this day, when I struggle with a lyric and find myself falling short, I am usually ignoring some very sound advice contained in these pages. And I read it again.

Gillian Welch
Nashville, Tennessee
April 2009

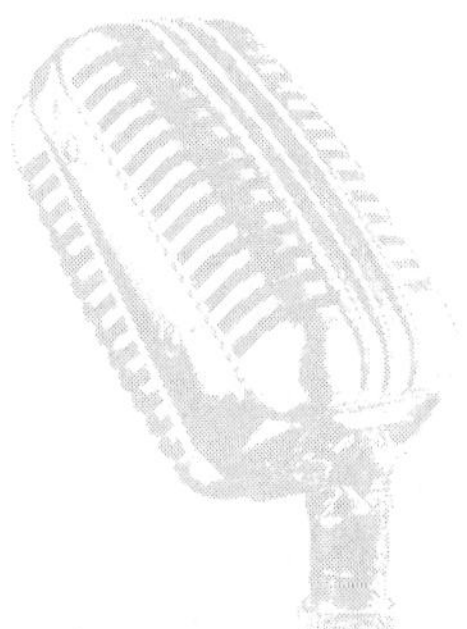

INTRODUCTION

I'm very happy that songwriters have found *Writing Better Lyrics* helpful, and I'm grateful to be writing an introduction to a second edition. It's been a while since the first publication in 1995, and I've learned a lot since then, thanks to my students at Berklee College of Music and the many songwriters I've met and worked with both in my traveling seminars and my online courses. Each time I teach, I learn something new from them—a real blessing in my life to be on such a journey.

This edition has added almost one hundred new pages and has expanded and revised some of the existing chapters.

I've enlarged the opening chapter on object writing with new (and, I think, more helpful) examples. Over the years, this exercise has proved to be a mainstay for many successful songwriters, including Grammy winners John Mayer and Gillian Welch. The additional material in this chapter incorporates some new and interesting ways to approach object writing, making it an even more useful way to brainstorm, open your senses, and discover unique ideas for your songs.

The chapters on verse development add examples and new material, introducing the concept of "boxes," which students over the years have found helpful. I think you will, too.

I've found an interesting and, I hope, helpful way of thinking about rhymes, treating them the way you treat chords in a song. It provides a clearer view of rhyme's function and will help you choose rhyme types for a reason.

The chapters on point of view also have a new look and suggest some interesting ways to approach the process of finding the right perspective for your song.

I've added several new chapters that reflect work I've been doing since the first publication of *Writing Better Lyrics*. There's a chapter on the productive use of repetition, a chapter on showing and telling, and several "in the trenches" chapters on structure to help you make more informed decisions while in the heat of writing.

There are two new chapters on handling couplets and common meter. Each will take you through a series of expansions and manipulations of these structures to show you some new options and possibilities, while still keeping to familiar territory.

I've also added a chapter on prosody, the most fundamental principle of songwriting and, indeed, of art in general: the concept that all the elements of a song—chords, melody, rhythm, words, and lyric structure—should work together for a common purpose.

The centerpiece of this new material is the chapter called "Understanding Motion," which explores the intersections of rhythm, rhyme, and phrase length, and their use in creating prosody, which is support for the ideas and emotion of the lyric. Motion creates *emotion*; knowing how to make structures move allows you to support your ideas on a whole new level. The chapter can also be used as a reference guide to stable and unstable structures.

I hope this edition will be helpful in making your lyrics work harder and better.

Write fearlessly. Have fun.
Pat Pattison, February 2009

CHAPTER ONE

OBJECT WRITING

THE ART OF THE DIVER

The native dives deep into the waters of his bay, holding his breath to reach the soft pink and blue glow below. Sleek through the water, churning up no cloud to disturb the bottom, he stretches and he opens the shell. Rising to the surface, he holds it aloft and shimmering in the sun: mother of all pearls, breathing light.

Like this pearl, your best writing lies somewhere deep within. It glows in fresh, interesting colors no one ever imagined in exactly that way before. Your most important job as a writer is to master the art of diving to those deep places, for there and only there will you find your own unique writing voice.

Remember this fundamental fact: You are absolutely unique. There never was, is not now, nor ever can be anyone exactly like you. The proof lies in the vaults of your senses, where you have been storing your sense memories all your life. They have come cascading in through your senses, randomly and mostly unnoticed, sinking to the bottom. Learn to dive for them. When you recover one, when you rise with it to the surface and hold it aloft, you will not only surprise your onlookers, you will surprise yourself.

Much of lyric writing is technical. The stronger your skills are, the better you can express your creative ideas. You must spend time on the technical areas of lyric writing, like rhyme, rhythm, contrast, balance, and repetition. Here, I want to focus on the most important part of all creative writing, and therefore surely of lyric writing: the art of deep diving—finding your own unique voice and vision.

OBJECT WRITING

The best diving technique I know is object writing. It's direct and simple. You arbitrarily pick an object—a real object—and focus your senses on it. Treat the object as a diving board to launch you inward to the vaults of your senses.

Although you understand your five senses, you could probably stand a few exercises to sharpen them, especially the four you don't normally use when you write. If I asked you to describe the room you're in, your answer would be primarily, if not completely, visual. Try spending a little time alone with each sense. What's there? How does the kitchen table smell? How would the rug feel if you rubbed your bare back on it? How big does the room sound? (What if it were twice as big? Half as big?) How would the table taste if you licked it? No, it's not silly. Remember this, it is important: The more senses you incorporate into your writing, the better it breathes and dances.

You have two additional senses that may need a little explanation:

1. Organic sense is your awareness of inner bodily functions, for example, heartbeat, pulse, muscle tension, stomachaches, cramps, and breathing. Athletes are most keenly focused on this sense, but you use it constantly, especially in responsive situations. I've been sitting here writing too long. I need a backrub.

2. Kinesthetic sense is, roughly, your sense of relation to the world around you. When you get seasick or drunk, the world around you blurs—like blurred vision. When the train you're on is standing still and the one next to it moves, your kinesthetic sense goes crazy. Children spin, roll down hills, or ride on tilt-a-whirls to stimulate this sense. Dancers and divers develop it most fully—they look onto a stage or down to the water and see spatial possibilities for their bodies. It makes me dizzy just thinking about it.

★ EXERCISE 1 ★

Pick an object at random and write about it. Dive into your sense memories and associations surrounding the object. Anything goes, as long as it is sense-bound. Write freely. No rhythm, no rhyme. No need for complete sentences. Use all seven senses: sight, hearing, smell, taste, touch, organic, and kinesthetic.

Here's an example of the above exercise:

Back Porch

> I must have been four. Memories from that time are a rare species—lobbing in like huge bumblebees on transparent wings, buzzing old Remington shavers torn free from those thick and brittle wires tangled in webs under our porch where I loved to crawl and hide; black snaking wires disappearing up through floors and humming into wall and socket. I still hear them.
>
> I hid under the back porch, smell of damp summer earth cool under my hands, ducking, scrunching my shoulders tight to avoid the rusty nails waiting patiently above for my back or skull to forget them. The tingling along my back and neck kept reminding me, don't stand up.
>
> Under the back porch, a place tinged with danger and smelling of earth, the air tastes faintly of mold and hollyhocks twining around the trellises that I see only the bottoms of, speckled gold by the shafts of sun slipping through high elm branches in the backyard, weaving shadows like Grandma's lace dresser doilies. When I squint, I can blur the sunlight into a bridge of green-gold. Crouching there fetal and content, I could feel Mom above me, could hear her high heels tap-tapping.

No one else has ever associated exactly those experiences with "back porch," yet anyone can understand them, relate to them. Because they are drawn from my senses, they will stimulate your senses. You will draw from your own sense reservoir, making my experiences yours. They take on a new look traveling from me into you. They get filtered through your senses and memories. They add to your uniqueness.

Look at the sense information in "Back Porch":

Sight: huge bumblebees on transparent wings; thick and brittle wires tangled in webs; black snaking wires disappearing up through floors; rusty nails; hollyhocks twining around the trellises I see only the bottoms of; speckled gold by shafts of sun; high elm branches in the backyard; weaving shadows like Grandma's lace dresser doilies; when I squint, I can blur the sunlight into a bridge of green-gold

Hearing: buzzing old Remington shavers; humming into wall and socket; I still hear them; could hear her high heels tap-tapping

Smell: smell of damp summer earth; smelling of earth

Taste: the air tastes faintly of mold and hollyhocks

Touch: thick and brittle wires; damp summer earth cool under my hands; tingling along my back and neck

Organic: crawl; crouching; ducking; scrunching shoulders tight; stand up quick; tingling along my back and neck; when I squint; crouching there fetal and content

Kinesthetic: lobbing in; tingling along my back and neck kept reminding me; avoid rusty nails waiting patiently above for my back or skull to forget them; don't stand up; I could feel Mom above me

TEN AND ONLY TEN MINUTES—A.M.

Object writing works best when you do it for ten minutes, first thing in the morning. Yes, I know—I'm brain-dead then, too. But you can always find ten minutes just by getting up a tad earlier, and the effort will pay huge dividends.

Two beings inhabit your body: you, who stumbles groggily to the coffeepot to start another day, and the writer in you, who could remain blissfully asleep and unaware for days, months, even years as you go on about your business. If your writer is anything like mine, "lazy," even "slug" is too kind. Always wake up your writer early, so you can spend the day together. It's amazing the fun the two of you can have watching the world go by. Your writer will be active beside you, sniffing and tasting, snooping for metaphors. It's like writing all day without moving your fingers.

If, instead, you waited until evening to wake your writer up, you'd float through the day alone, missing the wonderful worlds your writer sees. Old lazybones, meanwhile, would get up late and retire early.

Guarantee yourself ten minutes and only ten minutes. Set a timer, and stop the second it goes off. You're much more likely to sit down to a clearly limited commitment. But be sure you always stop at the buzzer. If you get on a roll some morning and let yourself write for thirty minutes, guess what you'll say the next morning:"Ugh, I don't have the energy to do it this morning (remembering how much energy you spent yesterday), and besides, I've already written my ten minutes for the next two days. I'll start again Thursday."

That's how most people stop morning writing altogether. Any good coach will tell you that more is gained practicing a short time each day than doing it all at once. Living with it day by day keeps writing on your mind and in your muscles.

Soon, something like this will happen: At minute six, you'll really get on a roll, diving, plunging, heading directly for the soft pink and blue glow below when beep! The timer goes off. Just stop. Wherever you are. Stop. Writus interruptus. All day, your frustrated writer will grumble, "Boy, what I might have said if you hadn't stopped me." Guaranteed, when you sit down the next morning, you will dive deeper faster. The bottom in three minutes flat. Next time, one minute. Finally, instantly. That is your goal: immediate access—speed and depth. So much information and experience tumbles by every minute of your life, the faster you can explore each bit, the faster you can sample the next. But, of course, speed doesn't count without depth. The ten-minute absolute limit is the key to building both. And it guarantees a manageable task.

Object writing prepares you for whatever other writing you do. It is not a substitute.

Loyalty

Forget it. There's no reason to stay loyal to the object that sets you on your path. Your senses are driving the bus—you can go wherever they take you. The object you begin with might only be your starting point. Full right turns or leaps to other places are not only allowed, but encouraged. Think of it as sense-bound free association. If you try to stay focused on the object you start with for the whole time, you may get bored with object writing after a few weeks. Let your hot morning shower with its rolling steam take you to thick clouds hanging overhead, to the taste of rain, to stomping through a puddle, splashing water up so it sprays like fireworks, to the boom in your chest and the smell of gunpowder and the taste of cotton candy.

Anywhere you go is okay. Try bouncing off of each sense-image to wherever else it might take you, using each new sense-image as a sort of pivot to the next, a kind of sensual free association. Always with your senses, all seven of them. All within ten minutes. Don't worry about story lines or "how it really happened." No rhyme or rhythm. Not even full sentences. No one needs to understand where you are or how you got there. Save more focused writing for your songs.

Of course, instead of association, you certainly can stay within the framework of a story or event if you like, like "Back Porch" above, but let your senses drive the bus. As you remember the events, remember with your senses. How did the park smell? Were children giggling over by the duck pond? Italian sausages with steaming onions? Let us experience it too by engaging our senses; stimulate us to see, smell, taste, hear, etc., to really experience the story for ourselves.

Even more important, your listeners will each fill your sense-bound words with their own sense memories:

> I remember stomping through puddles on Duluth Avenue in St. Paul when I was seven. I had a yellow slicker that smelled like my rubber boots, and my boot buckles jingled when I walked.

Where were you? Not on Duluth Avenue, I'll bet.

In this way, sense-bound language involves you; my words are filled with your experiences.

So practicing using sense-bound writing is a good thing. It's a powerful tool for involving your listeners in your song. It will often generate song ideas or interesting lines.

Object writing is about showing, not telling. It is an exercise, like a morning workout, that you use to stay in shape. And it happens to be really fun and challenging. It's not only worth the effort, it's a pleasure to do. You should stay with it, religiously, for at least six weeks. The record so far is Polk Shelton of Austin, Texas, who did his object writing every morning for five years straight. His writing skyrocketed.

Ten minutes every day for at least six weeks. You won't believe what happens.

★ EXERCISE 2 ★

Set a timer for ten minutes and try writing your own piece. Remember to stay inside your senses.

Ready?

Use the word "puddle" as a jumping-off point.

Go.

Good. Now let's look at some other ways you can use object writing to generate ideas.

GROUP WRITING

Object writing is great for a group. It's fascinating to hear other writers dive and roll off the same object. Get some people together, set a timer, then point to someone: "Pick an object." "Popsicle." Boom, you're all off. When time is up, each person reads. In larger groups (five to ten), shorten the time to five minutes so that, during readings, no one gets impatient. Do two or three at a sitting. Each one will be better because you feed off each other—each of you has something unique to offer. In a good group, the level of writing gets very high (or deep) very quickly. With smaller groups, write eight to ten minutes each time (never longer). Remember to pick real objects. Butter. Canary. The smell of split pea soup. Hanging ivy. Hot coffee.

Here is an example of group object writing, done by our online group using the same word we used for your exercise: "puddle".

> Yellow slickers and blue galoshes, each puddle like it's own hemisphere reflecting the blue sky and white clouds above, beached earthworms on wet asphalt, the whisper of tires through water, the spray rising up and fanning outwards like a peacock's feathers as the car rushes by, scent of lilac dazes the air, the blossoms heavy with raindrops droop and sag like an old woman's breasts, the slow metronome drip of water from the gutter onto the beaded hood of my car, tasting bitter spring on my lips, the oaky smell, the trunks of trees reaching like the walls of a cathedral up to the sky, the lace umbrella of leaves, patchwork squares of sunlight on the ferns below, a lizard skitters up the bark, its neck ballooning from green to translucent pink —***Susan Cattaneo***

> Puddle on the ground where the water will not drain between the sidewalk and the asphalt just a geometric stain, a water world, an escapee from the underworld of the storm drain where all is subsumed in a soup beneath the cast-iron teeth stamped with names like Chicago or Pittsburgh or St. Louis rusty and heavy and smelling of rotting leaves and piggy banks and cool damp cement. Sounds of underground torrents or secret creeks or gentle plunking like stalactites forming, depending on how much rain came down. But this little triangular puddle will never make it to the ocean, will never join the great descent to the Mississippi. Puddle of mosquito sex and gasoline rainbow and pollen scum brown and yellow, a tiny pond in the evolutionary gene pool, the very shallow end, it will be gone tomorrow. Evaporation, the Great Destroyer, will sneak in like a nurse with arsenic, unnoticed until it is too late. For you, not the muddy rolling wonder of Mark Twain, but the sky and the slow rising steam and clouds you are going to heaven, little puddle. —***Gillian Welch***

> Puddle staring up at the sky like a tinfoil hubcap. Raindrops plock plock across its cheek like the slap of typewriter palms against wet copier paper ... each raindrop forming instantaneous mountains of pinprick-sized acne that disappear like hooded wack-a-moles. I try and

leap across the puddle but my heel catches an edge. A black rubber first base that belly flop splashes my pant cuff with muddy shrapnel. I curse, another dry cleaning bill. I could have walked around, taken the longer easy way, but my puddle leap seemed like a road less traveled. My socks, soaked up to my calf, plastic wrap cling to my legs, almost buckling under the weight of the extra water. I can feel one sagging now, both teetering like the World Trade Center towers, collapsing into my shoe like the soggy black foreskin of a snapping turtle. —***Shane Adams***

I can see the reflections of the pines above in the sandy water. Scattered around the pavement like a minefield, I hop over each one in my new canvas shoes. A sweet smell of apple blossoms drifts through the neighborhood, and I hear Mr. Clemens revving up his lawn mower for the first mow of the season. My coarse nylon overcoat blocks the chill of the morning, but as I hop puddles, I feel the skin on my neck and back cool with sweat collecting under my cotton T-shirt. My gum has turned metallic—Mom says I always chew it too long. I don't mind. My jaw needs something to do now that the neighbor girl moved away and I don't have anyone to play with. The mailbox at the end of the drive gets closer every year as I inch upward, and it surprises me how quickly I'm able to pry open the rusty hinge and retrieve the mail. The mail truck always leaves tire grooves in the gravel that pools with muddy spring rain. I feel my rubber soles sink and suction to the natural concrete, and a shiver springs through my fingers as I consider the gravity of the situation. Carefully, I lift the weight onto my other foot and douse the bottoms in an overflowing pothole. Mom won't like too much that I've smudged my new shoes when I wasn't even supposed to be wearing them. I glance back down the main road and catch the glint of sunlight off a car just round the bend. A wheezing grind and then a steady hum, seems he's gotten that old mower going again. —***Andrea Stolpe***

Puddle collected tears as the old man stares at his shoes and fidgets with his shoe laces to look busy. He feels the strain on his back and neck, years lay heavy on him. He listens to the whispers of the car wheels misting through the rainy streets and he cries. It took him eighty years to be able to cry, and now he does it all the time. His sleeve has almost become a handkerchief and that old dog has become his therapist. They go everywhere together, the dog hates puddles, he sidesteps them, jumps over them, and sometimes bypasses his manhood by tiptoeing through them like a ballerina walking around land mines. He looks up and blinks hard to push away any evidence of crying and cups his tired hands over his knees and uses them to push himself up off that stranger's door step. He lights up a cigar, he never smokes it, he just likes the way it feels out of the corner of his mouth and he wobbles down the street pushing off of trees because he won't submit to a cane. He sees Lois in her garden and all of a subtle peering out between those wrinkle eyes of his is a fifteen-year-old schoolboy too shy to look up all the way. He tosses out a hello like he's flicking the ashes off his cigar letting the words float down, hoping she can hear his true intention. He loves to see her, she is a breeze to him, a sunny spot in a dark room when the sun is moving east. —***Scarlet Keys***

Tiny geysers, old faithful, as raindrops kerplunk into the puddle, a movie minefield exploding just behind the zigzagging runner, helmet raked to one side, pistols blazing, laughing off machine-gun chatter all around zinging as harmlessly as the dummy explosions. Taut film score conducting my breaths in staccato and shallow to match soldier's rampaging pulse and marching-band heartbeat. My boots smelled of rubber and clanked, steel buckles fashionably open, showing their teeth. Yellow slicker, hood up, rubbing against my cheek, the spatter of raindrops against the plastic whispering to me "Stomp down!" A God in this puddlewonderful world, I stomp a saucer of water, splattering my sister next to me. Giggling, she stomps back. Tiny microbes spill into the air, driven by thundering forces beyond their comprehension, unable. —***Pat Pattison***

There. Your first group writing experience.

Ready for one more?

EXERCISE 3

Set your timer for another ten minutes and write your own response before reading ahead. Ready?

"Pepper."

Go!

Now read these examples:

Coarse black pepper darkening the salmon filet, tamari and lemon and bake for ten minutes, still rare, wet with the sea to slide easily down my throat, singing its flavor all the way. Deep green water, diving, feeling the pull in the pit of his stomach—a leaning toward the far waters of home, shallow riverbed of his birth, eagles littering the treetops for miles awaiting the feast. Surging up the falls, against the current, leaping and shaking, rainbows of water droplets spilling of his polished skin, the bodies of his companions already torn open, flayed, fallen to bear, fox, and eagle. The dust of home, the smell of the big ditch behind Grandma's house and I exhale, shoulders relaxed, head clearing. The smell of home waters, the sound of grasshoppers winging from cornstalk to cornstalk, the smell of Carnation Instant Milk in the kitchen. ***—Pat Pattison***

Peppers shiny and red, oily and waxy little Christmas tree lights on all the pepper plants. So hot out here there is steam rising from the dark beds like fog off blacktop, but this heat is a perfume, chocolate brown soft soil smell everywhere, dead leaves wet and warm, new leaves light and crisp and lemony. Smell sweat and damp leather work gloves muddy canvas sneakers smell the peppers in the heavy air sharp tangy don't rub your eyes if you've been picking cause that shiny oil gets on your fingers and goes right into your skin. Smooth firm little teardrops plunking into my cardboard box as it gets hotter and closer and the buzzing little bugs zit round my ears. Moving irrigation pipe with the big men with the soft worn work boots the color of clay, the color of toast. Then later the dirt under my nails down in the cuticles down in the fingerprint and it won't come out. To have really beautiful hands, like the debs in the who's who columns holding crystal flutes like tender shoots, means to do nothing with them. The girls with the pretty fingers do nothing. I have been digging in the dirt all day making things grow and my hands look. ***—Gillian Welch***

Volcanic ash settles like freckles on the mangled yellow-white face of my breakfast eggs. Lounging strips of bacon are displaced equal signs or orphaned brown slats of a fallen horse pasture fence. I lift a pancake triangle to my mouth and bite into the xylophone tines of the fork and notice that my breakfast looks like chess pieces in jail through the tines of my fork ... misdemeanor toast, felony jelly, and a crime scene of half-full OJ glasses. Even though I'm sitting in the same spot as always, my belly seems closer to the table than I remember, like the table is trying to lean into me like a wooden elbow nudging me on its way out of an elevator. The egg pepper is brisk on my tongue and my nose crinkles in a mock pepper sneeze. My face becoming an accordion that implodes through a creosote chimney of crackly nose boogers that won't blow out. ***—Shane Adams***

Green waxy curves, so small it could be eaten whole. I'll never take a dare like that again. Inside, the seeds are white, and tiny, like little alien capsules ready to burst in my mouth and launch the war of the worlds. Outside the skin is better than government-grade protection, lead-lined or vacuum-sealed so that nothing disturbs the sleeping chaos within. My teeth etch the thin skin as I bite down, and for a moment I think, what's the big deal? It takes a moment for the chemical to seep through my gums, drift osmosis-like beyond the cell walls of my veins, and enter my bloodstream. I feel the hairs in my nose spring to life, as if every molecule and pore connecting them to the bare skin of my nostrils is suddenly inflamed. Moments later, my brain is sending SOS signals to every nerve north of my bellybutton, scolding them like a bad child for disobeying direct orders from my better judgment. I become a cartoon, stream engine-sized whistles pulsing from my ears, smoke billowing from the drums, eyes bulging with regret. My fingers bring in backup as they reach for a glass, a beer, water, anything to rip the sizzle from the skin of my tongue. That's the last time I try to impress a boy without high heels and a tube of ruby red lipstick. ***—Andrea Stolpe***

Pepper, black flakes snowing down, black speckles of ash, parachuter's landing on reluctant lettuce leaves. The salad is naked except for the oil and vinegar drowning it until it no longer tastes of lettuce but something more tolerable. She squeezes the lemon into her iced tea like a sailor with scurvy and mixes it in with her spoon imagining cake batter and a wooden spatula. "The diet, the diet, I must remember the diet," as she scoots and adjusts her newly acquired cellulite in the plastic-covered diner chair. She is embracing her new way of living, gently unfolding her napkin and draping it across her hopeful thighs. She smells a hamburger with fries and eyes it like a junkyard dog walking past a cookout. She is interrupted by the tall thin waitress as she sets down her grapefruit and once again focuses in on her goal. I can live without sugar she prays. —***Scarlet Keys***

Black seeds sprinkled on scrambled eggs, the bacon curling and spitting in the pan, smokes curls out of the toaster slot, the bread's white skin is branded from the toaster's red coils, fresh-squeezed orange juice, her hands are glazed with juice as shell pink nails bite into the rind and push down on the juicer, pulp floating like bloated rice, Christmas music frays the air, children squeal with excitement as they claw at the brightly wrapped presents, breathing in the scent of bacon and pine needles, the sound of tearing paper and laughter, toys in impossibly big boxes, imprisoned in hard cardboard with skin-like plastic and too many opaque twist-ties, children fidget and hop with anticipation as the grown-up tries to wrestle the toy from the cardboard's sandpaper. —***Susan Cattaneo***

Object Writing Parties

The best way to do group object writing is face to face. Gillian Welch had a group in Nashville that met for two and a half years, every Sunday afternoon from one to four. They'd warm up with a five-minute exercise and read their results to each other. The best writing of the round would set the bar for the next round. Then another five-minute warm-up. Read. Everyone dives a little deeper. Then ten minutes. Read. One more ten. Read. Then a ninety-second piece (suggested by Kami Lyle—I call it a Kami-kazi: you really approach it in a different way). Read. Then another five minutes to decompress from diving so deep. Read. And a break for munchies and conversation. After the break, they go back for one more ten minutes, then one for ninety seconds, and then one for five minutes before ending their weekly "object writing party." Welch says that object writing was one of the most important keys to her success—and she's had seven Grammy nominations, with three wins.

Cyber Writing

You can also try writing with a group over the Internet. Someone in the group is responsible for sending the morning word to the others, and, as each member completes the assignment, they send it to the group using "reply all." There's also an object writing site, objectwriting.com, where you can post and read what others have done with the daily word.

Expanded Object Writing

In her book, *Popular Lyric Writing: 10 Steps to Effective Storytelling*, Andrea Stolpe incorporates some commentary, some "telling," into her object writing, calling it "destination writing." She recognizes that good song ideas, especially titles, come just as easily from the "tell" side as the "show" side of your writing.

For example, I was tempted to add one more line to the passage I wrote about the yellow slicker for the "Puddle" exercise:

> I remember stomping through puddles on Duluth Avenue in St. Paul when I was seven. I had a yellow slicker that smelled like my rubber boots and my boot and buckles jingled when I walked. All the cool guys left their boots open.

Even though it isn't sense-bound, I like the last line, especially the tone it takes. It's a comment—a "tell." It might be a line in a song, maybe a comment after a few sense images set it up.

You might want to use some tells in your object writing, but you might wait a few weeks before you do—getting really sense-bound is hard work. You need to practice being specific and sense-bound to do it well in the context of building a song. Remember, showing is one of the most powerful ways of getting listeners involved in your song.

Neither object writing nor destination writing is journaling. In journaling, events, emotions, and "how I really feel" drive the bus. It's usually about self-exploration, not so much about writing. And that's fine. But object writing and destination writing are about writing. They are a preparation for writing songs. They have a specific purpose.

WHO, WHAT, WHEN, WHERE, WHY, HOW

It's fair to say that object writing is "what" writing. There are other possibilities, especially who, when, and where. One of the more interesting aspects of "destination writing" is its incorporation of these added elements.

"Who" is great for character development. In every song, you have to answer these questions: Who is talking? Who is she/he talking to? Sometimes the character is pretty much you, talking either to the audience or a particular person. Sometimes it's not. Either way, keep the character in focus. What is the song about? What is the character trying to say? Why? Be as specific as you can, using sense images that evoke something about the character. Try using the character's senses, even if the character is you. And remember, your song doesn't have to be an accurate autobiography. Never let reality get in the way of truth.

Practice using other perspectives. Your object writing can be from the perspective of an airline flight attendant, hurrying to serve drinks on a short flight. Or a volunteer at an animal rescue shelter. Sting's "Stolen Car" is told from the perspective of a car thief, and his "Tomorrow We'll See" is from the perspective of a male prostitute.

People watching is full of interesting possibilities. Ask yourself questions: Does she play golf? When did she learn? What was his favorite game when he was little? Of course, you'll be drawing on your own experiences as you answer your questions. And always stay close to your senses. Specifics. Sense images.

I also recommend this kind of storytelling when hanging out with other writers. You might even make a special trip to the mall or the airport to exercise your powers of observation. (I call it "the airport game.") As somebody passes you, ask your friend a question: Who did he take to his junior prom? Does she get along with her younger sister? Take turns asking questions.

"When" can be seasonal—"across the morning sky, all the birds are leaving." It can be a time of day—"midnight at the oasis." Or it can be a special occasion—"chestnuts roasting on an open fire." Play around with it. There's lots of stimulation available here. Try writing five minutes on "summer morning" or "dusk." Maybe "Christmas party" or "Thanksgiving dinner." Watch the ideas tumble out.

"Where" can be anywhere. That's its strength. The Wailing Wall, 42nd Street, a lake cabin, the Grand Canyon, a mountain path, the backseat of the school bus. The opportunities are endless.

Even "how" may be useful. "Forging a sword" or "learning to ride a bike," for example.

"Why" seems like it's more for telling. Maybe you can come up with a few ideas here.

CATALOGING THE GOOD STUFF

If you write on a computer, create a file for your gems. When an exciting image or idea drops into your object writing, mark it and save it in your file. (Mine is called "frag.") If you write in a notebook, leave the first five pages blank and transfer the gems there. The gem spot will be a good place to look for interesting stuff when you need stimulation.

Though object writing generates nifty lyric ideas, the main purpose is stimulation, deepening the world you swim in. Over time, your senses will take you places you never would have been as you see the world more and more through your writer's eyes.

Object writing makes the art of diving automatic, a sensible habit. Even when you start exploring abstractions like "friendship," you'll dive instinctively where the good stuff is—into your own unique sense pool, rather than into some ether of abstractions. Your lyric writing will benefit by drawing from a unique and provocative source, and everyone will listen. I promise.

CHAPTER TWO

RUSTY'S COLLAR

A LESSON IN SHOWING AND TELLING

★ ★ ★ ★ ★ ★ ★ ★ ★ ★ ★ ★ ★ ★ ★

Once you become adept in your object writing, with bushels of sense-bound images glittering on the kitchen table, what do you do with them? Here's some food for thought.

When I was in kindergarten, we got a new puppy.

I told Sister Mary Elizabeth, "I got a new puppy. His name is Rusty."

"That's nice," she smiled, in her kindergarten teacher sort of way.

"Can I bring Rusty to school for Show-and-Tell?"

"No, no," she said, shaking her finger (they always shake their fingers). "We don't bring our pets to school." (Who is we, anyway?)

I put on my best sad, irresistible face, and it had the usual effect. So she was quick to say, "But you could bring something of Rusty's, a picture, or his collar to show to the children. Then you could tell about him."

I walked home as fast as I could after school—making my way nine blocks down Jessamine Avenue to Duluth Avenue, then another three blocks down Duluth to our row of Quonset huts—a whole mile!

A little breathless, I asked my mom, "Can I bring Rusty's collar to school tomorrow for Show-and-Tell?"

"Of course."

I was excited all night. The next morning there was Rusty's collar laid out on the kitchen table next to my Superman lunchbox. What a good mom. I hurried through breakfast, pulled on my snowsuit, buckled my overshoes, wrapped my scarf around my face, yanked on my mittens, grabbed my lunchbox, and headed for St. Casimir's Grade School.

"I brought Rusty's collar for Show-and-Tell."

"That's nice," Sister Mary Elizabeth cooed, in her kindergarten teacher sort of way.

I hung my moon suit in the cloakroom and went to my desk to open my Superman lunchbox: a Spam sandwich with French's Mustard, a hard-boiled egg with salt wrapped in waxed paper, a banana, a celery stick with peanut butter in the groove, and Twinkies. No Rusty's collar.

Apparently, I had forgotten it in my hurry to leave. It was probably still on the kitchen table. I assumed that Mom had put it in my lunchbox.

"I forgot Rusty's collar. Mom didn't put it in my lunchbox."

"Oh, I'm sorry," said Sister Mary Elizabeth.

"Can I do Show-and-Tell anyway?"

"No, no," she said gently, shaking her finger (they always shake their fingers). "You can't tell unless you show first."

YOU CAN'T TELL UNLESS YOU SHOW FIRST.

To this day, I call that the "Sister Mary Elizabeth Rule of Songwriting." Show before you tell. Showing makes the telling more powerful because your senses and your mind are both engaged.

The Sister Mary Elizabeth Rule of Songwriting says: First, hold up Rusty's collar, and then say what you will. Look at this example:

> All the things we used to do
> Those dreamy teenage nights
> Nothing matters like it did
> Back when you were mine

Try showing Rusty's collar first:

> Hot rod hearts and high school rings
> Those dreamy teenage nights
> Nothing matters like it did
> Back when you were mine

Think of Rusty's collar this way: "Hot rod hearts and high school rings" is a bag of dye. Hang the dye on top of the section and let it drip its colors downward onto the other lines, giving them more interest and depth.

Even if you show Rusty's collar just a little later:

Nothing matters like it did
Those dreamy teenage nights
Hot rod hearts and high school rings
Back when you were mine

We still get colors, but the law of gravity says that they'll only drip downward, leaving us starting with:

Nothing matters like it did
Those dreamy teenage nights

This has less color than when we followed the Sister Mary Elizabeth Rule of Songwriting. Colors drip down, not up. Show first, and watch everything else gain impact:

Hot rod hearts and high school rings
Those dreamy teenage nights
Nothing matters like it did
Back when you were mine

The teenage nights get dreamier. We're really able to feel the emotion of:

Nothing matters like it did
Back when you were mine

Now, look at this example, from Gillian Welch's "One More Dollar":

A long time ago I left my home
For a job in the fruit trees
But I missed those hills with the windy pines
For their song seemed to suit me
So I sent my wages to my home
Said we'd soon be together
For the next good crop would pay my way
And I would come home forever

One more dime to show for my day
One more dollar and I'm on my way
When I reach those hills, boys

I'll never roam
One more dollar and I'm going home

Look what happens when we forget to bring Rusty's collar to school:

A long time ago I left my home
For a job in the city
But I miss that place and the things I did
Now it all seems so pretty
So I sent my wages to my home
Said we'd soon be together
For the next month's work would pay my way
And I would come home forever

One more dime to show for my day
One more dollar and I'm on my way
When I reach that place, boys
I'll never roam
One more dollar and I'm going home

Instant bland. David Rawlings, Welch's partner and an ardent student and practitioner of songwriting, called me with this beige version, remarking how he'd just turned the song into a disaster by trading the specific image for a cliché rhyme, city/pretty. "Look how completely it destroys a perfectly good work," he chuckled.

When you're writing, it's fine to just let things flow. But always be on the alert for potential "collars." Don't leave Rusty's collar on the kitchen table, no matter how excited you are to get to school and tell everyone about your new puppy.

The Sister Mary Elizabeth Rule of Songwriting: Show before you tell.

CHAPTER THREE

MAKING METAPHORS

★ ★ ★ ★ ★ ★ ★ ★ ★ ★ ★ ★ ★ ★ ★

Metaphors are not user-friendly. They are difficult to find and difficult to use well. Unfortunately, metaphors are a mainstay of good lyric writing—indeed, of most creative writing. From total snores like "break my heart" and "feel the emptiness inside" to awakening shocks like "the arc of a love affair" (Paul Simon), "feather canyons" (Joni Mitchell), "soul with no leak at the seam" (Peter Gabriel), and "brut and charisma poured from the shadow" (Steely Dan), metaphors support lyrics like bones. The trick is to know how to build them.

In its most basic form, a metaphor is a collision between ideas that don't belong together. It jams them together and leaves us to struggle with the consequences. For example, *an army is a rabid wolf.*

We watch the soldiers begin to snarl, grow snouts, and foam at the teeth. The army disappears, and we are left to face something red-eyed and dangerous. Of course, an army isn't a wolf. All metaphors must be literally false. If the things we identify are the same (e.g., a house is a dwelling place), there is no metaphor, only definition. Conflict is essential for metaphor. Put things that don't belong together in the same room and watch the friction: *dog* with *wind*; *torture* with *car*; *cloud* with *river*.

Interesting overtones. Let's take a closer look. There are three types of metaphor:

An **expressed identity metaphor** asserts an identity between two nouns (e.g., fear is a shadow, a cloud is a sailing ship). Expressed identity metaphors come in three forms:

"x is y" (fear is a shadow)
"the y of x" (the shadow of fear)
"x's y" (fear's shadow)

Run each of these through all three forms:

wind = yelping dog
wind = river
wind = highway

Now come up with a few of your own, and run them through all three forms. You might even try extending them into longer versions (e.g., clouds are sailing ships on rivers of wind).

A **qualifying metaphor** uses adjectives to qualify nouns, and adverbs to qualify verbs. Friction within these relationships creates a metaphor (e.g., hasty clouds, to sing blindly).

A **verbal metaphor** is formed by conflict between the verb and its subject and/or object (e.g., clouds sail, he tortured his clutch, frost gobbles summer down).

According to Aristotle, the ability to see one thing as another is the only truly creative human act. Most of us have the creative spark to make metaphors, we just need to train ourselves a bit and direct our energy properly.

Look at this metaphor from Percy Bysshe Shelley's "Ode to the West Wind": "A heavy *weight of hours* has chained and bowed / One too like thee..." Hours are links of a chain, accumulating weight and bending the old man's back lower and lower as each new hour is added, an interesting way to look at old age.

Great metaphors seem to come in a flare of inspiration—there is a moment of light and heat, and suddenly the writer sees the old man bent over, dragging a load of invisible hour-chains. But even if great metaphors come from inspiration, you can certainly prepare yourself for their flaring. The next section will help to train your vision, help you learn to look in the hot places, and help you nurture a spark that can erupt into something bright and wonderful.

PLAYING IN KEYS

Like musical notes, words can group together in close relationships, like belonging to the same key. Call this a diatonic relationship. For example, here are some random words that are diatonic to (in the same key as) *tide*: *ocean*, *moon*, *recede*, *power*, *beach*.

This is "playing in the key of *tide*," where *tide* is the fundamental tone. This is a way of creating collisions between elements that have at least some things in common—a fertile ground for metaphors. There are many other keys *tide* can belong to when something else is a fundamental tone—for example, *power*. Let's play in its key: *Muhammad Ali*, *avalanche*, *army*, *Wheaties*, *socket*, *tide*.

All these words are related to each other by virtue of their relationship to "power." If we combine them into little collisions, we can often discover metaphors:

> Muhammad Ali avalanched over his opponents.
> An avalanche is an army of snow.
> This army is the Wheaties of our revolution.
> Wheaties plug your morning into a socket.
> A socket holds back tides of electricity.

Try playing in the key of *moon*: *stars*, *harvest*, *lovers*, *crescent*, *astronauts*, *calendar*, *tide*.

> The New Mexico sky is a rich harvest of stars.
> Evening brings a harvest of lovers to the beach.
> The lovers' feelings waned to a mere crescent.
> The crescent of human knowledge grows with each astronaut's mission.
> Astronauts' flights are a calendar of human courage.
> A new calendar washes in a tide of opportunities.

Essentially, a metaphor works by revealing some third thing that two ideas share in common. One good way of finding metaphors is by asking these two questions:

1. What characteristics does my idea ("tide") have?
2. What else has those characteristics?

Answering the second question usually releases a veritable flood of possible metaphors.

Often, the relationship between two ideas is not clear. *Muhammad Ali* is hardly the first idea that comes to mind with *avalanche*, unless you recognize their linking term, *power*. In most contexts, *Muhammad Ali* and *avalanche* are non-diatonic, unrelated to each other. Only when you look to find a link do you come up with *power*, or *deadly*, or *try to keep quiet when you're in their territories*. Always asking the two questions above opens up these relationships and helps you develop metaphor-seeking habits. Here are several exercises to help you get hooked.

★ EXERCISE 4 ★

Get a group of at least four people. Divide the participants into two equal groups. Have each member of one group make an arbitrary list of five interesting adjectives. At the same time, have each member of the other group make an arbitrary list of five interesting nouns. Then combine their arbitrary lists. This usually results in some pretty strange combinations. For example:

adjectives	**nouns**
smoky	conversation
refried	railroad
decaffeinated	rainbow
hollow	rain forest
understated	eyebrows

Think about each combination for a minute; they evoke some interesting possibilities. Take any combination and try to write a sentence or short paragraph from it. Like this: "Since I got your phone call, everything seems dull. My day has been bleached of sound and color. Even the rainbow this afternoon has been decaffeinated."

★ EXERCISE 5 ★

Try writing a sentence or short paragraph for these combinations:

smoky conversation
refried railroad
hollow rain forest
understated eyebrows

Now jumble them up into different combinations (for example, smoky eyebrows) and write a sentence or short paragraph for each one. The point of the exercise is to see that overtones (linking ideas, metaphors) are released by this blind striking of notes. Wonderful accidents happen frequently.

★ EXERCISE 6 ★

Gather two groups of people. Have each member of one group make an arbitrary list of five interesting verbs. At the same time, have each member of the other group make an arbitrary list of five interesting nouns. Like these:

nouns	**verbs**
squirrel	preaches
wood stove	vomits
surfboard	cancels
reef	celebrates
aroma	palpitates

Again, take any combination and try to write a sentence or short paragraph from it. Like this: "The red squirrel scrambled onto the branch, rose to his haunches, and began preaching to us, apparently cautioning us to respect the silence of his woodlands."

Your turn:

wood stove vomits
surfboard cancels
reef celebrates
aroma palpitates

Jumbling up the list unveils new combinations. Write a sentence or short paragraph for each of the following combinations:

squirrel celebrates
wood stove palpitates
surfboard preaches
reef cancels
aroma vomits

If you don't already have a writers' group, these exercises might be a good reason to start one. Just get some people together (even numbers are best) and start making arbitrary lists. Put your lists together and see what your combinations suggest.

One thing will become clear right away: You get better results combining nouns and verbs than from combining adjectives and nouns. Verbs are the power amplifiers of language. They drive it; they set it in motion. Look at any of the great poets—Yeats, Frost, Sexton, Eliot. If you actually go through some poems and circle their verbs, you will see why the poems crackle with power. Great writers know where to look. They pay attention to their verbs.

EXERCISE 7

Have each member of one group make an arbitrary list of five interesting nouns. At the same time, have each member of the other group also make an arbitrary list of five interesting nouns. Like these:

nouns	**nouns**
summer	Rolls-Royce
ocean	savings account
thesaurus	paintbrush
Indian	beach ball
shipwreck	mattress

Remember the three forms of expressed identity, the first type of metaphor? Try these noun-noun collisions in each form. For example:

summer is a Rolls-Royce

the Rolls-Royce of summer
summer's Rolls-Royce

Summer is the Rolls-Royce of the seasons.
Winter is gone. Time for another ride in the Rolls-Royce of summer.
Once again, summer's Rolls-Royce has collapsed into the iceboat of winter.

Now it's your turn again. Use whatever form of expressed identity metaphor that seems to work best. Write a sentence or short paragraph for the other four noun combinations.

These are also great fun to jumble up. You can even jumble them within the same columns. Try a sentence for each of these:

summer mattress
ocean paintbrush
thesaurus beach ball
Indian Rolls-Royce
shipwreck savings account

★ EXERCISE 8 ★

After you have spent a few sessions discovering accidental metaphors through the previous exercises, you will be ready for the final method to activate the process: a five-step exercise guaranteed to open your metaphorical eyes and keep them open.

Step one: Make a list of five interesting adjectives. Then, for each one, find an interesting noun that creates a fresh, exciting metaphor. Take as long as you need for each adjective—hours, even days. Keep it in your vision. Push it against every noun you see until you create a breathtaking collision. Be patient. Developing a habit of looking takes time. It is the quality of your metaphors and the accumulated hours of practice that count here, not speed.

Remember that you can make vivid adjectives out of verbs: *to wrinkle* becomes the adjective *wrinkled* (wrinkled water) or *wrinkling* (the wrinkling hours). These are called participles.

Step two: Now make a list of five interesting nouns, and locate a terrific verb for each one. This will be more difficult, since you are used to looking at things in the world, not actions. Again, take your time. Develop a habit of mind that can see a doe stepping through the shallows as the water wrinkles into circles around her.

Step three: Make a list of five interesting verbs and track down a noun for each one. Most likely, you've never looked at the world from this angle before. You'll find it unnatural, challenging, and fun.

Step four: Make a list of five interesting nouns and find an adjective for each one. (Don't forget about participles.)

Step five: Make a list of five interesting nouns and find another noun for each one. Use whatever form of expressed identity metaphor you think works best.

This last step brings you full circle. You have looked at the world from the vantage point of nouns, verbs, and adjectives. (I left out adverbs as a matter of personal preference. I don't get much use out of them, especially when I am careful to find strong verbs. If you want to add them to the exercise, simply list five adverbs and find a verb for each one. Then reverse the process and start with a list of verbs.) This is a practical result: Because you have developed a habit of looking, you will see countless opportunities to create metaphors in your writing. After all, you run into nouns, verbs, and adjectives pretty frequently.

These exercises focus your creative attention on a practical way to find metaphors using expressed identity metaphors, qualifying metaphors, and verbal metaphors. You don't have to wait for a grand bolt of inspiration. Simply look at the word you're on, and ask: What characteristics does this idea have? What else has those characteristics?

Then watch ideas tumble out onto your page.

SIMILE

You learned in high school that the difference between metaphor and simile is that simile uses *like* or *as*. True enough, but that's like saying that measles are spots on your body. They are, but if you look deeper, the spots are there because a virus is present. There is something more fundamental going on. Remember the metaphor *an army is a rabid wolf*? Say it to yourself and let the pictures roll. You start with the army, but your focus transfers to the rabid wolf, something red-eyed and dangerous.

Simile doesn't transfer focus: An army is *like* a rabid wolf. Say it to yourself and let the pictures roll. The army refuses to budge. No snouts or foamy teeth. We sit waiting for an explanation while the army stands before us in full uniform.

Look at this from Kurt Thompson:

My love is an engine
It ain't run in years
Just took one kiss from you
to loosen up the gears

My heart needs to rev some
It's an old Chevrolet
You might think it's crazy
To want to race away

Who ever said
that love was smart

Baby won't you drive my heart
Won't you drive my heart

The metaphor sets up the car. The speaker is asking *baby* to get in and step on the accelerator. Now look at this version:

My love's **like** an engine
It ain't run in years
Just took one kiss from you
to loosen up these gears

My heart needs to rev some
Like an old Chevrolet
You might think it's crazy
To want to race away

Who ever said
that love was smart

Baby won't you drive my heart
Won't you drive my heart

Read it again and let the pictures roll. Now the focus stays on the speaker rather than transferring to the car. So the emphasis in "baby won't you drive my heart" is on *heart* rather than *drive*. It seems like a subtle difference, but it makes all the difference in how we hear the song. The metaphor creates a light, clever song. The simile is clever, too, but it's also more intimate, since we stay in the presence of the speaker throughout the song.

Because a simile refuses to transfer focus, it works in a totally different way than a metaphor does. A metaphor takes its second term (an army is a *rabid wolf*) very seriously—you must commit to it, because that's what everyone will end up looking at.

You needn't commit as deeply to the second term of a simile, since the first term gets most of the attention. This makes similes useful as a one-time event. In a line like "I'm as corny as Kansas in August," our focus stays on *I*. We have no further appetite for corn or Kansas. Good thing, since the rest of the song goes everywhere but Kansas. However, if the line had been "I am corn in Kansas in August," we'd expect to hear things about sun, rain, wind, and harvest in the upcoming lines.

As a rule of thumb, when you have a list of comparisons in mind, use a simile:

love is like rain
love is like planting
love is like the summer sun

When you're using only one comparison (e.g., *love is a rose*), and you want to commit to it throughout the song, use a metaphor. It only grows when it's on the vine.

CHAPTER FOUR

LEARNING TO SAY NO
BUILDING WORKSHEETS

Writing a lyric is like getting a gig: If you're grateful for any idea that comes along, you're probably not getting the best stuff. But if you have lots of legitimate choices, you won't end up playing six hours in Bangor, Maine, for twenty bucks. Look at it this way: The more often you can say no, the better your gigs get. That's why I suggest that you learn to build a worksheet—a specialized tool for brainstorming that produces bathtubs full of ideas and, at the same time, tailors the ideas specifically for a lyric.

Simply, a worksheet contains two things: a list of key ideas and a list of rhymes for each one. There are three stages to building a worksheet.

1. FOCUS YOUR LYRIC IDEA AS CLEARLY AS YOU CAN

Let's say you want to write about homelessness. Sometimes, you'll start the lyric from an emotion: "That old homeless woman with everything she owns in a shopping cart really touches me. I want to write a song about her." Sometimes you'll write from a cold, calculated idea: "I'm tired of writing love songs. I want to do one on a serious subject, maybe homelessness." Or, you may write from a title you like, maybe "Risky Business." Then the trick is to find an interesting angle on it, perhaps: "What do you do for a living?" "I survive on the streets." "That's a pretty risky business."

In each case, it's up to you to find the angle, brainstorm the idea, and create the world the idea will live in. Since you always bring your unique perspective to each experience, you will have something interesting to offer. But you'll have to look at enough ideas to find the best perspective.

Object writing is the key to developing choices. You must dive into your vaults of sense material—those unique and secret places—to find out what images you've stored away, in the present example, around the idea of homelessness.

★ EXERCISE 9 ★

Stop reading, get out a pen, and dive into homelessness for ten minutes. Stay sense-bound and very specific. How do you connect to the idea? Did you ever get lost in the woods as a child? Run away from home? Sleep in a car in New York?

Now, did you find an expressive image, like a broken wheel on a homeless woman's shopping cart, that can serve as a metaphor—a vehicle to carry your feelings? Did you see some situation, like your parents fighting, that seems to connect you with her situation? These expressive objects or situations are what T.S. Eliot calls "objective correlatives"—objects anyone can touch, smell, and see that correlate with the emotion you want to express. Broken wheels or parents fighting work nicely as objective correlatives.

Even if you find ideas that work well, keep looking a while longer. When you find a good idea, there is usually a bunch more behind it. (The gig opening for Aerosmith could be the next offer.) Jot down your good ideas on a separate sheet of paper.

2. MAKE A LIST OF WORDS THAT EXPRESS YOUR IDEA

You'll need to look further than the hot ideas from your object writing. Get out a thesaurus, one set up according to Roget's original plan according to the flow of ideas—a setup perfect for brainstorming. Dictionary-style versions (set up alphabetically) are useful only for finding synonyms and antonyms. They make brainstorming a cumbersome exercise in cross-referencing.

Your thesaurus is better than a good booking agent. It can churn up images and ideas you wouldn't ever get to by yourself, stimulating your diver to greater and greater depths until a wealth of choices litter the beaches.

Let's adopt the working title "Risky Business" and continue brainstorming the idea of homelessness. In the index (the last half of your thesaurus), locate a word the expresses the general idea, for example, *risk*. From the list below it, select the word most related to the lyric idea. My thesaurus lists these options for *risk: gambling 618n; possibility 469n; danger 661n; speculate 791vb*. The first notation should be read as follows: "You will find the word risk in the noun group of section 618 under the key word gambling."

Key words are always in italics. They set a general meaning for the section, like a key signature sets the tone center in a piece of music.

Probably the closest meaning for our purposes with "Risky Business" is *danger 661n*. Look in the text (front half) of the thesaurus for section 661 (or whatever number your thesaurus lists; numbers will appear at the tops of the pages). If you peruse the general area around danger for a minute, you will find several pages of related material. Here are the surrounding section headings in my thesaurus:

Ill health, disease	Insalubrity	Deterioration
Relapse	Bane	Danger
Pitfall	Danger signal	Escape
Salubrity (well-being)	Improvement	Restoration
Remedy	Safety	Refuge. Safeguard
Warning	Preservation	Deliverance

This related material runs for sixteen pages in double-column entries. Risk is totally surrounded by its relatives, so if you look around the neighborhood, you'll find a plethora of possibilities. Start building your list.

Look at these first few entries under danger: *N. danger, peril; ... shadow of death, jaws of d., dragon's mouth, dangerous situation, unhealthy s., desperate s., forlorn hope 700n. predicament; emergency 137n. crisis; insecurity, jeopardy, risk, hazard, ticklishness...*

Look actively. If you take each entry for a quick dive through your sense memories, you should have a host of new ideas within minutes. (Frequent object writing pays big dividends here. The more familiar you are with the process, the quicker these quick dives get. If you are slow at first, don't give up—you'll get faster. Just vow to do more object writing.) Jot down the best words on your list and keep at it until you're into serious overload.

Now the fun begins. Start saying no to words in your list until you've trimmed it to about ten or twelve words with different vowel sounds in their stressed syllables. Put these survivors in the middle of a blank sheet of paper, number them, and enclose them in a box for easy reference later on. Keep these guidelines in mind:

1. If you are working with a title, be sure to put its key vowel sounds in the list.
2. Most of your words should end in a stressed syllable, since they work best in rhyming position.
3. Put any interesting words that duplicate a vowel sound in parentheses.

Your goal is to create a list of words to look up in your rhyming dictionary. Here's what I got banging around in the thesaurus, looking through the lens of homelessness:

1. risk
2. business
3. left out
4. freeze (wheel, shield)
5. storm
6. dull (numb)
7. night (child)
8. change
9. defense
10. home (hope, broken, coat)

This is not a final list. Don't be afraid to switch, add, or take out words as the process continues.

3. LOOK UP EACH WORD IN YOUR RHYMING DICTIONARY

Be sure to extend your search to imperfect rhyme types, and to select only words that connect with your ideas. Above all, don't bother with cliché rhymes or other typical rhymes. First, a quick survey of rhyme types.

Perfect Rhyme

Don't let yourself be seduced by the word "perfect." It doesn't mean "better," it only means:

1. The syllables' vowel sounds are the same.
2. The consonant sounds after the vowels (if any) are the same.
3. The sounds before the vowels are different.

Remember, lyrics are sung, not read or spoken. When you sing, you exaggerate vowels. And since rhyme is a vowel connection, lyricists can make sonic connections in ways other than perfect rhyme.

Family Rhyme

1. The syllables' vowel sounds are the same.
2. The consonant sounds after the vowels belong to the same phonetic families.
3. The sounds before the vowels are different.

Here's a chart of the three important consonant families:

	↕ partners	PLOSIVES	FRICATIVES	NASALS	
VOICED		b d g	v TH z zh j	m n ng	← companions
UNVOICED		p t k	f th s sh ch	← companions	

Each of the three boxes—plosives, fricatives, and nasals—form a phonetic family. When a word ends in a consonant in one of the boxes, you can use the other members of the family to find perfect rhyme substitutes.

Rub/up/thud/putt/bug/stuck are members of the same family—plosives—so they are family rhymes.

Love/buzz/judge/fluff/fuss/hush/touch are members of the fricative family, so they also are family rhymes.

Strum/run/sung rhyme as members of the nasal family.

Say you want to rhyme this line:

I'm stuck in a rut

First, look up perfect rhymes for *rut: cut, glut, gut, hut, shut*.

The trick to saying something you mean is to expand your alternatives. Look at the table of family rhymes below and introduce yourself to t's relatives:

ud	**uk**	**ub**	**up**	**ug**
blood	buck	club	hard up	bug
flood	duck	hub	makeup	jug
mud	luck	pub	cup	unplug
stud	muck	scrub		plug
thud	stuck	tub		shrug
	truck			snug
				tug

That's much better. Now we find that we have a lot of interesting stuff to say no to.

What if you want to rhyme this:

There's nowhere I can feel safe

First, look up perfect rhymes for *safe* in your rhyming dictionary. All we get is *waif*. Not much.

Now look for family rhymes under f's family, the fricatives. We add these possibilities:

as	**av**	**az**	**aj**
case	behave	blaze	age

ace	brave	craze	cage
breathing-space	cave	daze	page
chase	grave	haze	rage
face	shave	phrase	stage
disgrace	slave	paraphrase	
embrace	wave	praise	
grace			
lace			
resting-place		**ath**	**aTH**
space		faith	bathe

Finally, nasals. The word "nasals" means what you think it means: All the sound comes out of your nose. Rhyme this line:

> My head is pounding like a drum

Look up perfect rhymes for *drum: hum, pendulum, numb, slum, strum.*

Go to the table of family rhymes and look at m's relatives:

un	**ung**
fun	hung
gun	flung
overrun	wrung
won	sung
jettison	
skeleton	

Finding family rhyme isn't difficult, so there's no reason to tie yourself in knots using only perfect rhyme. Family rhyme sounds so close that when sung, the ear won't know the difference.

Additive Rhyme

1. The syllables' vowel sounds are the same.
2. One of the syllables add extra consonants after the vowel.
3. The sounds before the vowels are different.

When the syllable you want to rhyme ends in a vowel (e.g., play, free, fly), the only way to generate alternatives is to add consonants after the vowel. The guideline is simple: The less sound you add, the closer you stay to perfect rhyme.

Look again at the table of family rhymes. Voiced plosives—b, d, g—put out the least sound. Use them first, rhyming, for example, *ricochet* with *paid*; then the unvoiced plosives, rhyming *free* with *treat*. Next, voiced fricatives, rhyming *fly* and *alive*. Then on to unvoiced fricatives, followed by the most noticeable consonants (aside from l and r), the nasals. You'd end up with a list moving from closest to perfect rhyme to furthest away from perfect rhyme. For example, for *free*, we find: *speed, cheap, sweet, grieve, belief, dream, clean, deal.*

You can also add consonants even if there are already consonants after the vowel, for example: street/sweets, alive/drives, dream/screamed, trick/risk.

You can even combine this technique with family rhymes, such as dream/cleaned, club/floods/shove/stuffed. This gives you even more options, making it easier to say what you mean.

Subtractive Rhyme

1. The syllables' vowel sounds are the same.
2. One of the syllables adds an extra consonant after the vowel.
3. The sounds before the vowels are different.

Subtractive rhyme is basically the same as additive rhyme. The difference is practical. If you start with *fast*, *class* is subtractive. If you start with *class*, *fast* is additive.

> Help me please, I'm sinking fast
> Girl, you're in a different class

For *fast*, you could also try: *glass, flat, mashed* (family), *laughed* (family), *crash* (fam. subt.).

The possibilities grow.

Assonance Rhyme

1. The syllables' vowel sounds are the same.

2. The consonant sounds after the vowels are unrelated.
3. The sounds before the vowels are different.

Assonance rhyme is the furthest you can get from perfect rhyme without changing vowel sounds. Consonants after the vowels have nothing in common. Try rhyming:

> I hope you're satisfied

For *satisfied*, we come up with: *life, trial, crime, sign, rise, survive, surprise.*

Use these rhyming techniques. You'll have much more leeway saying what you mean, and your rhymes will be fresh and useful. Again, look actively at each word. Use them to dive through your senses, as though you were object writing.

You'll find more on these rhyme types, including helpful exercises, in my book *Songwriting: Essential Guide to Rhyming.*

Rhymes and Chords

You can think about rhyme in the same way you think about chords. Go to the piano and play three chords: an F chord with an F as the bass note in the left hand, then G7 with G as the bass note, then, finally, C. Play the C chord with the notes C, E, and G in the right hand, and a C as a bass note in the left hand. Sing a C, too. It really feels like you've arrived home, doesn't it?

Next, do the same thing again with your right hand, singing a C when you get to the C chord, but this time, put a G in the left hand. It still feels like you're home, though not quite as solidly as when you played C in the bass. Still, it's difficult to notice the difference.

Do it all again, this time playing the third in the bass, an E. It still feels like a version of home, but less stable. It seems to have some discomfort at home—a very expressive chord.

Do it again, keeping the E in the bass, but this time take the C out of the chord in your right hand. Sing the C. This feels even less comfortable.

Last time, add a B to the right hand, still leaving the C out. Now, you're actually playing an E minor chord, the three minor in the key of

C, still singing the C. Now we have only a suggestion of home, rather than sitting down to the supper table.

All of these voicings are useful, and all of these voicings are tonic (home) functions. Some land solidly and bring motion to a complete halt. Others express a desire to keep moving somewhere else—a kind of wanderlust. Each has its own identity and emotion.

Rhymes work the same way. Some are stronger than others and express a desire to stay put; they are stable. Others may have a foot at home, but their minds are looking for the next place to go. They feel less stable.

Here are the rhyme types, listed like the chords you played, in a scale from most stable to least stable:

RHYME TYPES: SCALE OF RESOLUTION STRENGTHS

Most Resolved				Least Resolved
|	|	|	|	|
|	Family Rhyme	|	Assonance Rhyme	|
Perfect Rhyme		Additive/ Subtractive Rhyme		Consonance Rhyme

Look at the simple example below—a stable, four-stress couplet. With perfect rhyme, it feels very solid and resolved:

> A lovely day to have some fun
> Hit the beach, get some sun

As we move through the rhyme types, things feel less and less stable, even though the structure remains the same:

Family rhyme:

A lovely day to have some fun
Hit the beach, bring the rum (a lot like C with G in the bass)

Additive rhyme:

A lovely day to have some fun
Hit the beach, get some lunch (a lot like C with E in the bass)

Subtractive rhyme:

Hit the beach and get some lunch
A lovely day, have some fun (a lot like C with E in the bass)

Assonance rhyme:

A lovely day to have some fun
Hit the beach, fall in love (a lot like C with E in the bass, no C in the right hand)

Consonance rhyme:

A lovely day to have some fun
Hit the beach, bring it on (a lot like the E minor in the key of C)

Expanding your rhyming possibilities accomplishes three things:

1. It multiplies the possibility of saying what you mean (and still rhyming) exponentially.
2. It guarantees the rhymes will not be predictable or cliché.
3. Most important, it allows you to control, like chords do, how stable or unstable the rhyme feels, allowing you to support or even create emotion with your rhymes.

Together, these offer a pretty good argument against the proponents of "perfect rhyme only."

Baby baby take my hand
Let me know you__________

Ah yes, understand. Telegraphed and locked down. Mostly, I find it disappointing when I know what's coming. When it's already telegraphed and waltzing in your brain, why say it? If you instead said something different, you'd have both messages at the same time:

Baby baby take my hand
Let me know you'll take a stand (*understand*, the expected cliché, is still present.)

I like the perfect rhyme here. The full resolution seems to support the idea. Now, how about:

Baby baby take my hand
Let me know you'd like to dance

I love the surprise here. It also uses the telegraphing of *understand* as a second message. It's not a cliché rhyme. Pretty close, though, with n in common but d against c. That little bit of difference introduces something that perfect rhyme can't: a tinge of longing created by the difference at the end. The lack of perfect rhyme creates the same kind of instability as, say, the C major triad with a G in the bass. Almost, but not fully resolved. Just as a chord can create an emotional response, so can a less-perfect rhyme:

WORKSHEET: RISKY BUSINESS

1. risk	2. business	3. left out	4. freeze	5. storm
cliff	collisions	proud	grieve	reform
fist	visions	bound	leave	(re)born
kissed	frigid	count	peace	court
stiff	forgiveness	vowed	appeased	cord
itch	submissive	aloud	street	scorn
pitch	delicious	renowned	debris	divorce
drift	riches	aroused	diseased	reward
switch	suspicious	crowned	guarantee(s)	warm
shift	kisses		wheel	torn
pinched	finish		shield	ignored
chips	wind			

Baby baby take my hand
Let me know you're making plans

The same tinge of instability.

Baby baby take my hand
Let me know you want to laugh

What do you think the chances of hooking up are now? They seem about as remote as the assonance rhyme. Yup, the rhyme type really can affect and color the idea.

It's still a "tonic" function, but now it seems more like a C major triad with an E in the bass.

Finally:

Baby baby take my hand
Let me know I'm on your mind

6. dull	7. night	8. change	9. defense	10. home
sulk	flight	cage	expense	disowned
annulled	spite	slave	bench	blown
cult	bride	grave	trench	bone
pale	strike	safe	drenched	unknown
brawl	prize	faith	friend	stoned
numb	despised	castaway	revenge	dethroned
opium	deprived	ricochet	content	zone
martyrdom	child	haste	condemned	hope
crumbs	fault		contempt	coat
gun	crawl			throat
young				remote
				ghost
				Job
				load
				broken

Now there's curiosity and uncertainty, expressed completely and only by the consonance rhyme. Pretty neat, huh?

Brainstorming

Brainstorming with a rhyming dictionary prepares you to write a lyric. At the same time you are brainstorming your ideas, you are also finding sounds you can use later. With solid rhyming techniques that include family rhymes, additive and subtractive rhymes, assonance and even consonance rhymes (especially for l and r), using a rhyming dictionary can be as relaxed and easy as brainstorming with a friend, except it's more efficient than a friend, and it won't whine for a piece of the song if you get a hit.

A worksheet externalizes the inward process of lyric writing. It slows your writing process down so you can get to know it better, like slowing down when you play a new scale to help get it under your fingers. The more you do it, the faster and more efficient you'll get.

The sample worksheet on pages 44–45 includes both perfect and imperfect rhymes. Reading this worksheet should be stimulating. But doing your own worksheet will set you on fire. Decide now that you will do a complete worksheet for each of your next ten lyrics, then stick to it. The first one will be slow and painful, but full of new and interesting options. By the third one, ideas will be coming fast and furious. You will have too much to say, too many choices, and too many rhymes. Though getting to this point takes work, it will be well worth the effort. Think of all the times you'll get to say no. No more clichés. No more forced rhymes. No more helpless gratitude that some idea, any idea at all, came along. No more six-hour gigs in Bangor for twenty bucks. Trust me.

CHAPTER FIVE

CLICHÉS

THE SLEEPING PUPPY (A CASE STUDY)

The PBS documentary scene: A black puppy scampers across the lawn chasing a butterfly when, plop, she drops limp on her side, fast asleep. Moments later, she's up and romping. Then again, plop. "Narcolepsy," intones the narrator, "can strike its victim at any time. She'll sleep a few minutes then get up and move on, unaware that anything happened. Scientists cite a variety of possible causes."

The documentary fails to mention the radio playing in the background. Watch and listen closely—the puppy topples over at the lines. "You gotta take a chance / If you want a true romance." She sleeps until the song finishes, then gets up chasing her tail until she hears "Take my hand / Let me know you understand." Plop. I may not be *The New England Journal of Medicine*, but I know why the puppy is falling asleep: clichés. Cliché phrases. Cliché rhymes. Cliché images. Cliché metaphors. These viruses infect songs, television, movies, and commercials, not to mention everyday conversations. And if clichés can put puppies to sleep, think what they'll do to people who listen to your songs.

Clichés have been worn smooth by overuse. They no longer mean what they used to. *Strong as a bull*, *eats like a horse*, and *their ship came in* no longer evoke vivid images of bulls, horses, and ships. Overuse has made them generic. They suffer from the same malady that infects all generic language: They don't show—they can only tell. *How ya doin'? What's up? How's it goin'?* These phrases are interchangeable. So are *break my heart, cut me deep,* and *hurt me bad.* Your job as a writer isn't to point to a generic territory where images could be, but instead to go there, get one, and *show* it to your listeners. Clichés don't pump gasoline anymore.

Songs should be universal, but don't mistake universal for generic. Sense-bound is universal. When you stimulate your listeners' senses, they pick pictures from their own personal sense files. When you use generic language, they fall asleep. There's a difference between this:

1. Noise and confusion, there's no peace
   In the hustle and bustle of city streets
   It's time to get away from it all
   Deep inside I hear nature's call

and this, from William Butler Yeats:

2. I will arise and go now, for always night and day
   I hear lake water lapping with low sounds by the shore;
   While I stand on the roadway, or the pavements gray,
   I hear it in the deep heart's core.

Both express roughly the same sentiment, but the first, cliché and generic as it is, can only point to territories of meaning. Yeats takes you there.

Clichés are prefabricated. You can string them together as easily as a guitarist strings his favorite licks into a solo (two Claptons + one Hendrix + three Pages + one Stevie Ray, etc.). The problem is, it isn't *his* solo. Using other people's licks is an excellent way to learn, but there is a next step: finding your own way of saying it. Clichés are other people's licks. They don't come from *your* emotions.

Look at the sample lists of clichés below. They're all familiar—maybe uncomfortably familiar.

CLICHÉ PHRASES

(way down) deep inside	touch my (very) soul	take my hand
heart-to-heart	eye to eye	hand-in-hand

side by side	in and out	face-to-face
up and down	by my side	back and forth
we've just begun	hurts so bad	walk out (that) door
can't stand the pain	can't take it	feel the pain
give me half a chance	last chance	gotta take a chance
such a long time	night and day	take your time
all night long	the test of time	the rest of time
rest of my life	someone like you	end of time
no one can take your place	all my love	no one like you
lonely nights	say you'll be mine	losing sleep
I'll get along	how it used to be	made up my mind
calling out your name	it's gonna be all right	get down on my knees
more than friends	set me free	end it all
fooling around	work it out	had your fun
heaven above	true to you	done you wrong
break these chains	kiss your lips	back to me
take it easy	falling apart	make you stay
can't live without you	taken for granted	asking too much
somebody else	lost without you	no tomorrow
break my heart	safe and warm	give you my heart
try one more time	broken heart	aching heart
can't go on	all we've been through	want you / need you / love you
keep holding on	end of the line	now or never
always be true	hold on	over the hill
pay the price	never let you (me) go	know for sure
right or wrong	rise above	hold me tight

what we're fighting for
all we've done
tear me apart
you know it's true
worth fighting for
play the game
hold me close
nothing to lose
see the light
forget my foolish pride
losing sleep
oh baby
drive me crazy
treat me like a fool
all my dreams come true
going insane
rhyme or reason

Clichés come effortlessly. It's no sweat to string them together and feel like you've said something:

> She sits alone all day long
> The hours pass her by
> Every minute like the last
> A prisoner of time

It does say something, just nothing startling. It doesn't yank you by the hair into her room. No humming fluorescent lights. No faded lace curtains. You get to nap securely at a distance, untouched, uninvolved. Getting to the good stuff is harder work. Though clichés are great in a first or second draft as place markers for something better, don't ever mistake them for the real thing:

> She's wheeled into the hallway
> Till the sun moves down the floor
> Little squares of daylight
> Like a hundred times before

CLICHÉ RHYMES

When you hear one of these, no need to lose sleep wondering what's coming next. Plop. Naptime.

hand / understand / command
eyes / realize / sighs / lies
walk / talk
fire / desire / higher
kiss / miss
burn / yearn / learn
dance / chance / romance
forever / together / never

friend / end	ache / break
cry / die / try / lie / good-bye / deny	tears / fears
best / rest / test	door / before / more
love / above / dove	heart / start / apart / part
hide / inside / denied	wrong / strong / song / long
touch / much	word / heard
begun / done	arms / charms / harm / warm
blues / lose	true / blue / through
lover / discover / cover	pain / rain / same
light / night / sight / tight / fight /right	stronger / longer
take it / make it / fake it / shake it	maybe / baby
change / rearrange	knees / please

Most cliché rhymes are perfect rhymes, a good reason to stretch into other rhyme types—family rhyme, additive and subtractive rhyme, and even assonance rhyme. These imperfect rhyme types are guaranteed fresh, and most listeners won't notice the difference.

CLICHÉ IMAGES

These have been aired out so much they are mere whiffs of their former selves:

lips	eyes	smile	hands
face	hair	silky hair	voice
soft (smooth) skin	warmth of arms	kiss	moon
sky	light	sun going down	stars
shadow	bed	lying in bed	night
crying	knock	door	tears
key	door	wall	lock

chains	flowers	rose	cuts like a knife
glass of wine	fireplace	telephone	perfume
feel the beat	sweat	flashing lights	dance floor

The best cure for cliché images is to dive into your own sense pool and discover images that communicate *your* feelings. What did your lover say? Where were you? What kind of car? What was the texture of the upholstery in the backseat? You get the idea.

CLICHÉ METAPHORS

Review chapter three, "Making Metaphors." There's no reason to keep sleepwalking in these yellow fogs.

Storm for anger, including thunder, lightning, dark clouds, flashing, wind, hurricane, tornado

Darkness for ignorance, sadness, and loneliness, including night, blind, shadows

Fire for love or passion, including burn, spark, heat, flame, too hot, consumed, burned, ashes

Rain for tears

Seasons for stages of life or relationships

Prison, Prisoner used especially for love, includes chains, etc.

Cold for emotional indifference, including ice, freeze, frozen

Light for knowledge or happiness, including shine, sun, touch the sky, blinded by love, etc.

Walls for protection from harm, especially from love

Broken heart too numerous to mention

Drown in love

I've listed enough clichés to keep whole herds of puppies asleep for decades. If you have a barking dog in the neighborhood, instead of yelling or telephoning your neighbor, try reading aloud from these lists in its general direction.

FRIENDLY CLICHÉS

In some cases, you can use a cliché to your advantage. Put it in a context that brings out its original meaning or makes us see it in a new way. For example, *I'll be seeing you*, as a cliché, is a substitute for *so long* or *good-bye*. When Sammy Fain and Irving Kahal set it up, it's brand new:

> I'll be seeing you
> In all the old familiar places ...
> I'll be looking at the moon
> But I'll be seeing you

This passage implies *good-bye*, but only as an overtone of the primary meaning. The result is a combination: *After we say good-bye, I'll see you everywhere.*

David Wilcox slants *it's all downhill from here* to his advantage in "Top of the Roller Coaster" with this setup:

> Say good-bye to your twenties
> Tomorrow is the big Three-O
> For your birthday present
> I've got a place where we can go
> It's a lesson in motion
> We'll ride the wildest ride
> We're going to climb to the top of the roller coaster
> And look down the other side
>
> Let me ride in the front car
> You ride right behind
> And I'll click my snapshot camera
> At exactly the right time
> I'll shoot back over my shoulder
> Catch the fear no one can hide
> When we tip the top of the roller coaster
> And look down the other side
> Over the hill

So when the prints come back
We can look at that unmistakable birthday fear
Like your younger days are over now
And it's all downhill from here

He also gets a new look at *over the hill* and *tiptop* while he's at it. Neat.

Without a terrific setup, duck whenever you see a cliché. They come easy and from all directions, so it's difficult not to be infected. Your own senses and experiences are your best protection. So is brutal and resolute rewriting. I don't mean to sound revolutionary, but you might also try a diet of good literature and poetry. You are what you eat.

★ EXERCISE 10 ★

For fun, try these two experiments. First, come up with your own lists of clichés, at least as long as my list above. (It won't be difficult.) Second, string some of yours and mine together into a verse / chorus / verse / chorus lyric, making sure nothing original sneaks in.

Knowledge brings responsibility. Now that you know the fundamental cause of puppy narcolepsy, you have a special responsibility to keep your writing sense-bound and original. No one likes a person who puts puppies to sleep.

CHAPTER SIX

PRODUCTIVE REPETITION

★ ★ ★ ★ ★ ★ ★ ★ ★ ★ ★ ★ ★ ★ ★

In its simplest form, this is the basic rule of songwriting: Keep your listeners interested all the way through your song. Get them with you from the beginning with a strong opening line, then keep them with you the rest of the way. Whether they stay or go is up to you.

In most songs, you'll repeat a line (refrain) or a section (chorus) two or three times. The danger is that once your listeners have heard something once, it will be less interesting the second and third time—like telling the same person the same joke three times in a row: Once you've heard it, it doesn't give you anything more the second or third time.

Your job as a songwriter is to make your repetition interesting and productive so that the same words deliver more each time. A bit of a challenge, eh?

It might be helpful to think about a song as a stack of boxes that are connected to each other, each one getting progressively larger. Think of each one gaining more weight, the last being the heaviest of the lot.

The first box begins the flow of ideas, introducing us to the song's world. The second box continues the idea, but from a different angle, combining the weight of the first box with the weight of the second. The last box builds from the first two, introducing its own angle and combining its idea with the first two, resulting in the heaviest box.

Assume you're working with the idea "I'd just like to know."

Box 1: "Hi, it's nice to see you. You're looking good, and you're looking really happy. Are you? I hope you don't mind my asking. I'd just like to know."

Let's try to advance the idea and make the second box gain weight.

Box 2: "When you left, did you already know you were moving in with him? When I was out of town, did he come over to your place? Did you hide that picture of us you kept on your dresser? I suppose it doesn't matter now, but I'd just like to know."

See how the idea gains weight with the new information? It combines the first box, the meeting, with some history, giving the second box more weight and giving more impact to the title.

Box 3: "For me, a relationship is all about honesty. I want to be able to say everything to you, and for you to say everything to me. I don't want any secrets, no matter what. You could have told me about him. I wouldn't have tried to stop you. I'd just like to know."

Box 3 combines or resolves all the information, and delivers the point of the song. It's often the "why" of the song—why I'm saying all this to you. It weighs the most.

Now, it's simply a matter of actually writing the song, but writing it knowing where you're going. You have an outline, a scaffold to hang your song on. You can bang around inside each box without being afraid of getting lost.

And don't be afraid to call your six best friends—who, what, where, when, why, and how—to ask them for specific suggestions. They're always helpful, especially *when* and *where*.

VERSE DEVELOPMENT

Your verses are responsible for keeping listeners interested. The verses develop your idea; they are the basic tool to advance your concept, plot, or story. They get us ready to hear each chorus or refrain—they control the angle of entry and the way we see the repeated elements. Like the paragraphs of an essay, each one should focus on a separate idea.

Say you've written a song with only verses, and the verse summaries go something like:

Verse 1. The sheriff is the toughest man in town.
Verse 2. He is very strong and has a fast gun.

Verse 3. Everyone in town knows the sheriff is tough. They are afraid of him.

The ideas don't move much. These verses say pretty much the same thing in different words. Obviously, you'd probably have written it in more interesting language, using sense-bound images and metaphors, but no matter how you polished the language, it would only disguise the fact that something important is missing: development.

The only real fix is to take the idea new places:

Verse 1. The sheriff is the toughest man in town.

Verse 2. He is obsessed with a beautiful woman.

Verse 3. She is married to the weakest man in town.

The language is still bland and imageless. Yet now we want to know what happens next. We had no such curiosity about the first sequence.

REPETITION

When you add a repeated element to these verses (a refrain or chorus), development becomes even more important. Stagnant verses will make your repeated element stagnant, too. The boxes won't grow. Watch:

Box 1

The sheriff is the toughest man in town.
Beware, beware. All hands beware.

Box 2

He is very strong and has a fast gun.
Beware, beware. All hands beware.

Box 3

Everyone in town knows the sheriff is tough.
They are afraid of him.
Beware, beware. All hands beware.

The refrain suffers from the same disease as the verses: stagnation. Boredom is amplified. The boxes, at best, are all the same size—they don't gain any weight. More likely, the boxes lose weight. You can feel the letdown when you get to the second and third boxes. You can only fix stagnation by developing the ideas. Like this:

Box 1

The sheriff is the toughest man in town.
Beware, beware. All hands beware.

Box 2

He is obsessed with a beautiful woman.
Beware, beware. All hands beware.

Box 3

She is married to the weakest man in town.
Beware, beware. All hands beware.

Now each refrain gains weight. The boxes get progressively larger because the verse ideas move forward—they each introduce their own idea or angle. When a refrain (or chorus) attaches to verses that mean the same thing, the result is boredom. When it attaches to verses that develop the idea, it gains weight and impact. It dances.

What about changing the chorus each time? Some songs do exactly that, but the definition of a chorus is "many people singing together." If you change the words each time, you'll be the only one able to sing it the second and third time. One person singing alone is called a soloist, not a chorus. If you change the words to a refrain each time, it isn't a refrain, just additional material.

Remember, you fix a stagnant chorus or refrain by doing the same thing you do if you have only verses—you develop the idea.

Don't waste your verses. Don't let them sit idle waiting for the hook to come around and rescue them. Too often, there won't be anyone around to witness the rescue.

PUT SEPARATE IDEAS IN SEPARATE BOXES

Look at this lyric, "Strawberry Wine" by Matraca Berg and Gary Harrison:

He was working through college on my grandpa's farm
I was thirsting for knowledge and he had a car

I was caught somewhere between a woman and a child
One restless summer we found love growing wild
On the banks of the river on a well beaten path
It's funny how those memories they last

Like strawberry wine and seventeen
The hot July moon saw everything
My first taste of love oh bittersweet
Green on the vine
Like strawberry wine

I still remember when thirty was old
And my biggest fear was September when he had to go
A few cards and letters and one long distance call
We drifted away like the leaves in the fall
But year after year I come back to this place
Just to remember the taste

Of strawberry wine and seventeen
The hot July moon saw everything
My first taste of love oh bittersweet
Green on the vine
Like strawberry wine

The fields have grown over now
Years since they've seen a plow
There's nothing time hasn't touched
Is it really him or the loss of my innocence
I've been missing so much

Strawberry wine and seventeen
The hot July moon saw everything
My first taste of love oh bittersweet
Green on the vine
Like strawberry wine

What a nice lyric. The specific images really take you there, involve your own sense memories, involve you in the song. And I love the bridge, using the grandpa's fields as a metaphor for life and experience. And the chorus, from the title right on through until the end, grows each time we hear it.

Who drinks strawberry wine? Kids. Strawberry wine has both the taste of soda pop (childhood) and the danger of alcohol (adulthood). Besides which, it's cheap. It's the perfect vehicle for a song about coming of age, moving from childhood to adulthood.

Watch the boxes develop:

Each new verse idea builds on the last and adds weight to the song, enlarging the boxes. Each line gains weight each time we see it. The last chorus is the most powerful.

If we simply look at the line *the hot July moon saw everything*, we'll see the weight gain clearly:

Box 1: The hot July moon saw us down by the river having our first experience.

Box 2: The hot July moon knew that our love, like so many before ("well-beaten path"), wouldn't last.

Box 3: The hot July moon knew that, over time, we'd become unable to experience the innocence and power of first love—accumulated experiences would create too much awareness—"the fields have grown over now."

The moon grows from an observer to a prophet and predictor of the future. It becomes a bigger and bigger moon, needing bigger and bigger boxes. When you write a chorus, each line you include has the same responsibility: to be able to gain weight.

Now look at this lyric, "Between Fathers and Sons" from John Jarvis and Gary Nicholson:

> My father had so much to tell me
> Things he said I had to know
> Don't make my mistakes
> There are rules you can't break
> But I had to find out on my own
>
> Now when I look at my own son
> I know what my father went through
> There's only so much you can do
> You're proud when they walk
> Scared when they run
> That's how it always has been between fathers and sons

It's a bridge you can't cross
It's a cross you can't bear
It's the words you can't say
The things you can't change
No matter how much you care
So you do all you can
Then you've gotta let go
You're just part of the flow
Of the river that runs between fathers and sons

Your mother will try to protect you
Hold you as long as she can
But the higher you climb
The more you can see
That's something that I understand
One day you'll look at your own son
There'll be so much that you want to say
But he'll have to find his own way
On the road he must take
The course he must run
That's how it always has been between fathers and sons

It's a bridge you can't cross
It's a cross you can't bear
It's the words you can't say
The things you can't change
No matter how much you care
So you do all you can
Then you've gotta let go
You're just part of the flow
Of the river that runs between fathers and sons

Another nice lyric. For me, it really hits home, especially in the first chorus. It touches both the son and the father in me.

"Between Fathers and Sons" is made up of two boxes. Verses one and two plus the first chorus make up box one. Verses three and four plus the second chorus make the second box. Let's look at the first box:

My father had so much to tell me
Things he said I ought to know
Don't make my mistakes
There are rules you can't break
But I had to find out on my own

The speaker looks back at his father's attempts to help smooth the way ahead, and his own unwillingness to listen. Stubborn kid. Had to do it for himself when all that help was available.

Now when I look at my own son
I know what my father went through
There's only so much you can do
You're proud when they walk
Scared when they run
That's how it always has been between fathers and sons

Now the speaker is the father, going through the same things with his own son. He understands what he did to his father, but understands that it was necessary, perhaps even inevitable.

That's how it always has been between fathers and sons

I love the structure of the verse—how it tosses in an extra line (line three), refuses to rhyme lines four and five, then extends the last line to focus our attention on the title. Lovely moves. Now the chorus:

It's a bridge you can't cross
It's a cross you can't bear
It's the words you can't say
The things you can't change
No matter how much you care
So you do all you can
Then you've gotta let go
You're just part of the flow
Of the river that runs between fathers and sons

So far, very effective stuff. I've been interested the whole time. What a nifty chorus. I love the play on *cross*:

It's a bridge you can't cross
It's a cross you can't bear

and I love the metaphor

You're just part of the flow
Of the river that runs between fathers and sons

The river is a divider of generations, but it's also the connector of generations. *Between* means "separation," but it also means "from one to the other." The pattern repeats from father to son to father to son to father. Neat word play. Both the message and the fancy dancing sweep me along. Now look at the second box:

Your mother will try to protect you
Hold you as long as she can
But the higher you climb
The more you can see
That's something that I understand

This sounds familiar. Not that I've seen things from the mother's perspective yet, but I have seen the father—in fact, both fathers—trying to protect the child. I've also seen the child trying to go beyond the parents. Not that this information isn't interesting, it's just not new. The ideas (if not the exact perspectives—*she* and *you*) have been covered. This doesn't bode well for the second chorus. We'll need development rather than restatement to keep repetition interesting.

One day you'll look at your own son
There'll be so much that you want to say
But he'll have to find his own way
On the road he must take
The course he must run
That's how it always has been between fathers and sons

Oops. I know I've been here before. It's verse two with *I* changed to *you*. No need to try to universalize verse four with *you*. The idea was already universal. The second chorus is a goner. It can't help but say exactly the same thing as the first chorus.

It's a bridge you can't cross
It's a cross you can't bear
It's the words you can't say
The things you can't change
No matter how much you care
So you do all you can
Then you've gotta let go
You're just part of the flow
Of the river that runs between fathers and sons

It isn't so much that there is no advancement of the idea in verses three and four, there just isn't enough to give us a new look at the chorus when we get there. The power of this lovely chorus is diminished rather than enlarged the second time around, and we leave the song less interested than we were in the middle. Both boxes are the same size. Let's see if we can make the second box grow.

The song contains two perspectives: a son looking at his father, and the son as father. If the first box could focus only on the son looking at his father, saying:

My father had so much to tell me
Things he said I ought to know
Don't make my mistakes
There are rules you can't break
But I had to find out on my own

Verse two idea (in prose):

I kept him at arm's length.
I didn't want him interfering with my life.
He kept trying, but I wouldn't let him.
That's how it always has been between fathers and sons

Now move into the chorus:

It's a bridge you can't cross
It's a cross you can't bear
It's the words you can't say
The things you can't change

No matter how much you care
So you do all you can
Then you've gotta let go
You're just part of the flow
Of the river that runs between fathers and sons

We see the first chorus from the son's point of view, colored only by the son's eyes. Now the second box is free to look from the other side of the river:

Now when I look at my own son
I know what my father went through
There's only so much you can do
You're proud when they walk
Scared when they run
That's how it always has been between fathers and sons

It's a bridge you can't cross
It's a cross you can't bear
It's the words you can't say
The things you can't change
No matter how much you care
So you do all you can
Then you've gotta let go
You're just part of the flow
Of the river that runs between fathers and sons

The father's perspective colors the second chorus. It becomes—for me, at least—more interesting than the first chorus. Here is a simple principle for division of labor: Put separate ideas in separate boxes.

The problem in "Between Fathers and Sons" is that both ideas are in the first box, leaving the lyric no place new to go. Separating the ideas into separate boxes makes both choruses fresh.

DEVELOPMENT TIPS

The principle of division of labor has practical applications for your song. Say you've written a verse whose summary is:

You are really wonderful
And I've been looking for someone just like you
We should be together

Love Love Love
Love Love Love

It's difficult to see where to go next. It feels like everything's been covered. Perhaps it might help to separate the perspectives, dividing the idea into the three different perspectives: (1) you, (2) I (me), and (3) we.

Box 1: You are amazing. And beautiful. Your blonde hair flows over your milky-white complexion like chicken gravy over mashed potatoes...

Love Love Love
Love Love Love

Box 2: I've been looking for a codependent relationship for a long time. Someone who'll mother me and let me do whatever I want to...

Love Love Love
Love Love Love

Box 3: We'll always be together. Everyone I've ever loved is still with me...in the downstairs freezer...

Love Love Love
Love Love Love

Okay, just kidding. But you can see how the boxes gain weight by separating the perspectives. Call it the "you-I-we" formula for lyric development: Each verse focuses from a different perspective. It's a nice guideline for dividing your verses' jobs.

Or this—you write a verse that says:

We were so good together
But now everything's falling apart
What's going to happen to us?

Love Love Love
Love Love Love

This idea contains three tenses: past, present, and future. Try separating them into separate boxes:

Box 1: We used to smile and laugh together, etc., so much in...

> Love Love Love
> Love Love Love

Box 2: Everything's turned sour. What happened to...

> Love Love Love
> Love Love Love

Box 3: Can we work to stay together, or drift away, only remembering how it felt to be in...

> Love Love Love
> Love Love Love

So tense can also provide access to verse development, just like perspective can. Sometimes one or the other will be just what you need; other times, like any formula, they could take the freshness out of your writing. Be aware of these techniques, just beware of letting them become a habit in your writing.

One more tip: Just because you wrote a verse first doesn't mean it's your first verse. Give yourself two chances. Don't just ask "Where do I go next?" Try asking "What happened before this?"

Thinking about boxes from the outset, the minute an idea comes, is by far the best remedy for "second-verse hell" (songwriters' term for "Where do I go next?").

It's better when you find an idea that contains the DNA of its own development, or when plot does the development work. Look at this lyric, "One More Dollar" from Gillian Welch:

> A long time ago I left my home
> For a job in the fruit trees
> But I missed those hills with the windy pines
> For their song seemed to suit me

So I sent my wages to my home
Said we'd soon be together
For the next good crop would pay my way
And I would come home forever

One more dime to show for my day
One more dollar and I'm on my way
When I reach those hills, boys
I'll never roam
One more dollar and I'm going home

No work said the boss at the bunk house door
There's a freeze on the branches
So when the dice came out at the bar downtown
I rolled and I took my chances

One more dime to show for my day
One more dollar and I'm on my way
When I reach those hills, boys
I'll never roam
One more dollar and I'm going home

A long time ago I left my home
Just a boy passing twenty
Could you spare a coin and a Christian prayer
For my luck has turned against me

One more dime to show for my day
One more dollar and I'm on my way
When I reach those hills, boys
I'll never roam
One more dollar and I'm going home

Wonderful stuff. See how the lyric pulls us in with its sense-bound imagery, turning us into participants rather than observers? *Her* words are full of *our* stuff. And look at the lyrics using the box structure. Watch how the chorus gains weight, transforming the meaning of the chorus each time:

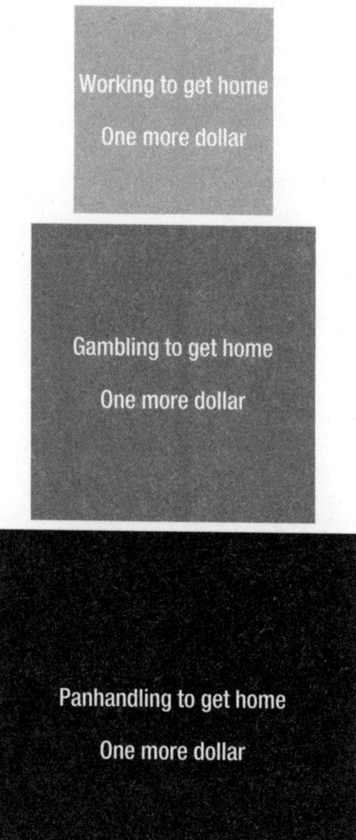

Each verse moves the story forward, making chances of getting home more and more remote. Great stuff!

Let's take a look at one last example, this one with a challenge in it. In this lyric, "Unanswered Prayers" written by Pat Alger, Garth Brooks, and Larry B. Bastian, the first two verses work to set up a clear situation:

> Just the other night at a hometown football game
> My wife and I ran into my old high school flame
> And as I introduced them the past came back to me
> And I couldn't help but think of the way things used to be

> She was the one that I'd wanted for all times
> And each night I'd spend prayin' that God would make her mine
> And if he'd only grant me that wish I'd wished back then
> I'd never ask for anything again

Now comes the punch line:

> Sometimes I thank God for unanswered prayers
> Remember when you're talkin' to the man upstairs
> That just because he doesn't answer doesn't mean he don't care
> Some of God's greatest gifts are unanswered prayers

With all the information we have so far, it's a little difficult to see how to develop the story much further. Here's verse three:

> She wasn't quite the angel that I remembered in my dreams
> And I could tell that time had changed me in her eyes too it seemed
> We tried to talk about the old days, there wasn't much we
> could recall
> I guess the Lord knows what he's doin' after all

Now follow it with the chorus:

> Sometimes I thank God for unanswered prayers
> Remember when you're talkin' to the man upstairs
> That just because he doesn't answer doesn't mean he don't care
> Some of God's greatest gifts are unanswered prayers

Is there anything gained? Not much. The boxes are roughly the same size. We already knew, from the combination of the first two verses and the chorus, how thankful he was not to be with his old girlfriend. This verse just elaborates on the same theme, giving us a few more details, including the old girlfriend's attitude. And the final line, *I guess the Lord knows what he's doin' after all*, just repeats the idea *just because he doesn't answer doesn't mean he don't care*.

In short, the second chorus is destined to die an ignominious death right there in front of everybody. Now the song moves into a bridge, followed by a third chorus:

And as she walked away I looked at my wife
And then and there I thanked the good Lord for the gifts in my life

Sometimes I thank God for unanswered prayers
Remember when you're talkin' to the man upstairs
That just because he doesn't answer doesn't mean he don't care
Some of God's greatest gifts are unanswered prayers

Much better. I had forgotten about the wife. The third chorus is interesting again; it gains weight by adding the wife. Go back and read the bridge followed by the whole chorus.

The wife becomes God's greatest gift. A lovely payoff.

Two out of three choruses work great, but the song sags at the second chorus. There isn't enough new information in verse three to make the chorus interesting. Other than leaving it alone as good enough (two out of three ain't bad ...), what would you do?

One possibility might be to reintroduce the wife in verse three and skip the bridge entirely, like this:

She wasn't quite the angel that I remembered in my dreams
And I could tell that time had changed me in her eyes too it seemed
As she turned and walked away I looked at my wife
And recognized the gift I'd been given in my life

Sometimes I thank God for unanswered prayers
Remember when you're talkin' to the man upstairs
That just because he doesn't answer doesn't mean he don't care
Some of God's greatest gifts are unanswered prayers

Now the song is a simple three verse, two chorus layout with both choruses doing their work. Read the entire lyric and watch how each chorus changes:

Just the other night at a hometown football game
My wife and I ran into my old high school flame
And as I introduced them the past came back to me
And I couldn't help but think of the way things used to be

She was the one that I'd wanted for all times
And each night I'd spend prayin' that God would make her mine
And if he'd only grant me that wish I'd wished back then
I'd never ask for anything again

Sometimes I thank God for unanswered prayers
Remember when you're talkin' to the man upstairs
That just because he doesn't answer doesn't mean he don't care
Some of God's greatest gifts are unanswered prayers

She wasn't quite the angel that I remembered in my dreams
And I could tell that time had changed me in her eyes too it seemed
As she turned and walked away I looked at my wife
And recognized the gift I'd been given in my life

Sometimes I thank God for unanswered prayers
Remember when you're talkin' to the man upstairs
That just because he doesn't answer doesn't mean he don't care
Some of God's greatest gifts are unanswered prayers

Very effective movement.

Okay, you caught me. I lied. The original version of the lyric that I gave you isn't the way the song was recorded. They did try to do it as verse / verse / chorus / verse / chorus / bridge / chorus, but it made the song, in Pat Alger's words, "feel too long." Another way of saying the song sagged, and listeners would lose interest. So what did they cut out?

Here's their solution, as recorded by Garth Brooks:

Just the other night at a hometown football game
My wife and I ran into my old high school flame
And as I introduced them the past came back to me
And I couldn't help but think of the way things used to be

She was the one that I'd wanted for all times
And each night I'd spend prayin' that God would make her mine
And if he'd only grant me that wish I'd wished back then
I'd never ask for anything again

Sometimes I thank God for unanswered prayers
Remember when you're talkin' to the man upstairs
That just because he doesn't answer doesn't mean he don't care
Some of God's greatest gifts are unanswered prayers

She wasn't quite the angel that I remembered in my dreams
And I could tell that time had changed me in her eyes too it seemed
We tried to talk about the old days, there wasn't much we could recall
I guess the Lord knows what he's doin' after all

And as she walked away I looked at my wife
And then and there I thanked the good Lord for the gifts in my life

Sometimes I thank God for unanswered prayers
Remember when you're talkin' to the man upstairs
That just because he doesn't answer doesn't mean he don't care
Some of God's greatest gifts are unanswered prayers

They left out the second chorus and went immediately to the bridge—an unusual formal move, especially in commercial music. But it works; both choruses shine, and we stay interested in the song all the way through.

Keeping the bridge gives the music a chance to breathe, since the verse lines are long and the tempo is slow. Creating a contrasting section helps the overall flow of the song. The formal risk pays off, creating interest and contrast at the same time. Put this move in your toolbox. It could come in handy.

Of course, there are no rules. The solution to the question "Where do I go now?" changes with every song. Sometimes it's even the wrong question. Just because you wrote a verse first doesn't mean it's the first verse. Instead of asking "Where do I go now?" it may help to ask "Where did I get here from?" Get used to juggling and trying new things.

★ EXERCISE 11 ★

Here's your assignment: Write three verses, each one ending with the line *ashes, ashes, all fall down.* (Call the line a refrain, because it's a part of the verse rather than a separate section.) You're writing a three-system song: verse / refrain / verse / refrain / verse / refrain.

Each verse / refrain system should advance the story line to the next place. Certainly *ashes, ashes, all fall down* has the element of childhood games in it. But where else could it go?

1. As a child, he sang in a circle with his playmates.
2. He volunteered to serve his country in the Great War. In the trenches, he suffered from shell shock and battle fatigue.
3. ?

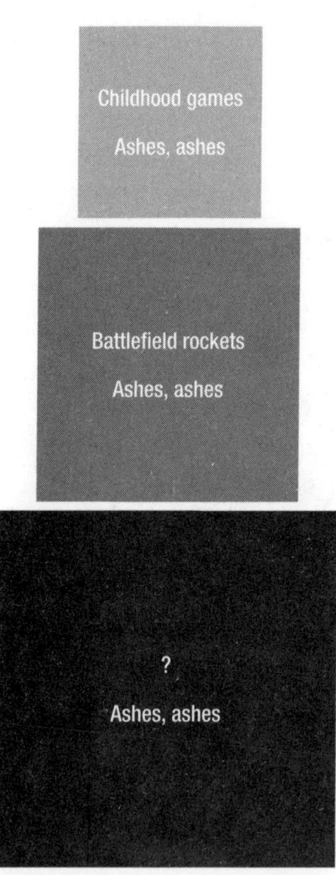

Maybe do some research on World War I and life in the trenches, looking for images and words that work both for childhood and for the war. Do some object writing to get something from your own sense pool. Try to see each idea you find as a metaphor for other parts of the lyric. For example, falling down certainly can go beyond the childhood game. Childhood dreams can fall. So can innocence. Bombs, rockets, and soldiers, too. What else?

Try to find ideas for the first box first, the childhood section. Then the second box, from the giggling child to the ashen face of the shell-shocked soldier, the dust from the rockets and gunpowder. Then find an angle for the third section—it shouldn't be too difficult. He certainly could tumble like a child whenever a door slams.

Go ahead and write the whole lyric. Remember that each verse should have its own job to do. Make the third box gain weight. Above all, take your time. This is a process. Enjoy it.

LINES WITHIN LINES

Generally speaking, as you write a song, you should be keeping your eyes peeled for something you can repeat. Something catchy or emotional. Something profound or funky, or something beautifully said. Something people might sing along to.

So how do you know what to repeat? Maybe the words just feel good in your mouth. Maybe there's a lot of internal sound making it easy and fun to sing, such as:

> Peaceful, easy feeling

There can be many reasons to repeat a line or a section, but let's take a look at one big one: The words we repeat stay interesting when we say them again. They gain something more when we repeat them, even gain something more *because* we repeat them.

Of course, that was the whole message of the boxes: Keep your listeners interested and engaged all the way through the song. You already know that the chorus should mean more the second time around. You're already a responsible citizen in the world of chorus repetition. You already practice productive repetition.

The second chorus of "Strawberry Wine" weighs more than the first chorus, because the second verse adds the weight of a fleeting summer romance to the first verse's picture of love on the riverbank. As we sing along, we feel something more than we did the first time. Productive repetition.

The second refrain of "Still Crazy After All These Years" adds the weight of cynicism and denial to the encounter with an old lover in verse one. We learn more about what kind of crazy he is, and how deep it runs. Productive repetition.

When we hear the repeated first verse at the end of Suzanne Vega's "Luka" or Joni Mitchell's "Roses Blue," we feel much more, having learned about the characters through the course of the songs. We know Luka's plight, though we didn't understand it the first time. We finally see the singer's predicament at the end of "Roses Blue." Productive repetition.

In each case, the repetition is productive because it gives the words more weight the second and third times than they had the first time. That's something useful. It keeps your listeners interested all the way through the song, and maybe even singing along.

Repetition can work on smaller scales, too. Not just when you repeat a section or a line, but inside a line itself.

Watch this, from Joni Mitchell's "Roses Blue":

> In sorrow she can lure you where she wants you
> Inside your own self-pity there you swim
> In sinking down to drown her voice still haunts you
> And only with your laughter can you win
> Can you win? Can you win?

In the last two lines, by simply isolating and repeating a portion of the line, *can you win*, she moves from a declarative sentence into a question, creating new energy and adding a new idea—in this case, the character's uncertainty whether winning (laughter) is possible.

Think of it as hunting for hidden treasures. Learn to start looking at sentences not just for meaning, but for little pieces of meaning that can be isolated and repeated, giving additional information or emphasis.

Look at this question:

Who do you love?

It starts with one of the interrogative pronouns (who, what, when, where, why, how). It also contains the auxiliary verb *do*. What if you drop *who*? It becomes:

Do you love?

Now you've got a brand new question. Simply repeat that smaller piece:

Who do you love? Do you love?

You've isolated a part of the sentence and repeated it, giving a new meaning. You can do it with the other interrogative pronouns, too:

What do you love? Do you love?
When do I love? Do I love?
Where do you go? Do you go?
Why do you laugh? Do you laugh?
How do you know? Do you know?

The auxiliary verb *do* can also introduce a question. That's what makes it work. You can do the same thing with the past and future tense, *did* and *will*:

Who did you love? Did you love?
What did you try? Did you try?
When did I know? Did I know?
Where did you go? Did you go?
Why did you laugh? Did you laugh?
How did you know? Did you know?

Who will you love? Will you love?
What will you try? Will you try?
When will I know? Will I know?
Where will you go? Will you go?
Why will you laugh? Will you laugh?
How will you know? Will you know?

How about the subjunctive (*can*, *could*, *should*, *would*) with the interrogative pronouns? Simply delete the pronoun:

> Who can you love? Can you love?
>
> Who could you love? Could you love?
>
> Who should you love? Should you love?
>
> Who would you love? Would you love?

(I'll leave it to you to fill out the other interrogative pronouns.)

You can find lots of opportunities for productive repetition. It's easy if you stay alert, as Joni Mitchell did when she discovered a question inside a statement:

> And only with your laughter can you win
> Can you win? Can you win?

Declarative sentences (or "statements") often can be easy prey for productive repetition. If the subject of the sentence is *you*, and the verb is present tense, there's usually a command (imperative) lurking, waiting to be isolated:

> You tell me that you want me.

Just delete the subject, isolating the verb, and presto, you have yourself a command:

> Tell me that you want me.

And even:

> Want me.

Note that this trick doesn't work in third person, since third person adds an *s* to the verb. You create only simple repetition—no command is isolated: *She tells me that she wants me. Tells me that she wants me. Wants me.*

Try it with:

You give me everything I need.

It becomes:

Give me everything I need.

You can isolate commands from questions using second-person direct address. For example:

Will you love me?
Love me.

Whenever you are working with present-tense verbs, look for the opportunity to repeat, starting from the verb, to create a command. Remember that this technique only works in first person and second person, not third person.

With past-tense or future-tense verbs, you can use the infinitive (*to*) form of the verb, so the verb can be isolated, creating a present-tense command:

Did (past) you want to win my heart? Win my heart.

He loved (past) to walk alone. Walk alone.

Won't (future) you try to walk alone?
Try to walk alone.
Walk alone.

Neat, huh?

When you move from one type of sentence to another, you create an energy boost that takes the emotion to a new level. It's just as a matter of practice. When you're writing a song, stay alert for chances to ask a question or give a command. It'll engage your listeners.

In general, be alert to the smaller grammatical units in your lines.
Sometimes they can do something really special.
Do something really special.
Would you like to be a better writer?
Be a better writer.

CHAPTER SEVEN

VERSE DEVELOPMENT AND POWER POSITIONS

Boxes represent the movement of ideas. They are form neutral. A series of three boxes can represent almost any formal movement:

- verse / chorus / verse / chorus / bridge / chorus
- verse / refrain / verse / refrain / bridge / verse / refrain (AABA)
- verse / pre-chorus / chorus / verse / pre-chorus / chorus / bridge / chorus
- verse / chorus / verse / chorus / verse / chorus

Boxes only show how the ideas evolve, regardless of the specific form you use. In this chapter, we'll look a little closer at the responsibility your verses have in making your boxes gain weight.

Think of your verses as colored spotlights. They shine their lights on their chorus or refrain. If two verses project exactly the same color, their choruses will look the same. If they project different or deeper colors, the choruses will look different.

When you keep your verses interesting and keep your idea moving forward, you'll have little trouble lighting up your chorus or refrain in different ways. You don't have to use formulas. You don't have to introduce a whole new cast of characters. You just have to pay attention.

Let's look at the verse development in Beth Nielsen Chapman's "Child Again." Each verse projects a deeper color on its chorus, enlarging our way of seeing it, keeping it interesting. We'll look at two areas of this lovely lyric:

1. Its use of repetition: Because of strong verse development, the chorus becomes a deeper and more interesting color each time we see it.
2. Its power positions light up the chorus with the right color from the right angle to put crucial ideas in the strongest focus.

Here is the full lyric of "Child Again":

Verse 1

She's wheeled into the hallway
Till the sun moves down the floor
Little squares of daylight
Like a hundred times before
She's taken to the garden
For the later afternoon
Just before her dinner
They return her to her room

Chorus

And inside her mind
She is running in the summer wind
Inside her mind
She is running in the summer wind
Like a child again

Verse 2

The family comes on Sunday
And they hover for a while
They fill her room with chatter
And they form a line of smiles
Children of her children
Bringing babies of their own
Sometimes she remembers
Then her mama calls her home

Chorus

And inside her mind
She is running in the summer wind
Inside her mind
She is running in the summer wind
Like a child again

Bridge (duet)

It's raining it's pouring	It's raining
The old man is snoring	Come out and play with me
Bumped his head on the edge of the bed	And bring your dollies three
And he never got up in the morning	Climb up my apple tree
Rain rain go away	Slide down my rain barrel
Come again another day	Into my cellar door
Little Johnny wants to play	And we'll be jolly friends
Some more	Forever more

Chorus

And inside her mind
She is running in the summer wind
Inside her mind
She is running in the summer wind
Like a child again

First Verse Focus

The first verse contains three scenes, each one showing the old woman being taken somewhere. She is physically helpless, a focus firmly established right away:

She's wheeled into the hallway
Till the sun moves down the floor
Little squares of daylight
Likes a hundred times before

This helplessness is reiterated by the following two scenes:

She's taken to the garden
For the later afternoon

Just before her dinner
They return her to her room

These scenes color the first chorus with helplessness. We see her helpless in the nursing home, being taken everywhere, but the chorus tells us:

Inside her mind
She is running in the summer wind
Inside her mind
She is running in the summer wind
Like a child again

We enter the chorus knowing her situation, and we are swept back to a time when she was *running in the summer wind / Like a child again*.

Since the verse puts her in a wheelchair, being taken and returned, we can't help but see running as a contrast. We interpret the chorus in the light of the verse.

Second Verse Focus

The second box turns the color of her relatives:

The family comes on Sunday
And they hover for a while
They fill her room with chatter
And they form a line of smiles

What terrific lines. Four generations are present in her room; no doubt she has little connection with the younger generations, nor do they have much with her:

Children of her children
Bringing babies of their own

She tries to pay attention, but her mind wanders off:

Sometimes she remembers
Then her mama calls her home

Chorus 2

And inside her mind
She is running in the summer wind

When the chorus repeats, we see her as a child with her own mother, a color carefully arranged by the second verse's focus on family. The emphasis is no longer on her running, but on the family (her mama) that she runs to, surrounded as she is by strangers. The second chorus lights up brilliantly, a new and different color made possible by strong verse development.

The bridge (an overlay of old-fashioned children's songs) is the coup de grâce. It shows us the colors of childhood inside her mind, or, more accurately, inside our own minds when we were children:

It's raining it's pouring	It's raining
The old man is snoring	Come out and play with me
Bumped his head on the edge of the bed	And bring your dollies three
And he couldn't get up in the morning	Climb up my apple tree
Rain rain go away	Slide down my rain barrel
Come again another day	Into my cellar door
Little Johnny wants to play	And we'll be jolly friends
Some more	Forever more

In our third and final look at the chorus, we see her with new eyes:

And inside her mind
She is running in the summer wind
Inside her mind
She is running in the summer wind
Like a child again

We see where she really is, back again with her mama, able to run home. Reality is doubled and reflected, colored by our knowledge that she is destined to follow her own mother all too soon, as inevitably as the generations crowding into her room will follow her. That is part of the point of showing us the children in the second verse, then showing her as a child running to her mama.

Many families visit relatives in nursing homes, and most leave saddened, often thinking, "She's losing it. She didn't even remember us." But to see their loved one in this new light for the first time *running in the summer wind / Like a child again* is an emotional revelation. It is this startling insight into the mind of the old woman that lights up radio station switchboards wherever "Child Again" is aired.

POWER POSITIONS

The opening and closing lines of any lyric section are naturally strong. They are bathed in spotlights. If you want people to notice an important idea, put it in the lights of a power position, and you will communicate the idea more forcefully. (For a full treatment of power positions, read my book *Songwriting: Essential Guide to Lyric Form and Structure.*) Look at the opening line of "Child Again": *She's wheeled into the hallway.*

Closing lines are also power positions, another place to light up an important idea. In "Child Again," the closing line prepares us to enter the chorus. I call it a trigger position, because it releases us into the chorus, carrying whatever the line says with us, and therefore we see the chorus in the light of the idea, *They return her to her room.*

Look at the first line and the last line of "Child Again" in combination, and you'll see how they focus the meaning of the chorus:

> She's wheeled into the hallway
> They return her to her room
>
> And inside her mind
> She is running in the summer wind ...
> Like a child again

Look at verse one carefully, and you'll see that it really contains two parts. The rhythm is basic common meter (like *Mary had a little lamb*), alternating first and third long phrases with shorter phrases in the second and fourth positions:

	rhyme	stresses
She's whéeled ínto the hállway	x	3+
While the sún moves dówn the flóor	a	3
Líttle squáres of dáylight	x	3+
Like a húndred tímes befóre	a	3

After these four lines, things are balanced. The structure has resolved. This creates a new beginning at line five—another power position. Look how it's used:

She's taken to the garden
For the later afternoon
Just before her dinner
They return her to her room

Taken is the first stressed syllable. Of the eight lines in the verse, two are opening positions, and two are closing positions. Look at the entire verse and see what messages the power positions communicate:

She's wheeled into the hallway
While the sun moves down the floor
Little squares of daylight
Like a hundred times before
She's taken to the garden
For the later afternoon
Just before her dinner
They return her to her room

Chapman makes sure we enter the first chorus from the angle of physical helplessness. She uses her power positions—the first and last positions of the verse, plus the ending and beginning of its subsections—to lock our focus in, forcing us to see the first chorus the color she wants us to. Neat.

Not So Powerful Power Positions

Look what happens with different ideas in the power positions:

While the sun moves down the hallway
She's wheeled out from her room

So many times she's been there
As the squares of daylight move
Then later in the garden
She's taken out of doors
They return her for her dinner
Down the hallway's polished floors

Chorus

And inside her mind
She is running in the summer wind...
Like a child again

Even though the beauty of the original verse has suffered, the ideas haven't really changed, only their placement has changed. Look at the information that's in the power positions now:

While the sun moves down the hallway
As the squares of daylight move
Then later in the garden
Down the hallway's polished floors

Chorus

And inside her mind
She is running in the summer wind...

Because the power positions focus us elsewhere, the chorus seems to stress her escape from routine rather than her physical disability.

Power Positions in Verse Two

The second verse introduces a different color with its opening and closing phrases:

The family comes on Sunday
Then her mama calls her home

This verse shifts focus to her room, where she is surrounded on Sunday by family visitors. They are external to her, shown by the brilliant metaphor closing the first subsection:

And they form a line of smiles

The family visits, mostly with each other. They are probably sad that she's "so out of touch," even though some of them are virtual strangers, four generations away.

The family seems almost oblivious as she seems to slip in and out of their reality. They don't have a clue of where she really is. The trigger line sets up the contrast between the external and the internal:

The family comes on Sunday
And they hover for a while
They fill her room with chatter
And they form a line of smiles
Children of her children
Bringing babies of their own
Sometimes she remembers
Then her mama calls her home

Chorus

And inside her mind
She is running in the summer wind ...
Like a child again

The power positions in this verse force the new color onto the chorus. Outside, the generations chatter on; inside lies a place of peace, memory, and happiness.

Each verse works beautifully to set up its special view of the chorus. The accumulation of the two systems delivers the knockout:

Verse 1

She's wheeled into the hallway
Like a hundred times before
She's taken to the garden
They return her to her room

Chorus

And inside her mind
She is running in the summer wind ...
Like a child again

Verse 2

The family comes on Sunday
And they form a line of smiles
Children of her children
Then her mama calls her home

Chorus

And inside her mind
She is running in the summer wind ...
Like a child again

Because her body is helpless, and because she is frustrated by the world her relatives seem so comfortable in, she seeks comfort in a kinder, gentler place away from boredom, routine, and frustration.

After the bridge shows us the colors of childhood again with her, old age becomes accessible; finally, we understand. That's the power of a perfectly developed song: It changes our way of looking at our lives and our surroundings.

More Power Positions

Opening and closing phrases are not the only way to create power positions. Wherever you create a special effect with your structure, you call attention to what you are saying. This extra focus gives the position its power. This one creates several power positions:

Mary had a little lamb
Its fleece was white as snow
And everywhere that Mary went
The lamb would go, indeed
He goes wherever Mary leads
He follows with devoted speed

The opening phrase, as usual, is a power position. So is the fourth phrase, since we expect it to close the section. But it gains extra punch by rhyming early, at the second rather than the third stress. Phrase five is unexpected, adding special interest. The final phrase is the most powerful of the bunch.

Look at all the power generated in this pretty structure in "Slow Healing Heart" by Jim Rushing:

When I left I left walking wounded	x
I made my escape from the rain	a
Still a prisoner of hurt	b
I had months worth of work	b
Freeing my mind of the pain	a
I had hours of sitting alone in the dark	c
Listening to sad songs and coming apart	c
Lords knows I made crying an art	c
Woe is a slow healing heart	c

When the third phrase ends short, the acceleration gets our attention. Then the fourth phrase chimes in, and the fifth phrase closes with a rhyme. Six is another opening and calls extra attention to its length. I could argue that seven is a power position as well, but I won't. Five out of nine is plenty of action, a tribute to interesting structures. We'll see more of this in later chapters.

Moral: First be aware of where your power positions are: opening positions, closing positions, and surprises, like shorter, longer, or extra lines. Pay attention as you create them, then put something important there. Everything will come up rosy, seafoam green, Tangiers blue, sun yellow ...

CHAPTER EIGHT

TRAVELOGUES

VERSE CONTINUITY

We've all seen travelogues. Ah, fabulous Hawaii—majestic mountains, pipeline surfing, luxury hotels, exotic cuisine. The places may be interesting, but as a film, a travelogue is dull, dull, dull. Its elements have no natural continuity. What do majestic mountains have to do with twenty-foot waves featuring pipeline surfing? What have either of these to do with elegant hotels and Oriental cuisine? Their only links are accidents of geography: They are all part of fabulous Hawaii!

A travelogue not only makes for a dull movie, it makes for dull verse development in a lyric. Look at this lyric summary:

Verse 1: Police brutality is a common problem in large cities.
Refrain: Streets are turning deadly in the dark.

Verse 2: Car bombs are becoming more common as a terrorist weapon.
Refrain: Streets are turning deadly in the dark.

Verse 3: More prostitutes carry the AIDS virus every year.
Refrain: Streets are turning deadly in the dark.

What's going on here? What does police brutality have to do with car bombs or prostitutes with AIDS? Nothing, except that they are all part of fabulous *Streets are turning deadly in the dark*. Aside from their connection to the refrain, the elements have no natural relationship—they don't belong together.

Verse development should mean verse relationship. Your verses should have a good reason to hang out together. When verses are in the same lyric only because you're taking a tour of the title, you likely have a travelogue on your hands.

Okay, so no one would actually write something like that, right? Wrong. In fact, it happens all the time—all too often in songs with serious political, ethical, or religious messages. This series of ideas is typical:

> **Verse 1:** We're screwing up our planet.
> **Refrain:** We're losing the human race.
>
> **Verse 2:** We're killing each other in stupid wars.
> **Refrain:** We're losing the human race.
>
> **Verse 3:** We ignore our poor and homeless.
> **Refrain:** We're losing the human race.

No matter how well written and interesting these verses get, the basic defect remains: The verses don't work together to accumulate power—they are simply a travelogue of human ineptitude. Important ideas deserve the most powerful presentation you can muster.

Your lyric accumulates power when your verses work together—using each verse to prepare what comes next. It's like starting avalanches. If you go a third of the way up the mountain and start three separate avalanches from different spots, you'll cause some damage to the town below, but not nearly as much as if you'd gone to the top and rolled one snowball all the way down. Speed and power accumulate and sweep everything away. The town is devastated. The boxes gain weight and power as the snow plummets down the mountain.

In a travelogue, all the boxes are the same size.

There's no real connection (other than the title) between the verses. The second box is isolated from the first and third. It's certainly a way to give us a new look at the title, but at the cost of forward momentum and accumulating power and weight. Although the strategy can work, it isn't optimum.

Let's get to work on verse development. We'll start by putting together a travelogue (on a serious subject), and then we'll try to fix it. Let's work with the idea of cycles of violence, using "Chain Reaction" as a title. Here's a starting verse and chorus:

Verse 1

Louis ducks behind the door
Patient as a stone
Listens, braces, hears the footsteps
Crip for sure and all alone
Steel barking, flashing, biting
Sinking to its home
Flesh to blood to heart to bone

Chorus

One more link in a chain reaction
Spinning round and round and round
A tiny step, a small subtraction
One more link in a chain reaction

Okay, gang warfare. One violent act will surely lead to another. But instead of using this scene to move us to the next act in the chain, we'll let the lyric make the easy move and randomly select another place. Here we are in some place like fabulous West Beirut:

Verse 2

Camille slips along the wall
Muslims stand their posts
Pulls the pin and lobs the metal
Perfect hook shot, crowd explodes
Spilling colors red and khaki
Gargles in their throats
Infidels and pagan hosts

Chorus

One more link in a chain reaction
Spinning round and round and round
A tiny step, a small subtraction
One more link in a chain reaction

However compelling the scene is, it is isolated; a single snowball a third of the way up the mountain. It's an equal-sized box, or at least a box that doesn't benefit from the weight of the first box. Because it relates to verse one only through the chorus, it doesn't build momentum. Its only power comes from what it is, not what it connects to. Verse one was a separate avalanche. It lent no power to verse two.

Now, one last stop in this travelogue of violence. How about racial hatred in fabulous old South Africa:

Verse 3

White boys rock the ancient Ford
Teeter-totter swing
Trapped inside, the children shudder
Afrikaner ditties ring
Drag the papa, slag the mama
Flames that lick and stink
Little buggers boil like ink

Chorus

One more link in a chain reaction
Spinning round and round and round
A tiny step, a small subtraction
One more link in a chain reaction

It's not that a lyric like this has no power, it just doesn't have the power it could have. Even when each scene in a travelogue is effectively presented, there is less total impact than there could have been if each verse had carried over into the next, accumulating power and momentum.

The test is to look at the verses without the chorus. Without knowing that all three events take place in fabulous "Chain Reaction," we wouldn't have a clue what's going on:

Verse 1

Louis ducks behind the door
Patient as a stone
Listens, braces, hears the footsteps

Crip for sure and all alone
Steel barking, flashing, biting
Sinking to its home
Flesh to blood to heart to bone

Verse 2

Camille slips along the wall
Muslims stand their posts
Pulls the pin and lobs the metal
Perfect hook shot, crowd explodes
Spilling colors red and khaki
Gargles in their throats
Infidels and pagan hosts

Verse 3

White boys rock the ancient Ford
Teeter-totter swing
Trapped inside, the children shudder
Afrikaner ditties ring
Drag the papa, slag the mama
Flames that lick and stink
Little buggers boil like ink

Now, instead, we'll try developing one continuous fabric. It doesn't matter which verse we pick, just so all the other verses roll down the same mountain with it. Let's start with verse one and develop from there:

Verse 1

Louis ducks behind the door
Patient as a stone
Listens, braces, hears the footsteps
Crip for sure and all alone
Steel barking, flashing, biting
Sinking to its home
Flesh to blood to heart to bone

Chorus

One more link in a chain reaction
Spinning round and round and round

A tiny step, a small subtraction
One more link in a chain reaction

Verse 2

Straightens up now cool and thin
Checking out his score
That's for Iggy, dirty bastard
Gargled blood in memory's roar
Circle turf in hasty exit
One more hero born
Mamas screaming dark and torn

Chorus

One more link in a chain reaction
Spinning round and round and round
Another turn, another fraction
One more link in a chain reaction

Verse 3

Gathered hands in rings of steel
They weld a sacred vow
Swing down low, chariot wheeling
Rolling dark across the town
Mad archangel's scabbard flashing
Cut another down
Driving by on bloody ground

Chorus

One more link in a chain reaction
Spinning round and round and round
Another turn, another fraction
One more link in a chain reaction

The linking of the verses gives the whole lyric momentum. Each box lends weight to the next box. Look at the results when we leave out the chorus:

Verse 1

Louis ducks behind the door
Patient as a stone

Listens, braces, hears the footsteps
Crip for sure and all alone
Steel barking, flashing, biting
Sinking to its home
Flesh to blood to heart to bone

Verse 2

Straightens up now cool and thin
Checking out his score
That's for Iggy, dirty bastard
Gargled blood in memory's roar
Circle turf in hasty exit
One more hero born
Mamas screaming dark and torn

Verse 3

Gathered hands in rings of steel
They weld a sacred vow
Swing down low, chariot wheeling
Rolling dark across the town
Mad archangel's scabbard flashing
Cut another down
Driving by on bloody ground

Now the verses show the circle of violence, and the chorus gains power each time because the information carries over from verse to verse, adding weight and momentum to each scene.

★ EXERCISE 12 ★

Start with either verse two or verse three of the original and write two more verses to make a story. (Keep the same chorus, and be sure to follow the current verse rhyme scheme and rhythm.) You'll notice the power and momentum your lyric develops as the verses accumulate into one full-blown strategy.

Verse development is probably a lyricist's trickiest job. Verse ideas must advance enough, but can't move too much. If the ideas are too close, the repetition of the chorus will become static and boring. If the verses' ideas are too far apart, you might end up in fabulous Hawaii. Hawaii is a nice place, but songwriters beware how you get there. The best trip is paid for by royalty checks from great songs.

CHAPTER NINE

STRIPPING YOUR REPETITION FOR REPAINTING

Strong verse development is crucial to deepening the colors of your refrain or chorus. Just as important, however, is making sure your refrain chorus *can* be recolored. Sometimes it can resist recoloring, no matter how well your verses develop. Look at this example:

Exploding from the starting blocks
Again he set the pace
Though he was crowned by laurel wreaths
As thousands cheered he came to grief
He lost the human race

Yessirree, what a refrain: *He lost the human race*. Even a double meaning! Of course, now you have to figure out what to say next so the refrain will be as interesting the second time as it was the first. Let's try:

It's hard see through miles ahead
To shoulders bent by age
With crowds of whispers drawing tight
He'll tilt his head one final night

Oops! You can't say *He lost the human race*. It won't go with the future tense in *He'll tilt his head one final night*. The refrain has to change:

It's hard see through miles ahead
To shoulders bent by age
With crowds of whispers drawing tight
He'll tilt his head one final night
He'll lose the human race

Though this isn't the kiss of death, it would be preferable to avoid changing the refrain if you can. Then everyone can sing along each time.

A good lyric works hard for interesting verse development that colors the same refrain a new shade each time, so it's frustrating when a refrain or chorus proves to be color resistant—the words in the refrain or chorus won't work with the next verse without changing the words somehow because they're protected from receiving the next verse's color by coats and coats of verbal polyurethane.

Too often, a problem with verb tense or an inconsistent point of view (POV) blocks effective recoloring.

You can often solve the problem by neutralizing the refrain's tense and POV—stripping away protective coatings so your refrain can accept the colors the verses try to paint.

NEUTRALIZING TENSES

Verbs determine tenses:

> **Past:** He lost the human race.
> **Present:** He loses the human race.
> **Future:** He'll lose the human race.

Controlling verbs is the key to controlling tense. Here are three ways:

1. Use the *-ing* form of the verb (e.g., *losing*). Omit any helping verbs (*losing* instead of *is losing, was losing, will be losing*). Don't mistake the *-ing* verb form for verbal adjectives (participles), e.g., *a losing strategy*, or for verbal nouns (gerunds), e.g., *losing builds character.*
2. Use the *to* form of the verb (infinitive) and omit the main verb, e.g., *to lose* rather than *I hate to lose*.
3. Omit verbs altogether.

A tense-neutral refrain will accept whatever tense the verse throws at it. Look at what the *-ing* verb form does for our refrain, no matter what tense the verse takes:

Past tense

Exploding from the starting blocks
Again he set the pace
Though
he was crowned by laurel wreaths
As thousands cheered he came to grief
Losing the human race

Present tense

Exploding from the starting blocks
Again he sets the pace
Although he's crowned by laurel wreaths
As thousands cheer he comes to grief
Losing the human race

Future tense

Exploding from the starting blocks
Again he'll set the pace
Though he'll be crowned by laurel wreaths
As thousands cheer he'll come to grief
Losing the human race

Now let's add our second verse:

Present tense

Exploding from the starting blocks
Again he sets the pace
Although he's crowned by laurel wreaths
As thousands cheer he comes to grief
Losing the human race

Future tense

It's hard see through miles ahead
To shoulders bent by age
With crowds of whispers drawing tight
He'll tilt his head one final night
Losing the human race

The neutralized refrain works with the tense of both verses. Let's try the infinitive:

Present tense

Exploding from the starting blocks
Again he sets the pace
Although he's crowned by laurel wreaths
As thousands cheer he comes to grief
To lose the human race

Future tense

It's hard see through miles ahead
To shoulders bent by age
With crowds of whispers drawing tight
He'll tilt his head one final night
To lose the human race

Again, the neutralized refrain accepts any tense. Whichever results you like better, the *-ing* form or the infinitive, it's nice to have the option. Let's try the third technique—leaving out the verb altogether. In this case, it makes the refrain sound like a commentary:

Present tense

Exploding from the starting blocks
Again he sets the pace
Although he's crowned by laurel wreaths
As thousands cheer he comes to grief
A loss in the human race

Future tense

It's hard see through miles ahead
To shoulders bent by age
With crowds of whispers drawing tight
He'll tilt his head one final night
A loss in the human race

Always try all three options. Use whichever feels best.

NEUTRALIZING POINT OF VIEW

Pronouns determine POV:

> **First person:** I lose the human race
> **Second person:** You lose the human race
> **Third person:** She loses the human race

To strip your refrain's POV, omit pronouns. Sometimes you'll have to neutralize verb tenses, too. We'll look at that later.

Look back at our tense-neutral refrain, *Losing the human race*. It not only neutralizes the verb, it also omits pronouns, freeing each verse to set its own POV. The neutral refrain accepts them all:

First person (singular)

Exploding from the starting blocks
Again I set the pace
Although I'm crowned by laurel wreaths
As thousands cheer I'll come to grief
Losing the human race

First person (plural)

Exploding from the starting blocks
Again we set the pace
Although we're crowned by laurel wreaths
As thousands cheer we'll come to grief
Losing the human race

Second person

Exploding from the starting blocks
Again you set the pace
Although you're crowned by laurel wreaths
As thousands cheer you'll come to grief
Losing the human race

Third person (singular)

Exploding from the starting blocks
Again she sets the pace
Although she's crowned by laurel wreaths

As thousands cheer she'll come to grief
Losing the human race

Third person (plural)

Exploding from the starting blocks
Again they set the pace
Although they're crowned by laurel wreaths
As thousands cheer they'll come to grief
Losing the human race

When you use third person with present tense, the verb adds an *s*: She loses. If you don't use *he*, *she*, or *it* in your lyric, none of your verbs will add an *s*, so your verbs will all already by POV neutral. You won't need to neutralize the verbs—you just need to drop the pronouns:

First person (singular)

Exploding from the starting blocks
Again I set the pace
Although I'm crowned by laurel wreaths
As thousands cheer I'll come to grief
And lose the human race

First person (plural)

Exploding from the starting blocks
Again we set the pace
Although we're crowned by laurel wreaths
As thousands cheer we'll come to grief
And lose the human race

Second person

Exploding from the starting blocks
Again you set the pace
Although you're crowned by laurel wreaths
As thousands cheer you'll come to grief
And lose the human race

Third person (plural)

Exploding from the starting blocks
Again they set the pace

Although they're crowned by laurel wreaths
As thousands cheer they'll come to grief
And lose the human race

Be careful, though. *And lose the human race* works only in present tense. If you change to past, you're in trouble:

Third person (plural)

Exploding from the starting blocks
Again they set the pace
Though they were crowned by laurel wreaths
As thousands cheered they came to grief
And lose the human race

You'd need to neutralize the verb tense, too, back to *losing the human race.*

Now, the real thing. Paul Simon's refrain in "Still Crazy After All These Years" has no pronouns and no verb. The result is a refrain that can accept the POV and tense from each verse:

I met my old lover on the street last night
She seemed so glad to see me, I just smiled
And we talked about some old times
And we drank ourselves some beers
Still crazy after all these years

I'm not the kind of man who tends to socialize
I seem to lean on old familiar ways
And I ain't no fool for love songs
That whisper in my ears
Still crazy after all these years...

Now I sit by my window and I watch the cars
I fear I'll do some damage one fine day
But I would not be convicted
By a jury of my peers
Still crazy after all these years

Because the refrain is stripped of action, the first verse is able to color it with three different POVs:

I am still crazy after all these years
She was still crazy after all these years
We were still crazy after all these years

All three work fine. The result is a productive ambiguity that adds to the spell of the lyric.

Verse two's possible interpretations of the refrain include: *I am* still crazy after all these years, and *you are* still crazy after all these years.

We can almost hear the jukebox whispering "Hey fella, you're still crazy about her after all these years." Again, the POV swabs multiple colors on the refrain, creating depth. In the third verse, my peers wouldn't convict me because *I would be* still crazy after all these years, or *they would be* still crazy after all these years. *I* could cop a plea of insanity. *They* would understand, being, as my peers, crazy themselves. Again, the neutral refrain contributes productivity to the ambiguity.

STRIPPING YOUR CHORUS

Neutralize a chorus the same way you neutralize a refrain: Don't use a tense or POV. Here's a prototype neutral chorus:

Losing the human race
Losing the human race
Yeah, yeah, yeah
Losing the human race

See how easy it works with a verse:

Exploding from the starting blocks
Again he sets the pace
Although he's crowned by laurel wreaths
As thousands cheer he comes to grief
No reprieve

Chorus

Losing the human race
Losing the human race
Yeah, yeah, yeah
Losing the human race

Like a refrain, a neutral chorus will accept the verse's tense and POV, no matter how many times you change them in the lyric. Remember as a rule of thumb that verses show, chorus tells. Keep your verses specific and interesting.

Okay, the prototype chorus is pretty dumb. But you could add more lines and find interesting rhymes. Make it as specific and artistic as you want to, just don't commit to a tense or a POV. Like this:

Chorus

Losing the human race
Falling from heaven's grace
No way to stop it
Only a dot in space
Losing the human race

None of the lines commit to tense or POV. They either use *-ing* (lines one, two, and five), the infinitive (line three), or omit the verb altogether (line four). This stripped chorus will accept any POV and tense:

Exploding from the starting blocks
Again he sets the pace
Although he's crowned by laurel wreaths
As thousands cheer he comes to grief
No reprieve

Chorus

Losing the human race
Falling from heaven's grace
No way to stop it
Only a dot in space
Losing the human race

He doesn't see the miles ahead
Shoulders bent by age
With crowds of whispers drawing tight
He'll tilt his head one final night
Slip from sight

Chorus

Losing the human race
Falling from heaven's grace
No way to stop it
Only a dot in space
Losing the human race

Try it with a verse using second person, past tense:

Exploding from the starting blocks
Again you set the pace
Though you were crowned by laurel wreaths
As thousands cheer you came to grief
There was no reprieve

Chorus

Losing the human race
Falling from heaven's grace
No way to stop it
Only a dot in space
Losing the human race

The same chorus works fine. You don't have to neutralize your refrain or chorus for every lyric, but when your verses change tense and POV, it's good to know how to get your repetitive section ready for the new colors. Stripping away tense and POV, is often the key to success.

EXERCISE 13

Neutralize the refrain *I fell too hard.* Don't read ahead until you're finished. You should have three versions, something like these: *falling too hard*, *to fall too hard*, and *too hard a fall.* Let your verses establish the tense and POV, and any of the three would work just fine. Here's a chorus to neutralize:

I'm ready for love
I search for the good stuff
I hope I can find enough
I'm ready for love

Have fun.

CHAPTER TEN

PERSPECTIVES

Whenever you put pen to paper, you must answer a few fundamental questions: Who is doing the talking? Is it you personally? Is it a character you're creating? What should that character's relationship to the audience be? A storyteller? A confessor? Something else?

You write for an instrument—a singer (maybe you) who faces the audience and delivers your words. The point of view you choose controls the relationship between the singer and the audience. It sets the context for your ideas.

You control this choice. You control the singer's role (and, therefore, your audience's relationship to the singer) by choosing between the four possible points of view: third-person narrative, second-person narrative, first-person narrative, and direct address.

Point of view controls our distance from the world of the song. Think of it as a movie camera, allowing the audience to look at the song's world from various distances, from long shots to close-ups. Roughly, it looks like this:

POINT OF VIEW: CAMERA ANGLES

Most Intimate (Close-up: Feelings)			Most Objective (Long Range: Facts)
Direct Address	Second Person Narrative	First Person Narrative	Third Person Narrative

Let's look at the three main points of view: third-person narrative, first-person narrative, and direct address. We'll deal with second-person narrative separately in chapter twelve.

THIRD-PERSON NARRATIVE

In third-person narrative, the singer acts as a storyteller who simply directs the audience's attention to an objective world neither the singer nor the audience is a part of. They look together at a third thing, an objective, independent world. If you think in terms of film, this is the long-distance, panoramic view. We, the audience, are simply observing the song's world. We are not participants.

You can tell third person by its pronouns:

	Singular	**Plural**
Subject:	he, she, it	they
Direct object:	him, her, it	them
Possessive adjective:	his, her, its	their
Possessive predicate:	his, hers, its	theirs

e.g. Possessive adjective: "That is *her* responsibility."
Possessive predicate: "The responsibility is *hers*."

In third-person narrative, both the singer and the audience turn together to look at the song's world. The singer functions as storyteller or narrator, and the audience observes. Take a look at Buck Ram's "The Great Pretender," in third-person narrative:

Yes, she's the great pretender
Pretending that she's doing well
Her need is such, she pretends too much
She's lonely but no one can tell

Yes, she's the great pretender
Adrift in a world of her own
She plays the game, but to her real shame
He's left her to dream all alone

Too real is her feeling of make-believe
Too real when she feels what her heart can't conceal

Yes, she's the great pretender
Just laughing and gay like a clown
She seems to be what she's not, you see
She's wearing her heart like a crown
Pretending that he's still around

Imagine watching a singer perform the song. Either gender could sing it, no problem. As an audience, we would look at the pretender along with the singer. Neither we nor the singer participates in the world. Here's another example of third-person narrative:

Sentimental Lady

The sidewalk runs from late day rainfall
Washes scraps of paper up against the grate
Backing up in shallow puddles
Oil floats like dirty rainbows
She hardly seems to notice as she steps across the street

Knows where she's headed for
She goes inside
Shuts the door

Chorus

Sentimental lady
Doesn't mind it when it's raining
Doesn't seem to matter when it ends
Sentimental lady
Sips her tea in perfect safety
Smiles her secret smile and pretends

Polished floors of blonde and amber
Hanging ivies lace her windows smooth and green
Soft inside these graceful patterns
Lost in thought she reads his letters
All that matters kept inside in memories and dreams

Knows where she has to be
Tucked away
Alone and free

Chorus

Sentimental lady
Doesn't mind it when it's raining
Doesn't seem to matter when it ends
Sentimental lady
Sips her tea in perfect safety
Smiles her secret smile and pretends

She made her mind up long ago
Not to look again
Her life was full
She sits content
Knows she's had its best

Chorus

Sentimental lady
Doesn't mind it when it's raining
Doesn't seem to matter when it ends
Sentimental lady
Sips her tea in perfect safety
Smiles her secret smile and pretends

FIRST-PERSON

A first-person narrative is also a storytelling mode, but instead of being separate from the action, the singer participates. There is some intimacy here. The audience knows something about the singer, who speaks directly *to* the audience *about* other people and events. The other people and events are still at a distance from the audience.

Here are the first-person pronouns:

	Singular	**Plural**
Subject:	I	we
Direct object:	me	us
Possessive adjective:	my	our
Possessive predicate:	mine	ours

In a first-person narrative, the first-person pronouns mix with third-person pronouns. There is no *you*.

The Great Pretender

Oh yes, I'm the great pretender
Pretending that I'm doing well
My need is such, I pretend too much
I'm lonely but no one can tell

Yes, I'm the great pretender
Adrift in a world of my own
I play the game, but to my real shame
He's (or she's) left me to dream all alone

Too real is this feeling of make-believe
Too real when I feel what my heart can't conceal

Yes, I'm the great pretender
Just laughing and gay like a clown
I seem to be what I'm not, you see
I'm wearing my heart like a crown
Pretending that he's (or she's) still around

We, the audience, have some level of intimacy with the singer, but we are still observers to the rest of the song's world. The singer is a participant, revealing something about himself or herself, so the gender of the singer and the pronouns will now make a difference. In film terms, this is the middle-distance shot. Look at this:

Digging for the Line

My daddy loved the greyhounds
Oh he lived to watch 'em run
Breathless as they slow danced past
Like bullets from a gun
Muscles wound like springs of steel
Aching to unwind
Caught up in their rhythm
Daddy swayed in perfect time
Even when the chains of age
Left him weak and blind
He still could feel their rhythm
Digging for the line

Even as a child I knew
The greyhounds never won
Though one of them might finish first
It wasn't why they'd run
Sliding on a rail of steel
A rabbit made of clay
Stayed up just ahead of them
Led the dancers all the way
Circle after circle
Panting just behind
They ran with grace and beauty
Digging for the line

It hurt to see them run
A race they'd never win
But daddy smiled and made me see
This is what he said to me

A greyhound lives for running
It's the strongest drive he has
And though he never wins the race
The losing's not so bad
If he never ran at all
In time he'd surely die
The only world he cares to know
Is one that's always streaking by
It isn't what runs up ahead
It isn't what's behind
The beauty's in the way it feels
Digging for the line

The narrator tells the story, but includes him/herself in it. In the last verse, daddy is quoted by the narrator while we are allowed to eavesdrop.

First-Person Narrative

Let's see what happens when we change "Sentimental Lady" into first-person narrative:

The sidewalk runs from late day rainfall
Washes scraps of paper up against the grate
Backing up in shallow puddles
Oil floats like dirty rainbows
I hardly seem to notice as I step across the street

I know where I'm headed for
I go inside
I shut the door

Chorus

Sentimental lady
I don't mind it when it's raining
Doesn't seem to matter when it ends
Sentimental lady
I sip my tea in perfect safety
Smile my secret smile and pretend

This sounds odd. She's saying external or descriptive things about herself, like "I hardly seem to notice as I step across the street." Observations like this are best left to a third-person narrator.

Polished floors of blonde and amber
Hanging ivies lace my windows smooth and green
Soft inside these graceful patterns
Lost in thought I read his letters
All that matters kept inside in memories and dreams

Know where I have to be
Tucked away
Alone and free

Chorus

Sentimental lady
I don't mind it when it's raining
Doesn't seem to matter when it ends
Sentimental lady
I sip my tea in perfect safety
Smile my secret smile and pretend

Again it sounds unnatural for her to say, "Lost in thought I read his letters." The language is more appropriate from the mouth of an observer than from the mouth of a participant. Finally, the bridge:

I made my mind up long ago
Not to look again
My life was full
I'll sit content
Knowing I've had its best

Chorus

Sentimental lady
I don't mind it when it's raining
Doesn't seem to matter when it ends
Sentimental lady
I sip my tea in perfect safety
Smile my secret smile and pretend

The bridge sounds natural in first person, since she's telling us something about herself we couldn't know from simply looking. Of course, looking into a character's mind is also perfectly appropriate in third-person narrative.

If we really were to make sense of "Sentimental Lady" as a first-person narrative, the perspective would have to shift in several places:

The sidewalk runs from late day rainfall
Washes scraps of paper up against the grate
Backing up in shallow puddles
Oil floats like dirty rainbows
Splashed by cooling raindrops as I step across the street

I know what I'm headed for
Slip inside
Shut the door

Chorus

I'm a sentimental lady
I don't mind it when it's raining
Doesn't *really* matter when it ends

A sentimental lady
Sipping tea in perfect safety
Tucked away in secret with a friend

I love these floors of blonde and amber
Hanging ivies lace my windows smooth and green
I live inside these graceful patterns
Afternoons I read his letters
All that matters here inside my memories and dreams

I know where I *need* to be
Tucked away
Alone and free

Chorus

I'm a sentimental lady
I don't mind it when it's raining
Doesn't really matter when it ends
A sentimental lady
Sipping tea in perfect safety
Tucked away in secret with a friend

I made my mind up long ago
Not to look again
My life was full
I sit content
Knowing I've had its best

Chorus

I'm a sentimental lady
I don't mind it when it's raining
Doesn't really matter when it ends
A sentimental lady
Sipping tea in perfect safety
Tucked away in secret with a friend

Okay, so the rewrite could be more elegant. The point is that it works better. The trick is to put yourself in her mind—look from her perspective, and say what comes naturally.

Back to Third-Person Narrative

As a further exercise, go back and try changing "Digging for the Line" into a third-person narrative. It's an interesting problem, isn't it? First there's the pronoun problem: you have to make daddy's child *she* to keep the *he*s from getting all jumbled together. Instead of:

His daddy loved the greyhounds
Oh he(?) lived to watch 'em run

You have to say:

Her daddy loved the greyhounds
Oh he lived to watch 'em run

Even with that problem solved, you end up with a story about a father telling a story to his daughter. Seems a little complicated:

Her daddy loved the greyhounds
Oh he lived to watch 'em run
Breathless as they slow danced past
Like bullets from a gun
Muscles wound like springs of steel
Aching to unwind
Caught up in their rhythm
He swayed in perfect time
Even when the chains of age
Left him weak and blind
He still could feel their rhythm
Digging for the line

Even as a child *she* knew
The greyhounds never won
Though one of them might finish first
It wasn't why they'd run
Sliding on a rail of steel
A rabbit made of clay
Stayed up just ahead of them
Led the dancers all the way
Circle after circle

Panting just behind
They ran with grace and beauty
Digging for the line

It hurt to see them run
A race they'd never win
But her daddy smiled and made her see
What it really means

He said, a greyhound lives for running
It's the strongest drive he has
And though he never wins the race
The losing's not so bad
If he never ran at all
In time he'd surely die
The only world he cares to know
Is one that's always streaking by
It isn't what runs up ahead
It isn't what's behind
The beauty's in the way it feels
Digging for the line

Daddy told me this story is an acceptable premise for a song, but *here's a story about someone telling a story* seems more remote. The playwright Henrik Ibsen said, "If you put a gun in Act I, it damn well better go off by the end of the play!" This is more than a principle about effective use of props. It says that you should have a reason for each element in your work. Nothing without its purpose. No duplication of function.

Maybe the daughter is a gun that isn't going off. Let's see what happens if we eliminate her altogether:

Edwin loved the greyhounds
He lived to watch 'em run
Breathless as they slow danced past
Like bullets from a gun
Muscles wound like springs of steel
Aching to unwind
Caught up in their rhythm

He swayed in perfect time
Even when the chains of age
Left him weak and blind
He still could feel their rhythm
Digging for the line

Even as a child *he* knew
The greyhounds never won
Though one of them might finish first
It wasn't why they ran
Sliding on a rail of steel
A rabbit made of clay
Stayed up just ahead of them
Led the dancers all the way
Circle after circle
Panting just behind
They ran with grace and beauty
Digging for the line

It hurt to see them run
A race they'd never win
But as he grew old he learned to see
What it really means

A greyhound lives for running
It's the strongest drive he has
And though he never wins the race
The losing's not so bad
If he never ran at all
In time he'd surely die
The only world he cares to know
Is one that's always streaking by
It isn't what runs up ahead
It isn't what's behind
The beauty's in the way it feels
Digging for the line

Much cleaner than with two characters. Simplify, simplify, simplify. The only question now is: Which do you prefer, the first-person narrative or the third-person narrative? The key will be in the third verse. We will choose between listening in a more intimate situation to the singer telling us what he/she learned from daddy, or observing Edwin from a distance as he discovers the meaning of running:

FIRST-PERSON NARRATIVE	THIRD-PERSON NARRATIVE
But daddy smiled and made me see	But as he grew old he learned to see
This is what he said to me	What it really means
Son, a greyhound lives for running	A greyhound lives for running
It's the strongest drive he has	It's the strongest drive he has
And though he never wins the race	And though he never wins the race
The losing's not so bad	The losing's not so bad
If he never ran at all	If he never ran at all
In time he'd surely die	In time he'd surely die
The only world he cares to know	The only world he cares to know
Is one that's always streaking by	Is one that's always streaking by
It isn't what runs up ahead	It isn't what runs up ahead
It isn't what's behind	It isn't what's behind
The beauty's in the way it feels	The beauty's in the way it feels
Digging for the line	Digging for the line

In first person, the singer as character/storyteller is right in front of us. We feel like we know him/her. But third person is cleaner and more focused in this case, because it eliminates a character. Your call.

DIRECT ADDRESS

In direct address (sometimes inaccurately called second person), the singer (the first person, I) is talking to some second person (you), or maybe even right to the audience.

This is the close-up, the most intimate a song can be. You can see the lip quivering and the jaw muscles tightening with emotion. This is about feelings, not facts.

Here are the pronouns for direct address:

	Singular	**Plural**
Subject:	you	you
Direct object:	you	you
Possessive adjective:	your	your
Possessive predicate:	yours	yours

Second-person pronouns are mixed with first-person pronouns to produce direct address—contact between *I* and *you*.

The Great Pretender
Yes, I'm the great pretender
Adrift in a world of my own
I play the game, but to my real shame
You've left *me* to dream all alone

Too real is this feeling of make-believe
Too real when I feel what my heart can't conceal

Yes, I'm the great pretender
Just laughing and gay like a clown
I seem to be what I'm not, you see
I'm wearing my heart like a crown
Pretending that *you're* still around

This is the camera close-up. The singer sings directly to another person or people. (In English, there is no difference between singular and plural *you*, unless we resort to *y'all* or *youse* as plural forms, both forms intended as sophistications in a barren language that forgot to make the distinction.) Because of the direct contact, second person is the most intimate of the points of view. As a listener:

- I imagine the singer is singing to me, or
- I watch the singer singing directly to someone else, real or imagined by the singer, or

- I can imagine that the singer is someone I know singing to me, or
- I can identify with the singer and sing to someone I know.

However I do it, it's pretty intimate. Below, the singer speaks to the image of someone in his past:

As Each Year Ends

Becky Rose, you stole the night
Body dark, a sash of light
Soft you slippered from my bed
Not to wake me, dressing slow
How I watched I still don't know
I should have knelt and bowed to you instead

Chorus

As each year ends and one more breaks
I'll raise my wineglass high
To praise your beauty, you who touched my life
Though seasons bend, and colors fade
The memories still remain
I'll taste them once again as each year ends

Becky, how you broke my faith
Tearful as you pulled away
Dust of years and miles apart
Storms of summer rolled in slow
So hard it was, our letting go
That even now its shadows cross my heart

Chorus

As each year ends and one more breaks
I'll raise my wineglass high
To praise your beauty, you who touched my life
Though seasons bend, and colors fade
The memories still remain
I'll taste them once again as each year ends

Years like water join and run
Faces fade, too soon become

A taste of sadness on the tongue

Chorus

As each year ends and one more breaks
I'll raise my wineglass high
To praise your beauty, you who touched my life
Though seasons bend, and colors fade
The memories still remain
I'll taste them once again as each year ends

Even though Becky Rose is not in the singer's presence, it's still pretty intimate stuff. Compare it to a system of first-person narrative:

Becky Rose stole the night
Her body dark, a sash of light
Soft *she* slippered from my bed
Not to wake me, dressing slow
How I watched I still don't know
I should have knelt and bowed to *her* instead

Chorus

As each year ends and one more breaks
I'll raise my wineglass high
To praise *her* beauty, *she* who touched my life
Though seasons bend, and colors fade
The memories still remain
I'll taste them once again as each year ends

Now look at the system as a third-person narrative:

Becky Rose stole the night
Her body dark, a sash of light
Soft she slippered from *his* bed
Not to wake *him*, dressing slow
How *he* watched *he* doesn't know
He should have knelt and bowed to her instead

Chorus

As each year ends and one more breaks
He raises his wineglass high

To praise her beauty, she who touched *his* life
Though seasons bend, and colors fade
The memories still remain
He tastes them once again as each year ends

What do you lose? Are there any gains? One thing changes: The chorus can be in present rather than future tense. A third-person narrative can have a larger overview of time, stating simply, *He tastes them once again as each year ends.*

From the first person, the singer promises to continue raising his glass: *I'll taste them once again as each year ends.*

I don't have a problem making a choice here. I prefer the intimacy of direct address. Does that mean we should always go for intimacy?

★ EXERCISE 14 ★

Try rewriting "Sentimental Lady" and "Digging for the Line" in direct address before you answer the question above. Go on, do it.

It's impossible to make a rule about when to use each point of view. The only way to make sure your point of view is working the most effectively it can is to do a point of view check on every lyric you write. Check once during the process, and then also at the end of the process. Every lyric. You'll find that a different point of view works better often enough to make checking every time worth it. It only takes a little practice and not much time, and sometimes it will turn a good lyric into a killer one.

But as you've seen, direct address can get pretty complicated. The next two chapters will deal with some of its challenges.

CHAPTER ELEVEN

POINT OF VIEW:

SECOND PERSON AND THE HANGMAN

"Just wait till your father gets home, young man!" said Mom, rolling her eyes in exasperation.

I was really going to get it. She'd tell Dad and I'd be lucky to see anything but my bedroom walls for weeks. More likely, this time I'd probably swing, twisting slowly in the wind.

Hours crawled by. Finally, the whirr of his Pontiac sliding into the driveway. Please God, let him suddenly remember something back at the office. Slam. Clomp clomp clomp.

Murmurs downstairs, then: "Come down for dinner, children." False sweetness in my executioner's voice. They're always nice right before they stretch your neck and watch your eyeballs pop. My sisters and I slid into our chairs, me reluctantly, them bright with expectation.

A casserole had never looked so gray, maybe tinged a little green. She let the minutes stack as Dad doused his cottage cheese with Tabasco sauce. I could hear the rope being flung over a high branch, checked for strength, the noose tested. Finally, she spoke: "Well, young man, you've had quite a day today, haven't you?"

Aarrgh. That tightening sensation, breath coming harder.

"You're eleven years old, and should know better, shouldn't you?"

They always start by telling you how old you are.

"First, you sneak the BB gun out of the closet, where it is supposed to stay unless you have supervision!"

Dad chewed his cottage cheese and scowled, a dot of Tabasco sauce on his chin.

Why doesn't she just tell *him*? Why does she always have to say it to me?

"You could have stayed inside," she continued. "But oh no, mister smarty pants, mister grown-up. You have to take it outside and shoot it! Were you aiming at Mister Nelson's window, trying to break it?"

Actually, I was trying to kill a bird. Never even noticed the window.

"You hit his living room mirror, too, didn't you?"

Dad sat bolt upright, as though he felt someone going after his wallet.

She knew the facts, and I knew the facts. The girls knew the facts. Dad was the only one who didn't know, so why was she telling me instead of him? More pleasure in the execution?

"And what did he say it would cost? *One hundred and seventy-two dollars*, that's what!" She sat back, sagging and weak from the burden of having me for a son. My sisters flushed with delight, pulling for the hangman.

Dad reddening and rising. The feeling of my feet leaving the floor, a tightening in my throat, and the sound of the wind in the trees ...

Sometimes, lyrics sound like Mom. They seem to be talking directly to you, but are really telling someone else what you already know. Like this:

> I met you on a Saturday
> Your hair was wound in braids
> You walked up and you said hello
> And then you asked my name

This sounds unnatural because *you* already knows all this stuff. The verse is trying to do two things at once: Tell the audience the facts, while pretending to carry on a conversation with *you*. Technically, we have a point of view problem: second person trying to do first or third person's job. Don't give the facts to someone who already should know them!

Though it's tempting to try to give the audience facts by letting them eavesdrop on a conversation, be careful. You might end up with something as stilted and unnatural sounding as the little gem above. First-person narrative would sound closer to what's really happening:

I met her on a Saturday
Her hair was wound in braids
She walked up and she said hello
And then she asked my name

Third-person narrative is better, too:

He met her on a Saturday
Her hair was wound in braids
She walked up and she said hello
And then she asked his name

Moving into first- or third-person narrative is one way to solve the problem. But sometimes you may be committed to second person. In that case, you have to find a way to make the conversation sound more natural. Do you really want the audience to know that it was Saturday and she had braids and she made the first move? If not, just drop the unnatural verse and write a better, more natural one. If the facts are important, you have to say them naturally, like you would in a real conversation:

I never felt anything quite as strong
As I did that Saturday night we met
You looked so fresh with your hair in braids
And I felt like singing
When you walked right up and asked my name

Including personal information that *you* couldn't have known makes the conversation more natural. Or this:

I still remember the Saturday night we met
Your hair so pretty, up in braids
You blew me away when you said hello
And asked me, "What's your name?"

Both of these versions work because they include the singer's reactions to the facts. Okay, so it's not great writing. Even so, it still sounds more natural, and once you know what approach to take, you can always polish up the language. The second version also includes the old "do you remember" ploy for introducing information. Put it in your own bag of tricks.

No matter what the point of view is, mothers will always have their modes of torment. This natural use of second person is maddeningly effective. Any mother would be proud to use it.

The point is simple: Make second person conversational. If you want to give the audience a history lesson, either put it in third person or find a natural way to list your facts. If you've gotta swing, make it quick and natural.

As a matter of habit, you should try out all three points of view—first, second, and third person—for each lyric you write from now until you die, just to make sure you are using the best possible one for each song. Read your lyric aloud, each time substituting the different pronouns to see which you like best. Sometimes, a change in point of view will raise a bland lyric from the dead.

CHAPTER TWELVE

POINT OF VIEW:
SECOND PERSON AS NARRATIVE

When you tell a story, it is usually narrative, either first person or third person. As we've seen, first-person narrative includes the storyteller in the story, using first-person and third-person pronouns. Third-person narrative uses only third-person pronouns: *he*, *she*, *it*, *they*. There is no *I*.

The following lyric, "The Fire Inside" by Bob Seger, took me by surprise, because it has all the qualities of a narrative, but it uses second person (*you*):

> There's a hard moon risin' on the streets tonight
> There's a reckless feeling in your heart as you head out tonight
> Through the concrete canyons to the midtown light
> Where the latest neon promises are burning bright
> Past the open windows on the darker streets
> Where unseen angry voices flash and children cry
> Past the phony posers with their worn out lines
> The tired new money dressed to the nines
> The lowlife dealers with their bad designs
> And the dilettantes with their open minds
> You're out on the town
> Safe in the crowd
> Ready to go for the ride
> Searching the eyes
> Looking for clues

There's no way you can hide
The fire inside

Well you've been to the clubs and the discotheques
Where they deal one another from the bottom of the deck of promises
Where the cautious loners and emotional wrecks
Do an acting stretch as a way to hide the obvious
And the lights go down and they dance real close
And for one brief instant they pretend they're safe and warm
Then the beat gets louder and the mood is gone
The darkness scatters as the lights flash on
They hold one another just a little too long
And they move apart and then move on
On to the street
On to the next
Safe in the knowledge that they tried
Faking the smile, hiding the pain
Never satisfied
The fire inside

Now the hour is late and he thinks you're asleep
And you listen to him dress and you listen to him leave like you knew
he would
You hear his car pull away in the street
Then you move to the door and you lock it
When he's gone for good
Then you walk to the window
And you stare at the moon
Riding high and lonesome through the starlit sky
And it comes to you how it all slips away
Youth and beauty are gone one day
No matter what you dream or feel or say
It ends in dust and disarray
Like wind on the plains
Sand through the glass
Waves rolling in with the tide
Dreams die hard
And we watch them erode

But we cannot be denied
The fire inside

What's going on with Seger's use of second person? Second person is usually direct address—*I* talking to *you*. But there's no *I*. Sometimes *you* can be used as a substitute for first person. That's the way I sometimes talk to myself: "Come on, Pat, can't you be clear for once?" instead of "I wish I could be clear for once."

Try reading through the whole first verse in first-person narrative:

There's a hard moon risin' on the streets tonight
There's a reckless feeling in my heart as I head out tonight
Through the concrete canyons to the midtown lights
Where the latest neon promises are burning bright
Past the open windows on the darker streets
Where unseen angry voices flash and children cry
Past the phony posers with their worn out lines
The tired new money dressed to the nines
The lowlife dealers with their bad designs
And the dilettantes with their open minds
I'm out on the town
Safe in the crowd
Ready to go for the ride
Searching the eyes
Looking for clues
There's no way I can hide
The fire inside

Clearly, Seger is not using *you* as a disguise for *I*.

Continue the first-person substitution until you finish the whole lyric. Of course, the pronouns have to change in verse three (at least with a Seger lead vocal):

Now the hour is late and *she* thinks I'm asleep
And I listen to *her* dress and I listen to *her* leave like I knew she would
I hear *her* car pull away in the street
Then I move to the door and I lock it
When *she's* gone for good

Then *I* walk to the window
And *I* stare at the moon
Riding high and lonesome through the starlit sky
And it comes to *me* how it all slips away
Youth and beauty are gone one day
No matter what *I* dream or feel or say
It ends in dust and disarray
Like wind on the plains
Sand through the glass
Waves rolling in with the tide
Dreams die hard
And we watch them erode
But we cannot be denied
The fire inside

The result is a clear first-person narrative. But something gets lost: a kind of universal feeling that *you* seems to add.

Let's try the lyric in third person:

There's a hard moon risin' on the streets tonight
There's a reckless feeling in *her* heart as *she* heads out tonight
Through the concrete canyons to the midtown lights
Where the latest neon promises are burning bright
Past the open windows on the darker streets
Where unseen angry voices flash and children cry
Past the phony posers with their worn out lines
The tired new money dressed to the nines
The lowlife dealers with their bad designs
And the dilettantes with their open minds
She's out on the town
Safe in the crowd
Ready to go for the ride
Searching the eyes
Looking for clues
There's no way she can hide
The fire inside

Continue reading the whole lyric in third person. Take your time. Now it's a clear third-person narrative, landing squarely in storytelling mode.

Second-person narrative serves up a tricky combination of third-person narrative (where we watch the character) and direct address (talking right to the character). Part of it works like using *you* as a substitute for *one* (e.g., "You get what you pay for" is the same as "One gets what one pays for").

> There's a hard moon risin' on the streets tonight
> There's a reckless feeling in one's heart as one heads out tonight

Now stir in the illusion of direct address by using *you* instead of *one*:

> There's a hard moon risin' on the streets tonight
> There's a reckless feeling in *your* heart as *you* head out tonight

Think back to our point of view scale (see page 111). The intimacy of second-person narrative comes from its suggestion of direct address. We expect *I* to appear from behind the curtain at any moment. It just never happens.

Second-person narrative actively forces us to say, "This character could easily be me." The universal theme set up in the lovely third verse helps, too. One key to the lyric's success is the move to first-person plural at the end:

> And it comes to you how it all slips away
> Youth and beauty are gone one day
> No matter what you dream or feel or say
> It ends in dust and disarray
> Like wind on the plains
> Sand through the glass
> Waves rolling in with the tide
> Dreams die hard
> And *we* watch them erode
> But *we* cannot be denied
> The fire inside

We forces the listener into the emotion.

One test for second-person narrative: Does it translate easily into third person? Try it with another second-person narrative, Steely Dan's "Kid Charlemagne":

> While the music played
> *You* worked by candlelight
> Those San Francisco nights
> *You* were the best in town
> Just by chance *you* crossed the diamond with the pearl
> *You* turned it on the world
> That's when *you* turned the world around

★ EXERCISE 15 ★

Go ahead and translate it into third person:

> While the music played
> *He* worked by candlelight …

Finish it.

And now, translate it into first-person narrative:

> While the music played
> *I* worked by candlelight …

Finish it.

Each narrative mode makes you look at the lyric differently. Which do you like better for "Kid Charlemagne"? Yup. I like second-person narrative best here too. But a cautionary note: Don't dash out and turn all your third-person narratives into second person. Beware of the hangman: Don't tell facts to someone who should already know them!

You can also leave the narrative mode, using second person as a substitute for *I*, as in, "C'mon, can't you be clear for once?" Or as an internal command: "C'mon, be clear for once!" Leonard Cohen's "Dress Rehearsal Rag" is a good example. In it, the character is standing in front of a mirror getting ready to shave:

... Look at your body now, there's nothing much to save
And a bitter voice in the mirror cries "Hey, Prince, you need a shave"
Now, if you can manage to get your trembling fingers to behave
Why don't you try unwrapping a stainless steel razor blade ...
... Cover up your face with soap, there, now you're Santa Claus
And you've got an "A" for anyone who will give you his applause ...

I suppose we could call it an internal monologue or dialogue. One thing is clear: Narrative it ain't.

Practice with points of view. Get in the habit of checking every lyric you write from each point of view. Sometimes a change will make all the difference. Mostly, you'll get your best results with direct address and with standard first- and third-person narratives. But don't let that keep you from checking out second-person narrative. When it works, it works big time.

CHAPTER THIRTEEN

DIALOGUE AND POINT OF VIEW

Conversation overheard in a country home, using a surveillance microphone:

> **Alphonse:** What gifts can I bring you to prove that my love for you is true? I want to make you mine forever. There's nothing on this Earth I would not do.
>
> **Emma Rae:** Anything I have wanted, you have given willingly. So now there's only one more thing I need: If you love me, give me wings. Don't be afraid if I fly. A bird in a cage will forget how to sing; if you love me, give me wings.
>
> **Alphonse** (walking over to the window, staring into space)**:** I just want to protect you, because this world is a dangerous place.
>
> **Emma Rae** (putting her arms around him)**:** I know you mean well, but there's lessons I must learn for myself. If you love me, give me wings. Don't be afraid if I fly. A bird in a cage will forget how to sing; if you trust me, give me wings. Up above the clouds you can see forever, and I know you and I could learn to fly together. If you love me, give me wings. Don't be afraid if I fly. A bird in a cage will forget how to sing; if you trust me, give me wings. If you really love me, give me wings.

Gosh, what a nice conversation. It even rhymes. How would you turn this dialogue into a song? Think about it for a minute. Go back, read it again, and try it.

No, it probably isn't a duet. Duets need equal characters, both of whom can say the same chorus. Emma Rae is the only one here who can say "Give me wings." Unless you're writing opera (sung dialogue), you're better off having one singer tell us about the conversation, complete with quotes. The real trick is selecting a point of view to set the whole thing up.

Here are your options:

1. FIRST-PERSON NARRATIVE

I asked her, "What gifts can I bring you
To prove that my love for you is true?"

Or:

He asked me, "What gifts can I bring you
To prove that my love for you is true?"

In first-person narrative, the singer tells us about a conversation he/she actually had with some third party. Like someone coming in to work and saying, "Guess who I talked to yesterday. You'll never believe who he was with!" And then telling you the story.

2. DIRECT ADDRESS

I asked you, "What gifts can I bring you
To prove that my love for you is true?"

In direct address, the singer is talking either directly to us, or to some unseen you. We're watching him/her have a conversation with a second person.

3. THIRD-PERSON NARRATIVE

He asked her, "What gifts can I bring you
To prove that my love for you is true?"

Now our singer is a storyteller, pointing to a scene in the distance. The singer isn't in the story, and neither are we.

Let's try all three.

First-Person Narrative

I asked her, "What gifts can I bring you
To prove that my love for you is true?

Want to make you mine forever
There's nothing on this Earth I would not do"

She said, "Anything I have wanted
You have given willingly
So now there's only one more thing I need

If you love me, give me wings
Don't be afraid if I fly
A bird in a cage will forget how to sing
If you love me, give me wings"

I walked over to the window
Silently stared into space
And said, "I just want to protect you
'Cause this world is a dangerous place"

She put her arms around me
She said "I know you mean well,
But there's lessons I must learn for myself

If you love me, give me wings
Don't be afraid if I fly
A bird in a cage will forget how to sing
If you trust me, give me wings"

She said, "Up above the clouds you can see forever
And I know you and I could learn to fly together

If you love me, give me wings
Don't be afraid if I fly
A bird in a cage will forget how to sing
If you trust me, give me wings
If you really love me, give me wings"

The point of view works okay, but something is askew. The emotion feels off balance, a little forced. Why is this guy standing up there with his microphone telling us the story, anyway? What's his point?

Maybe the source of the problem is that the lyric is about *her*, not *I*. Our first version of first-person narrative shines the spotlight on the wrong person. In order for the male character to sing the song, he'd have to have something important to say about the story at the end, like in the final line of Don Schlitz's "The Gambler": *But in his final words I found an ace that I could keep*. Maybe something like: *I gave her her freedom, and we've been great ever since / Soaring together, lovers and friends.*

So let's try it the other way. Since it is her story, maybe she should be the narrator:

He asked me, "What gifts can I bring you
To prove that my love for you is true?
Want to make you mine forever
There's nothing on this Earth I would not do"

I said, "Anything I have wanted
You have given willingly
So now there's only one more thing I need

If you love me, give me wings
Don't be afraid if I fly
A bird in a cage will forget how to sing
If you love me, give me wings"

Go back to the first version and make the rest of the changes.

This point of view is better, but not terrific. Again, why is she raising the microphone and telling us these facts? We'd still need something like: *He gave me my freedom, and we've been great ever since / Soaring together, lovers and friends.*

Moral: If the singer is the *I* in the story, you've got to give him/her a good reason for telling it.

Direct Address

Next, let's get up close and personal:

> I asked you, "What gifts can I bring you
> To prove that my love for you is true?
> Want to make you mine forever
> There's nothing on this Earth I would not do"
>
> You said, "Anything I have wanted
> You have given willingly
> So now there's only one more thing I need
>
> If you love me, give me wings
> Don't be afraid if I fly
> A bird in a cage will forget how to sing
> If you love me, give me wings"
>
> I walked over to the window
> Silently stared into space
> I said, "I just want to protect you
> 'Cause this world is a dangerous place"
>
> You put your arms around me
> Said "I know you mean well,
> But there's lessons I must learn for myself
>
> If you love me, give me wings ..."

Total disaster—the worst of history lessons. The *you* of the song was already there during the conversation, so what's the point of telling her about it again? The same is true if the woman sings the song:

> You asked me, "What gifts can I bring you
> To prove that my love for you is true?"

As we saw in chapter eleven, "Second Person and the Hangman," simply telling people what they already know doesn't make for credible dialogue.

Third-Person Narrative

Finally, look at the point of view of the actual lyric of this song, "Give Me Wings," by Don Schlitz and Rhonda Kye Fleming:

He asked her, "What gifts can I bring you
To prove that my love for you is true?
I want to make you mine forever
There's nothing on this Earth I would not do"

She said, "Anything I have wanted
You have given willingly
So now there's only one more thing I need

If you love me, give me wings
Don't be afraid if I fly
A bird in a cage will forget how to sing
If you love me, give me wings"

He walked over to the window
Silently stared into space
He said, "I just want to protect you
'Cause this world is a dangerous place"

She put her arms around him
She said, "I know you mean well,
But there's lessons I must learn for myself

If you love me, give me wings
Don't be afraid if I fly
A bird in a cage will forget how to sing
If you trust me, give me wings"

She said, "Up above the clouds you can see forever
And I know you and I could learn to fly together

If you love me, give me wings
Don't be afraid if I fly
A bird in a cage will forget how to sing
If you trust me, give me wings
If you really love me, give me wings"

Nifty. It doesn't matter if the singer is male or female, the dialogue seems complete and natural. This doesn't mean that third-person narrative is always the right answer for every lyric that uses dialogue. You should read every lyric you write in each point of view. See how each one feels, then decide which one works best.

Something on structure while we're here.

There's more to like about this little gem of a lyric, so while we're here, let's take a quick look at its structure, a really nice display of technical savvy.

The verses are fairly balanced—four lines in common meter, rhyming xaxa:

	Rhyme	**Stresses**
He asked her, "What gifts can I bring you	x	3+
To prove that my love for you is true?	a	3
Want to make you mine forever	x	3+
There's nothing on this Earth I would not do"	a	3

Pretty standard stuff. But beware, it's a setup to lull you into a false sense of security.

The section between the verse and chorus (call it whatever you want to—vest, pre-chorus, prime, lift, channel, runway, climb—I call it a transitional bridge) throws us off balance with its three lines:

> She said, "Anything I have wanted
> You have given willingly
> So now there's only one more thing I need"

Or, if you like, two lines of wickedly unequal length:

> She said, "Anything I have wanted you have given willingly
> So now there's only one more thing I need"

We are toppled into the chorus, praying to find a secure landing. Perfect. That's what a transitional bridge is supposed to do.

Once we're securely into the chorus, things seem okay. The first two lines feel sturdy, balancing each other with three stresses:

If you love me, give me wings
Don't be afraid if I fly

Then a four-stress line sets up a little more tension:

A bird in a cage will forget how to sing

Boy, do we ever want a three-stress line rhyming with *fly*. How come? The aba rhyme scheme, wings/fly/sing, begs for a pairing with the unrhymed word. What do you want to hear? Maybe something like:

If you love me, give me wings
Don't be afraid if I fly
A bird in a cage will forget how to sing
I must soar beyond the sky

Okay, my line is pretty cheesy, but even so, it does the job, resolving the tension nicely, both structurally and emotionally. The rhyme structure, wings/fly/sing/sky, feels much more resolved than the situation of the song intends. She's asking for, not getting, wings. That's why the real chorus's rhyme scheme, abaa, is so perfect:

If you love me, give me wings
Don't be afraid if I fly
A bird in a cage will forget how to sing
If you love me, give me wings

The last line fools you (I call it a deceptive cadence), and in doing so, it accomplishes three things: (1) it repeats the title—a good commercial move; (2) the structural surprise spotlights the title; and (3) it resolves the chorus, though not as solidly as a rhyme for *fly* would have. The surprise rhyme is emotionally better suited to the intent of the chorus since it's a little less secure.

Neat structure. It lights up the title and supports the emotion of the lines with perfect prosody. I'm glad we looked.

CHAPTER FOURTEEN

METER:
SOMETHING IN COMMON

The sea captain of Western popular music is the eight-bar musical section, subdivided into two- and four-bar units. Expressed in quarter notes, old salty looks like this:

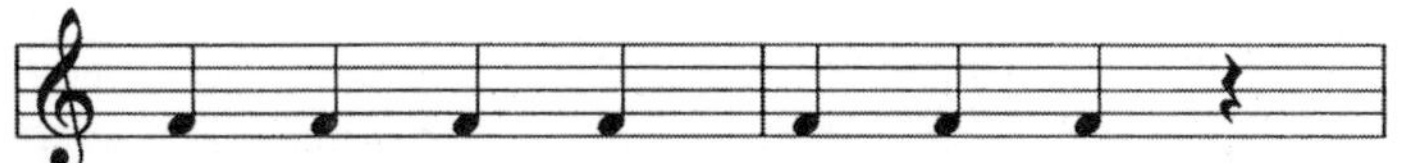

The eight-bar system is really one piece. Each of the subdivisions is a landmark along the voyage, giving directions and charting relationships. The end of bar two rests:

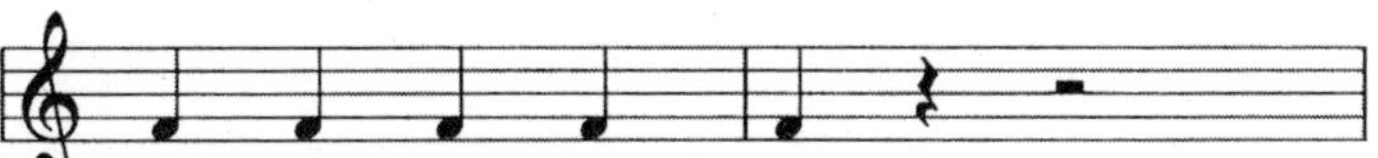

Then we tack into bars three and four:

What a different trip this section is (probably headed into the wind). Though we're at the end of four bars, we certainly feel unbalanced, and must continue:

That's better; now we're in familiar territory. Not only that, but we know exactly what to expect next. Because of the match between bars one and two and bars five and six, we expect bars seven and eight to match bars three and four. When they do, we have arrived at the end of the trip. We feel stable:

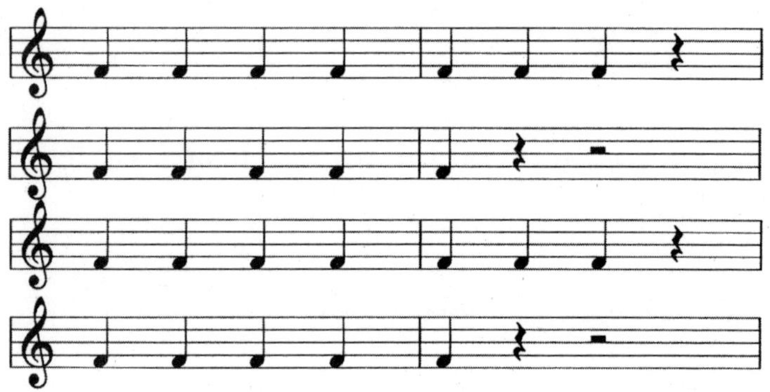

Of course, this has been a very simple trip, but you'd be surprised how basic it is to Western music, from Bach to Berry. Go back and take another look at the complete thing, and, while you're at it, mark the strong and weak notes in each two-bar group:

DUM da DUM da DUM da DUM	4 stresses
DUM da DUM da DUM	3 stresses
DUM da DUM da DUM da DUM	4 stresses
DUM da DUM da DUM	3 stresses

The continuous voyage is organized according to a very simple principle: longer / shorter / longer / shorter.

You can't stop until you get to port. Now look at this simple nursery rhyme:

Máry hád a líttle lámb	4 stresses
Its fléece was whíte as snów	3 stresses

And éverywhére that Máry wént	4 stresses
The lámb was súre to gó	3 stresses

Yup, it has something in common with the voyage we just took:

DUM da DUM da DUM da DUM	4 stresses
DUM da DUM da DUM	3 stresses
DUM da DUM da DUM da DUM	4 stresses
DUM da DUM da DUM	3 stresses

Like the eight-bar unit, this meter is the staple of songwriters, from the early troubadours to Tom Waits. It is even called common meter, partly because of its pervasiveness (the basis of nursery rhymes—e.g., "Mary, Mary, Quite Contrary," "Old Mother Hubbard"), and partly because of its relationship to musical form. Imagine our old seafarer singing:

O Western wind, when wilt thou blow	4 stresses
The small rain down can rain?	3 stresses
Christ, that my love were in my arms	4 stresses
And I in my bed again	3 stresses

Since common meter is based on strong stresses, it doesn't really matter where the unstressed syllables fall. Like this:

If Máry hád a líttle lámb	4 stresses
Whose fléece was whíte as snów	3 stresses
Then éverywhére Máry wént	4 stresses
The lámb would be súre to gó	3 stresses

Or even this:

It was Máry who hád the líttlest lámb	4 stresses
With fléece just as whíte as the snów	3 stresses
O and éverywhére that Máry might chánce	4 stresses
The lámb would most súrely gó	3 stresses

Sometimes, common meter omits a strong stress. The most usual variation shortens the four-stress lines to three stresses, and adds an unstressed syllable at the end:

Sátan rídes the fréeway	3+ stresses
Pláying róck and róll	3 stresses
Gíve him lánes of léeway	3+ stresses
He lóngs to dríve your sóul	3 stresses

It still works the same way: longer / shorter / longer / shorter.

The important point is that the first and second phrases don't match; three-plus stresses is still longer than three stresses.

Sometimes a strong stress isn't really that strong, as seen in this selection from Emily Dickinson:

I heard a fly buzz when I died	4 stresses (2 adjacent)
The stillness in the room	2 stresses (*in* is pretty wimpy)
Was like the stillness in the air	4 stresses (2 of which are pretty wimpy)
Between the heaves of storm	3 stresses

Common meter is nothing if not flexible. Sometimes the four-stress lines divide into two phrases. Sometimes the four-stress and three-stress lines add up to one complete phrase. Here are both events in one verse (written in triple meter) from Gordon Lightfoot's "The Wreck of the Edmund Fitzgerald":

They might ´a split up or they might ´a capsized	2 phrases, each 2 stresses
They might have broke deep and took water	
And all that remains is the faces and names	
Of the wives and the sons and the daughters	2 lines equal one phrase of 7 stresses

Common meter is a great starting point for creating a lyric, and for assuring a musical match. But remember, I said *starting point*. Writing in common meter is not a *goal*, it is a *tool*. Since common meter creates expectations, you can learn to create nice little surprises. Watch Paul Simon work his magic in these two lovely unbalanced bridges.

First, from "Still Crazy After All These Years":

Foúr in the mórning, craṕped out, yaẃning	4 stresses
Lonǵing my life awaý	3 stresses
I'ĺl never worŕy, why should Ì	4 stresses
It's al̓l gonna fad́e	2 stresses (unbalanced)

The short ending leaves us hanging, supporting the emotion of the bridge. (What? Structure can be used to support emotion? Yup. Structure can be used to support emotion.)

Next, from "Train in the Distance":

Tẃo disappoińted beliévers	3+ stresses
Twó people pláying the gaḿe	3 stresses (*people* set on weak beats)
Negótiátions and lov́esongs	3+ stresses (*songs* is weak in *lovesongs*)
Are of́ten mistáken for ońe and the saḿe	4 stresses

The last line unbalances the section and turns spotlights on the idea. A neat and effective ploy: If you want people to notice something, put it in spotlights. Ergo, put your important ideas in spotlights. Corollary: Don't turn on spotlights just to be cute.

Learn to cram your ideas into alternating four-stress and three-stress phrases. If they resist, let them, and see whether the results create any nifty little surprises, especially if the surprises help the meaning. The exercise will do you good; it will help you chart your course more clearly, and in stages that are foreseeable and easy to accomplish. If you need to take a detour, you will know where you are when you leave, and it will help you keep safely under control. A simple detour:

You've never felt what lonely is	4 stresses
Till you've flown the night alone	3 stresses
And the wind has blown you almost to despair	5 stresses
The sky runs black as midnight	3+ stresses
And the strip is hard to see	3 stresses
Heading into Charlotte on a prayer	5 stresses

Organizing your ideas into common meter may take a little work, but probably not that much, since, with rhymes like "Old King Cole" and "Little Miss Muffet," it is ingrained from your earliest childhood. You can practice with any idea—a telemarketing call for example:

I had to call to say hello
I hope you're gonna buy
Times are tough and rent is due
And I've got songs to write

Or deciding whether to call for a date:

I wanna call, I wanna call
I know I'll sound too scared
My self-esteem is plunging fast
O do I do I dare?

★ EXERCISE 16 ★

Try doing this with your grocery list. Try one in duples—da DUM da DUM—and one in triples—da da DUM da da DUM.

Learn to think in common meter. It will give you plenty in common with every Billboard chart in history, and plenty in common with the language of song from its earliest chartings. You will be sailing through it and its variations as long as you write lyrics. It's a strong map to work from; it will help you chart a manageable course to keep you from getting lost when those prosodic zigs and zags take you into lovely and unexpected waters.

CHAPTER FIFTEEN

SPOTLIGHTING WITH COMMON METER

★ ★ ★ ★ ★ ★ ★ ★ ★ ★ ★ ★ ★ ★ ★

Don't be depressed because people are nodding off during your best song, their eyes crossing, their faces drooping inexorably toward the tabletops at your best lines. Don't bother spending big bucks on an exotic vacation pilgrimage to find "inspiration" again. Before you call your travel agent, try a little juggling. It could be a simple case of dull, lifeless lyric structure, and a little excitement might be all you need to put your ideas in a nice, bright spotlight.

Let's start with a common meter structure and see if we can get your listeners' faces off the table:

	Rhyme	**Stresses**
I hitched to Tulsa worn and soaked	a	4
Stopped to get a bite	b	3
The waitress stared before she spoke	a	4
Then asked me what I'd like	b	3

Both the rhyme and the rhythm move in an abab (alternating) structure, giving double power to our expectations, and making the expected fourth line resolve completely, though a bit dully.

But just because you expect something to happen doesn't mean it has to happen. Expectations can be used to make structures more interesting. A surprise can add color and interest to your songs. First, let your listeners expect something, then surprise them with something different.

★ EXERCISE 17 ★

Stop reading and create your own four-line common meter structure. Then, as I manipulate our original Tulsa structure throughout the chapter, make the same changes to your own version.

Okay, let's start with something we've seen already. Remember the bridge from Paul Simon's "Still Crazy After All These Years" with the shortened fourth line? Let's try that same trick here:

	Rhyme	**Stresses**
I hitched to Tulsa worn and soaked	a	4
Stopped to get a bite	b	3
The waitress stared before she spoke	a	4
I felt the vibe	b	2

This throws us off balance. We wonder what the vibe is, but it doesn't seem all that promising, given the feeling of instability the shortened line creates.

Do the same thing to your section of common meter.

Now let's make another easy move: Extend line four by another strong stress (including an unstressed syllable). I've added the extra stressed syllable inside the line to keep the end line rhyming with line two:

	Rhyme	**Stresses**
I hitched to Tulsa worn and soaked	a	4
I stopped to get a bite	b	3
The waitress stared before she spoke	a	4
Then **smiled and** asked me what I'd like	b	**4**

Do the same thing to yours.

Extending the last line creates a surprise—a deceptive rhythmic closure. Your listeners were innocently expecting a three-stress line rhyming with line two.

You've turned spotlights on both the third and the fourth stressed syllables of line four—the third because it doesn't rhyme with the third stressed syllable of line two, where you expected the rhyme, and at the fourth stressed syllable because it's sticking out of the end where it wasn't expected to be:

	Rhyme	Stresses
Then smiled and asked me **what** I'd **like**	a	**4**

The spotlighted positions exaggerate the innuendo in her question. What a simple technique. All it takes is an extra two syllables inserted inside the line, one unstressed and one stressed. You can do it anytime you want. Uncross your listeners' eyes.

You could stop here and have a more interesting structure, but let's keep this effect and try something more.

Let's take what we have so far and rhyme line four with lines one and three instead of line two:

	Rhyme	Stresses
I hitched to Tulsa worn and **soaked**	a	4
I stopped to get a bite	b	3
The waitress stared before she **spoke**	a	4
Then smiled and flashed her petti**coats**	**a**	4

Now we've added a surprise. Let's call it a deceptive closure in this case because it fools us. We expected something else.

The fourth-line rhyme fools us and the spotlights blaze on. Plus there's a little more to see here, since the language is suddenly very specific. And once again, you can do this simple spotlighting maneuver any time you pick up your rhyming dictionary. By the way, this structure leaves the end line sound of line two lingering in the ear; this is discussed more in chapter nineteen, "Understanding Motion."

So far you've juggled phrase length and rhyme scheme. Again, you could stop here and have a more interesting structure, but you can make it even more exciting.

Let's add another line to what we already have. Make the additional line a four-stress line that rhymes with lines one, three, and four:

	Rhyme	Stresses
I hitched to Tulsa worn and soaked	a	4
Stopped to get a bite	x	3
The waitress stared before she spoke	a	4
Then smiled and flashed her petticoats	a	4
I grinned and told her I was broke	a	4

Now we've added another kind of surprise. Let's call it unexpected closure because it came out of the blue. It's not like being fooled, where we expected something else (deceptive closure). Here, we had no expectations at all. Pretty neat, huh?

Your listeners are sitting up straighter, paying close attention to the stuff in spotlights:

> Then smiled and **flashed** her **petticoats**
> I **grinned** and **told** her **I** was **broke**

But the added line seems a little thin for all those spotlights. *Told* and *I* are in stressed positions, yet they don't really deliver much. If this line were in an ordinary position, it wouldn't make much difference, but we've set up the line specifically to get extra attention, so something important should go there. Maybe even the title. When you turn on spotlights, use them:

	Rhyme	Stresses
I hitched to Tulsa worn and soaked	a	4
I stopped to get a bite	x	3
The waitress stared before she spoke	a	4
Then smiled and flashed her **petticoats**	a	4
And vanished like some ancient ghost	a	4

Better. Some drama for the spotlights. I don't mind the rhymes—almost perfect, so they keep the ear on track, despite the tomfoolery with structure.

Once more, we could stop here and have a more interesting structure. But let's see what happens if we add even more.

Let's add yet another line to what we already have. Make it a four-stress line, and rhyme it with lines one, three, four, and five. Add it *inside* the structure if you want to. Don't look ahead until you've done yours.

I got:

	Rhyme	Stresses
I hitched to Tulsa worn and soaked	a	4
I stopped to get a bite	x	3
The waitress stared before she spoke	a	4
Smiled and flashed her petticoats	a	4
Then rising in a curl of smoke	a	4
She vanished like some ancient ghost	a	4

Pretty interesting, huh? We're able to sustain all these lines, building pressure and excitement with each step without losing momentum. All this just because we're expecting a rhyme for *bite*.

Let's take one more step. Since your listeners (now giving you complete attention bordering on adoration) have been expecting a rhyme for *bite* all along, let's see what will happen if, in the blaze of all these spotlights, you actually produce it. Finish your section with a three-stress line, rhyming it with line two. Use your rhyming dictionary and find either perfect rhymes or family rhymes. Since you have to pick up a sound five lines earlier, the rhyme has to be as near as possible to perfect. That's also why you'll want to match the rhythm of the three-stress line.

Here's my final result:

	Rhyme	Stresses
I hitched to Tulsa worn and soaked	a	4
I stopped to get a bite	**b**	3
The waitress stared before she spoke	a	4
Smiled and flashed her petticoats	a	4
Then rising in a curl of smoke	a	4
She vanished like some ancient ghost	a	4
A phantom in the night	**b**	**3**

All of the extra lines are lit up. Your listeners are wide awake.

Smiled and flashed her **petticoats**	**a**	**4**
Then rising in a curl of smoke	**a**	**4**
She vanished like some ancient ghost	**a**	**4**
A phantom in the night	**b**	**3**

As you might have guessed, the final line could have been delivered anywhere in the earlier versions, resulting in any of these structures:

1.

Rhyme	Stresses
a	4
b	3
a	4
a	4
b	3
b	3

2.

Rhyme	Stresses
a	4
b	3
a	4
a	4
a	4

★ EXERCISE 18 ★

Go back with your version and adjust it to each of these structures.

See how easy it is to create interesting structure? You simply have to know what the possibilities are and, *crack*, you're off!

XAXA RHYME SCHEME

All of these same moves are available if you start with the other form of common meter, xaxa, which doesn't rhyme the first and third lines. Revise your piece of common meter so lines one and three don't rhyme, and manipulate yours as I manipulate mine:

	Rhyme	Stresses
I hitched to Tulsa worn and **frayed**	**x***	4
I stopped to get a bite	a	3
The waitress stared before she **spoke**	**x**	4
Then asked me what I'd like	a	3

*x stands for any unrhymed line

The structure is slightly more relaxed, but, as you will see, the same surprises are possible:

	Rhyme	Stresses
I hitched to Tulsa worn and frayed	x	4
I stopped to get a bite	a	3
The waitress stared before she spoke	x	4
Then **smiled and** asked me what I'd like	a	**4**

Our old friend, the additional stressed syllable. Now, rhyme lines three and four instead of two and four:

	Rhyme	Stresses
I hitched to Tulsa worn and frayed	x	4
I stopped to get a bite	x	3
The waitress stared before she **spoke**	a	4
Then smiled and flashed her petti**coats**	a	4

Only the last two lines rhyme, again turning on spotlights, but this time the rhyme comes out of nowhere, so the structure is as surprising (unexpected closure) as her petticoats. In the full abab, her petticoats fool us. In the looser structure, they surprise us—a subtle but interesting difference.

Now the rest of the added lines are the same as the ones from our original abab exercise:

	Rhyme	Stresses
I hitched to Tulsa worn and frayed	x	4
I stopped to get a bite	a	3
The waitress stared before she spoke	b	4
Smiled and flashed her petticoats	b	4
Then rising in a curl of smoke	b	4
She vanished like some ancient ghost	b	4
A phantom in the night	a	3

Either version of common meter can create interesting structure. The more interesting your structure is, the more visible those wonderful ideas are. The more visible the ideas are, the stronger the interest from your listeners will be: heads up, eyes uncrossed, lives transformed.

Okay, so my last line, *a phantom in the night*, is pretty cheesy, and the cheese really, really shows up in this heavily spotlighted position. It would be a great place to put the song's title, wouldn't it?

★ EXERCISE 19 ★

Go find a final line that's better than mine. Go to your rhyming dictionary under *IT* or *ID*. Remember, at this distance between rhymes, the sonic bond has to be pretty strong.

Learn to turn on spotlights. Then be sure to put something interesting where they shine.

CHAPTER SIXTEEN

METER:
TWO BY TWO

As we saw in chapter fourteen, common meter typically organizes music into a single eight-bar unit, running (two bars + two bars) + (two bars + two bars). The second line of common meter, comprising bars three and four, contains only three stresses, keeping the entire system moving until it is matched at line four (bars seven and eight).

When you want to organize into four-bar units rather than eight-bar units, all you have to do is match bars one and two with bars three and four. Here's the paradigm:

Eénie méenie míney móe	4 stresses
Cátch a tíger ón the tóe	4 stresses
If he hóllers máke him páy	4 stresses
Fífty dóllars évery dáy	4 stresses

The lines are four-stress balanced lines called couplets. They move differently. There's no problem stopping after line two:

Eénie méenie míney móe	4 stresses
Cátch a tíger ón the tóe	4 stresses

Not so with common meter:

Máry hád a líttle lámb	4 stresses
Fléece as whíte as snów	3 stresses

Think of line length as a traffic cop: It tells you when to stop, and when to go. Matched line lengths are stable. Unmatched lines create instability and make us move forward, looking for a place to rest. And when you rhyme matched lines, the stop sign is even stronger.

Here's a real one from A.E. Housman's "To an Athlete Dying Young":

The tíme you wón your tówn the ráce
We cháired you thróugh the márket pláce
Mán and bóy stood chéering by
And hóme we bróught you shóulder hígh

USING COUPLETS

Couplets usually rhyme, marking stopping places for the ear. They form a lyrical and musical unit, typically four bars long. They move us forward in regular, balanced steps with four stressed notes in each two-bar section.

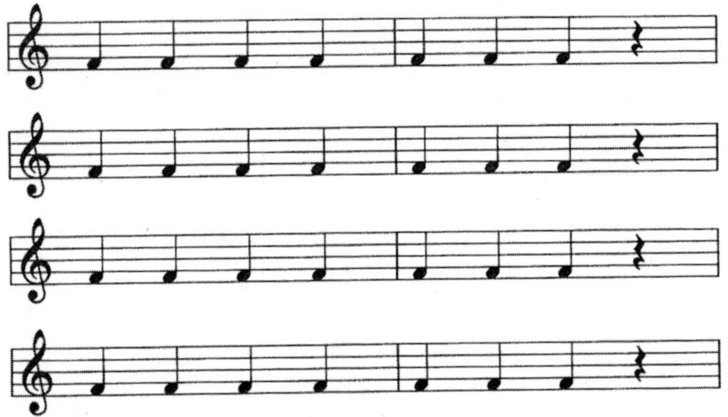

You can easily extend from four lines to six without getting too far off balance. Look at the first verse of "Where've You Been" by Don Henry and Jon Vezner:

Claire had all but given up
When she and Edwin fell in love
She touched his face and shook her head
In disbelief she sighed and said
In many dreams I've held you near
Now at last you're really here

The feeling is slightly unstable, since we have an odd number of couplets, yet an even number of lines, a subtle and interesting verse structure. You can use it to create a strong sense of center, yet raise expectations that something else is coming.

You can also use a couplet at the end of a section of common meter for acceleration and contrast:

Claire had all but given up
Then fell in love with Ed
She touched his face and closed her eyes
In disbelief she said
In many dreams I've held you near
Now at last you're finally here

The ending couplet creates a real sense of interest and arrival.

You can use couplets to set up an expectation of balance, then take a different route. Like this, from David Wilcox's "Eye of the Hurricane":

Tank is full, switch is on	4 stresses
Night is warm, cops are gone	4 stresses
Rocket bike is all her own	4 stresses
It's called a hurricane	3 stresses
She told me once it's quite a ride	4 stresses
It's shaped so there's this place inside	4 stresses
Where, if you're moving you can hide	4 stresses
Safe within the rain	3 stresses

Neat structure! The odd fourth line stands out because we expected a four-stress rhymed couplet. Instead, we get a three-stress unrhymed line, handing us an IOU that isn't cashed in until line eight. It's a good way to create a seamless eight-line (sixteen-bar) section.

WITHOUT COUPLETS

What happens when four-stress lines aren't rhymed in couplets? Look at this section of "The End of the Innocence" by Don Henley and Bruce Hornsby:

Remember when the days were long	4 stresses
And rolled beneath a deep blue sky	4 stresses
Didn't have a care in the world	4 stresses
With mommy and daddy standin' by	4 stresses

This is a more leisurely trip, with balanced four-bar phrases that settle gently, rather than asking for forward motion. After we've seen only the first two lines,

Remember when the days were long	4 stresses
And rolled beneath a deep blue sky	4 stresses

there is no urgent push forward, as there would have been if the lines were unmatched.

Mary had a little lamb	4 stresses
Whose fleece was white as snow	3 stresses

pushes forward, while the four-stress couplets don't:

Mary had a little lamb	4 stresses
Whose fleece was white as deepest snow	4 stresses

Instead, we just roll smoothly along, in no particular hurry.

	rhyme scheme	
Remember when the days were long	x	4 stresses
And rolled beneath a deep blue sky	a	4 stresses
Didn't have a care in the world	x	4 stresses
With mommy and daddy standin' by	a	4 stresses

When the next three lines come along in rhyme, we can feel the acceleration, a strong pressure building forward:

	rhyme scheme	
But "happily ever after" fails	b	4 stresses
And we've been poisoned by these fairy tales	b	4 stresses

The lawyers dwell on small details	b	4 stresses
Since daddy had to fly	c	3 stresses

Seven four-stress lines in a row, and after three rhymed lines in a row, an unrhymed three-stress line! It's a huge IOU that you can actually hear being cashed in sixteen lines later, after a pre-chorus, a chorus, and the entire second verse have come in between. That's the power of the expectations these balanced lines are able to create.

It's interesting that the last line of the verse, *since daddy had to fly*, sounds unrhymed. It should rhyme with *sky* and *by* in lines two and four, but since the first four lines close off to form a unit, we won't hear the connection.

The next four lines move into common meter. After all the four-stress couplets in the verse, the contrast is startling:

	rhyme scheme	
But I know a place where we can go	x	4 stresses
That's still untouched by men	d	3 stresses
We'll sit and watch the clouds roll by	x	4 stresses
And the tall grass wave in the wind	d	3 stresses

The section moves in a completely different way—in a four-line unit rather than two by two. We get a simultaneous effect of speeding up (with shorter second and fourth lines) and slowing down (less frequent rhymes). It's a great contrast to use for this transitional section (pre-chorus), preparing us to go back to four-stress lines:

	rhyme scheme	
You can lay your head back on the ground	a	4 stresses
And let your hair fall all around me	a	4 stresses
Offer up your best defense	b	4 stresses
But this is the end	b	2 stresses
This is *The End of the Innocence*	b	4 stresses

All the mixing and matching of four-stress couplets and common meter has led to this chorus. Here's the payoff for all the balanced lines and even numbers of bars. With a maddeningly simple move of inserting only a piece of the last line, *but this is the end*, everything is thrown off balance. There are now an odd number of lines in the chorus. There is an odd rhyme scheme. There is a two-stress line for the first time. And the chorus stretches beyond the eight-bar units we saw in the verse and pre-chorus into eleven bars. An effective way to showcase the title. This is *The End of the Innocence*.

Throwing it off balance keeps it from closing solidly; it supports the emotion of the idea—a sort of bittersweet longing that feels a little airy and suspended, matching the unstable structural perfectly. Very impressive. And all done in couplets and common meter.

★ EXERCISE 20 ★

Here are a few exercises to get you moving. Write a section for each of the following models and watch it in action. Then put a few of the more unusual rhyme schemes in your toolbox for later use. Offer your listeners some nice surprises.

	rhyme scheme		rhyme scheme
1. 4 stresses	a	2. 4 stresses	a
4 stresses	a	4 stresses	a
4 stresses	b	4 stresses	a
4 stresses	b	4 stresses	a
	rhyme scheme		**rhyme scheme**
3. 4 stresses	a	4. 4 stresses	a
4 stresses	a	3 stresses	b
4 stresses	b	4 stresses	c
4 stresses	a	4 stresses	b
	rhyme scheme		**rhyme scheme**
5. 4 stresses	a	6. 4 stresses	a
3 stresses	b	3 stresses	b

	rhyme scheme		rhyme scheme
4 stresses	c	4 stresses	a
4 stresses	c	4 stresses	a

	rhyme scheme		rhyme scheme
7. 4 stresses	a	8. 4 stresses	a
3 stresses	b	4 stresses	a
4 stresses	a	4 stresses	a
3 stresses	b	3 stresses	b
4 stresses	c	4 stresses	c
4 stresses	c	4 stresses	c
		4 stresses	c
		3 stresses	b

	rhyme scheme
9. 4 stresses	a
4 stresses	b
4 stresses	a
4 stresses	b
4 stresses	c
4 stresses	c
4 stresses	c
4 stresses	c

Pretty easy stuff, step by step. But you can build interesting structures by mixing and matching couplets and common meter. Obviously, there are more lines available in the universe than are found in these two philosophies, but they, with their combinations and variations, can take us a long way without stopping anywhere else. We'll look at more of the essential building blocks later, in chapter nineteen, "Understanding Motion."

CHAPTER SEVENTEEN

MANAGING COUPLETS

Let's do some work with four-stress couplets. Couplets are dangerous because too many of them can march lockstep in small, repetitive units that make your song feel too long and old before its time. When your lines are all the same length and rhyme in pairs, your structure is probably working against you—no matter how interesting your ideas may be, they have to work harder to overcome the interruption of stopping and starting, stopping and starting, over and over again.

I'll bet you've done this a lot in your lyrics. I know I have:

	Rhyme	**Stresses**
I hitched to Tulsa worn and frayed	a	4
Stopped inside a small café	a	4
The waitress stared before she spoke	b	4
Then smiled and showed her petticoats	b	4

Not so bad for just four lines. But admit it, you have songs that march lockstep from beginning to end in matched couplets: aa bb cc dd ee ff gg, etc. ad nauseam. Those are probably the songs that feel too long. It doesn't have to be that way if you remember that structure doesn't happen *to* you. *You* can make interesting things happen in your songs. You have choices.

Here's a tip: The more words there are in your lyric section, the larger your structure should make it feel. Couplets are units of two lines. If you have couplets in your verse, you can expand them into something larger. Size can make all the difference.

★ EXERCISE 21 ★

Write your own four lines of matched, four-stress couplets. Then, as I manipulate my Tulsa example, follow along by changing yours.

Okay, first, let's build our pair of couplets into something larger in one easy stroke: Unrhyme the first couplet and leave the second one rhymed. Like this:

	Rhyme	**Stresses**
I hitched to Tulsa worn and tired	x	4
Stopped inside a small café	x	4
The waitress stared before she spoke	a	4
Then smiled and showed her petticoats	a	4

Rather than a section that subdivides into two units of two, we've created a section that doesn't end until the final line. It feels better, more interesting.

★ EXERCISE 22 ★

Now, shorten the second line to a three-stress line, like this:

	Rhyme	**Stresses**
I hitched to Tulsa worn and tired	x	4
Found a small café	x	**3**
The waitress stared before she spoke	a	4
Then smiled and showed her petticoats	a	4

Doing this, you unleash all the techniques we saw in chapter fifteen on spotlighting. You can also add extra lines.

Now, using your version, add a five-stress line between lines two and three, and add another five-stress line that rhymes with it at the end. The rhyme scheme will be xxaxxa. Your line lengths should be 435435. Don't look ahead unless you absolutely have to.

This is what I came up with for my lyric:

	Rhyme	Stresses
I hitched to Tulsa worn and tired	x	4
Found a small café	x	3
The pláce was cóld, the wáitress cáme at lást	a	5
She stopped and stared before she grínned	x	4
Then flashed her petticoats	x	3
And disappeared, a vision from the past	a	5

Now the long third and sixth lines provide the main glue, creating a six-line section that keeps moving all the way to the end. Of course, you can use more rhymes, too.

★ EXERCISE 23 ★

Now rhyme line two with five, as well as three with six. Don't look ahead.

Here's what I did:

	Rhyme	Stresses
I hitched to Tulsa worn and tired	x	4
Found a small café	a	3
The pláce was cóld, the wáitress came at lást	b	5
She stopped and stared before she grínned	x	4
Then quickly turned away	a	3
And disappeared, a vision from the past	b	5

The movement feels stronger, not quite so loose.

★ EXERCISE 24 ★

Now rhyme line one with four so the section rhymes abcabc. Again, take your time and write something you like. It's good practice.

Mine is:

	Rhyme	Stresses
I hitched to Tulsa worn and tired	a	4
Found a small café	b	3
The pláce was cóld, the wáitress came at lást	c	5
She stopped and stared before she smiled	a	4
Then quickly turned away	b	3
And disappeared, a vision from the past	c	5

Now the motion is even more organized and precise, even with the imperfect rhymes. Which rhyme scheme should you use? It depends on what you're saying. If the lyric's emotion deals with uncertainty or loss (unstable), keep it looser. If its ideas are more factual or resolved (stable), tighten it up. Make your structure reflect the emotion of the lyric. Prosody.

Here's another way to approach the process. When you have something already written with matched couplets, like my beginning lyric:

	Rhyme	Stresses
I hitched to Tulsa worn and frayed	a	4
Stopped inside a small café	a	4
She stared a while before she spoke	b	4
Then smiled and showed her petticoats	b	4

You can "clean it out" by first unrhyming both couplets. Then, insert five-stress lines in the middle and end. It should be easy. Do it to your matched couplets first.

Here's what I did. First, I unrhymed them:

	Rhyme	Stresses
I hitched to Tulsa worn and tired	x	4
Stopped inside a small café	x	4
She stared at me before she turned	x	4
Then smiled and flashed her petticoats	x	4

Then I inserted rhyming five-stress lines:

	Rhyme	Stresses
I hitched to Tulsa worn and tired	x	4
Stopped inside a small café	x	4

The pláce was cóld, the wáitress came at lást	a	5
She stopped and stared before she grínned	x	4
Then smiled and flashed her petticoats	x	4
And disappeared, a vision from the past	a	5

Pretty easy, huh? And the structure has become a lot more interesting.

★ EXERCISE 25 ★

Now try keeping your four-stress couplets intact and adding the rhymed five-stress lines into the lyric. Like this:

	Rhyme	**Stresses**
I hitched to Tulsa worn and frayed	a	4
Stopped inside a small café	a	4
The pláce was émpty, shé appéared at lást	b	5
The waitress stared before she spoke	c	4
Then smiled and flashed her petticoats	c	4
And disappeared, a vision from the past	b	5

Here's one more way to escape the deadly march of couplets: Create an eight-line structure using four-stress rhymed lines with shorter fourth and eighth lines.

Here's mine:

	Rhyme	**Stresses**
I hitched to Tulsa worn and frayed	a	4
Stopped inside a small café	a	4
Then she appeared, an angel's face	a	4
I sat there hypnotized	b	3
She stared at me before she spoke	c	4
Then smiled and flashed her petticoats	c	4
And vanished like some ancient ghost	c	4
A phantom from the night	b	3

This rhyme scheme, unrhyming line four and matching it at line eight, was David Wilcox's move from "Eye of the Hurricane." Without the rhyme scheme's organizing larger motion, the eight lines could really have been dull city:

	Rhyme	Stresses
I hitched to Tulsa worn and frayed	a	4
Stopped inside a small café	a	4
When she appeared with angel's eyes	b	4
I knew she had me hypnotized	b	4
She stared at me before she spoke	c	4
Then smiled and flashed her petticoats	c	4
She turned away and disappeared	d	4
A phantom who was never there	d	4

With couplets, the lines themselves have to work hard to keep the song interesting; the structure isn't helping a bit. Any weakness in the lines is exaggerated. Even if the lines were great (which those above clearly aren't), the message would still be stronger if the *structure* helped, too. Any of the structures we went through earlier in the chapter could be useful alternatives.

Once you rearrange your couplets into larger units, you can invent new and more exciting possibilities. Look at these lines from Leonard Cohen's "Closing Time":

	Rhyme
Well we're drinking and we're dancing	a
And the band is really happening	a
And the Johnnie Walker wisdom's running high	b
And my very sweet companion	a
She's the angel of compassion	a
And she's rubbing half the world against her thigh	b

Okay, so it's a little quirky. What did you expect from Cohen? He's built a six-line structure using longer third and sixth lines (with five stresses each) contrasting with shorter lines (basically three-stress lines with weak syllable endings). The structure is interesting enough, and the language is interesting, too. A nice combination. But wait, there's more:

	Rhyme
Well we're drinking and we're dancing	a
And the band is really happening	a
And the Johnnie Walker wisdom's running high	b
And my very sweet companion	a
She's the angel of compassion	a
And she's rubbing half the world against her thigh	b
Every drinker every dancer	c
Lifts a happy face to thank her	c
And the fiddler fiddles something so sublime	b

These three new lines make listeners expect another three, ending in an *-ime* rhyme. They're waiting for another first six-line structure to match the first six lines. Of course, once you raise their expectations, you are free to play tricks that turn on spotlights:

	Rhyme
Well we're drinking and we're dancing	a
And the band is really happening	a
And the Johnnie Walker wisdom's running high	**b**
And my very sweet companion	a
She's the angel of compassion	a
And she's rubbing half the world against her thigh	**b**
Every drinker every dancer	c
Lifts a happy face to thank her	c
And the fiddler fiddles something so sublime	**b**
All the women tear their blouses off	d
And the men they dance on the polka dots	d

Now we have five of the six lines we're expecting. All that's missing is a five-stress line with an *-ime* rhyme. The new lines aren't *quite* matched with what came before, since they end with strong stressed syllables rather than weak, but they're close enough to prepare our ear for the final line with its *-ime* rhyme. Instead, though, we get:

It's partner found and it's partner lost	d

This line delays the resolution and leaves the structure unbalanced; we still want to hear the *-ime* rhyme. At this point, you could produce the expected line, satisfying the listeners *and* spotlighting the final idea (because you have made the listeners wait for the resolution). But not Leonard Cohen. His next move is:

And it's hell to pay when the fiddler stops	d

This extra delay builds even more pressure for a resolution. But it's like stretching a rubber band (Minnesotans call them "binders", New Englanders call them "elastics"... weird): You don't want to stretch them too far or they'll break. If you don't stretch it far enough, though, they won't hurt when you snap someone with them.

The delay is maddening. Spotlights are flashing on. We still want the *-ime* rhyme, and we're right at the brink of the whole thing falling apart when he finally gives it to us:

It's closing time	b

Whew! Look at the whole thing now:

	Rhyme
Well we're drinking and we're dancing	a
And the band is really happening	a
And the Johnnie Walker wisdom's running high	**b**
And my very sweet companion	a
She's the angel of compassion	a
And she's rubbing half the world against her thigh	**b**
Every drinker every dancer	c
Lifts a happy face to thank her	c
And the fiddler fiddles something so sublime	**b**
All the women tear their blouses off	d
And the men they dance on polka dots	d
It's partner found and partner lost	d
And it's hell to pay when the fiddler stops	d
It's closing time	**b**

He keeps us dangling for two extra lines before giving is the *-ime* rhyme in a blaze of spotlights, spotlights created by building the structure carefully—raising our expectations, satisfying them, then raising them again. The second time is the charm. It's another great example of what expectations can do to make your journey through a series of ideas more interesting. Look at what the section could have been:

	Rhyme
Well we're drinking and we're dancing	a
And the band is really happening	a
And my very sweet companion	b
She's the angel of compassion	b
Rubs the world against her thigh	c
The Johnnie Walker wisdom's high	c
Every drinker every dancer	d
Lifts their face to thank her	d
And the women shed their blouses	e
And the men all dance around them	e
It's partner found and lost	f
And hell when the fiddler stops	f
'Cause he fiddles so sublime	g
But alas it's closing time	g

The relentless march of couplets sinks the whole enterprise. More has been lost than just some neat words and a couple of nice turns of phrase. The dance of ideas has lost its partner. When the interesting structure decides to sit this one out, the ideas stumble into a partner with two left feet. What was elegant and interesting becomes something almost embarrassing; rather than looking on with pleasure, we avert our eyes. Such is the power of the dance between structure and ideas.

Interesting structure isn't something that just happens. You create it. And usually out of the simplest of starting places: matched couplets and/or common meter. None of these techniques are difficult to use—you can create wonderful partnerships any time you choose to. It's always up to you. Just work hard. Pay attention. Write well.

CHAPTER EIGHTEEN

PROSODY:
STRUCTURE AS FILM SCORE

Now that you have some tools for manipulating common meter and matched couplets, let's take a closer look at the power you have at your fingertips when you use your tools effectively. Look at this lyric, "Can't Be Really Gone" by Gary Burr (recorded by Tim McGraw):

Her hat is hanging by the door
The one she bought in Mexico
It blocked the wind and stopped the rain
She'd never leave that one
So she can't be really gone

The shoes she bought on Christmas Eve
She laughed and said they called her name
It's like they're waiting in the hall
For her to slip them on
So, she can't be really gone

I don't know when she'll come back
She must intend to come back
And I've seen the error of my ways
Don't waste the tears on me
What more proof do you need
Just look around the room
So much of her remains

Her book is lying on the bed
The two of hearts to mark her page

Now, who could ever walk away
At chapter twenty-one
So, she can't be really gone

Just look around this room
So much of her remains

Her book is lying on the bed
The two of hearts to mark her page
Now, who could ever walk away
With so much left undone
So, she can't be really gone

No, she can't be really gone

Okay. How soon did you know that she isn't coming back?

Right. At the end of the first verse. Of course, that's only because we're smart, intuitive beings—we just *know* these things. Poor guy. He has no idea. While this poor slob is looking for reasons to prove that she's coming back, we, with our deeper understanding of life and the ways of the world, know the real truth.

Kinda like watching a movie where the beautiful couple is running in slow motion toward each other through a golden sunlit field, smiling. There's a soft lens. The film score is full of romantic strings, swelling in a major key. But as they float closer to each other and our chests swell in anticipation of the long-awaited embrace, an oboe cuts through the film score in a nasty minor second, and our bodies stiffen a little. We don't really notice the music, but something tells us that something bad is about to happen. Suddenly, the guys with the shotguns leap up from their hiding places and blow the couple away. We knew it! We knew something bad was going to happen! Of course, that's because we're smart, intuitive beings—we just know these things.

Of course, the film score, which is created to stand behind the action, gave it away. Most folks don't really notice it—they just react. The composer is pulling the strings and we, like puppets, react predictably, feeling just what the score makes us feel.

That's what's going on in "Can't Be Really Gone," but this time it's not the music that creates the film score. It's the structure of the lyric, acting, just like a film score, on our emotions.

Look at the first verse:

> Her hat is hanging by the door
> The one she bought in Mexico
> It blocked the wind and stopped the rain
> She'd never leave that one
> So she can't be really gone

Though the character is giving us evidence that she's not gone for good, we don't believe him. Something just doesn't feel right. The verse itself feels funny—unstable.

PROSODY

Aristotle said that every great work of art contains the same feature: unity. Everything in the work belongs—it all works to support every other element. Another word for unity is *prosody*, which is the "appropriate relationship between elements, whatever they may be." Some examples of prosody in songs might be:

- Between words and music: A minor key could support or even create a feeling of sadness in an idea.
- Between syllables and notes: An appropriate relationship between stressed syllables and stressed notes is a really big deal in songwriting—when they are lined up properly, the shape of the melody matches the natural shape of the language.
- Between rhythm and meaning: Obvious examples like "you gotta stop! ... (pause) ... look and listen" or writing a song about galloping horses in a triplet feel.

The elements all join together to support the central intent, idea, and emotion of the work. Everything fits. Prosody: the appropriate relationship between elements.

Stable vs. Unstable

Looking at your sections through the lens of stablility or instability is a practical tool for creating prosody because you'll be able to use it for every aspect of your song: the idea, the melody, the rhythm, the chords, the lyric structure—everything. It governs the choices you make. Ask yourself: Is the emotion in this section stable or unstable? Once you answer that question, you have a standard for making all your other choices.

The Five Elements of Structure

Every section of every lyric you write uses five elements—always the same five elements—of structure. These elements conspire to act like a film score and, in and of themselves, create motion. And motion always creates emotion, completely independent of what is being said. Ideally, structure should create prosody—support what is being said—strengthening the message, making it more powerful.

The five elements of lyric structure are:

1. number of lines
2. length of lines
3. rhythm of lines
4. rhyme scheme
5. rhyme type

In "Can't Be Really Gone," we'll look at the prosody—the relationship between its structure and its meaning. Let's take a look at each of these five elements and what they do in the first verse.

1. Number of Lines

Every section you'll ever write—verses, choruses, pre-choruses, bridges—will have (here it comes, get ready) some number of lines or other. Okay, not much of a revelation. But more specifically, every section you'll ever write will have either an even number of lines, or an odd number of lines. Wow. Even more of a revelation.

Let's talk a bit about lyrics with an odd number of lines. An odd number of lines feels odd—off balance, unresolved, incomplete, *unstable*. Let's say you're writing a verse where the idea is something like: "Baby, since you left me I've been feeling lost, odd, off balance, unresolved, incomplete, unstable." Just theoretically, do you think this verse would be better with an even number of lines or an odd number of lines? Right. An odd number of lines.

This changes everything. You've recognized, maybe for the first time, that there can be a relationship between what you say and how many lines you use to say it. You're feeling unstable, and the odd, or unstable, number of lines supports that feeling. Prosody. Your structure (in this case, your number of lines) can support meaning.

An even number of lines tends to feel, well, even—solid, resolved, balanced, *stable*. Let's say that your message is something like: "Baby, you're the answer to all my prayers. I'll be with you forever. I'm your rock. You can count on me." How many lines should you use? Odd or even? Right. Even. You want a solid feeling in the structure to support the emotion you're trying to communicate. "I mean it. You can trust me." Prosody.

Now, for a really interesting case. What if you say, "Baby, you're the answer to all my prayers. I'll be with you forever. I'm your rock. You can count on me," and you say it in an *odd* number of lines? Do you trust this guy? I don't think so. Something doesn't feel right—there's a mismatch between *what* is being said and *how* it's put together, how it moves. Though the message promises stability, the *motion* creates instability, which pulls the rug out from under the narrator. It creates irony.

Let's look at the first verse again:

> Her hat is hanging by the door
> The one she bought in Mexico
> It blocked the wind and stopped the rain
> She'd never leave that one
> So she can't be really gone

This feels unstable, though the message is: "Look at the evidence—it proves that she'll be coming back." But the feeling we get from the unstable structure (which is acting like a film score) is that he's wrong and perhaps a bit hysterical or, at least, in denial.

So the number of lines can make a big difference.

What if the verse had been:

> Her hat is hanging by the door
> From Mexico, that funny store
> I know she'd take her hat along
> So I know she can't be really gone

Since the section feels balanced, we'd probably be convinced—there's a sense of resolution, balance, and completeness that we feel here. Go ahead, have some breakfast. Take the dog for a walk. She'll be home when you get back.

So an even number of lines supports stability and resolution, while an odd number of lines support the opposite.

2. Length of Lines

Line length is the traffic cop in your lyric. Two lines of equal length, because they're balanced, tell you to stop. (Note, for future reference, that the length of a line is not determined by the number of syllables, but by the number of *stressed* syllables, because the number of stressed syllables helps determine the number of musical bars.)

> Her hat is hanging by the door
> The one she bought in Mexico

The two four-stress lines feel balanced. It feels like we're finished with one thing and ready to start something new. Of course, we would feel even more stability if the lines rhymed, too. More on this later.

Lines of unequal length, because they do not reach a point of balance, tell you to keep moving:

> It blocked the wind and stopped the rain
> She'd never leave that one

Now we feel unbalanced and unresolved, and the traffic cop tells us to keep moving forward. Simple, but very effective.

The first three lines are equal length:

	Stresses
Her **hat** is **hang**ing **by** the **door**	**4**
The **one** she **bought** in **Mex**ico	**4**
It **blocked** the **wind** and **stopped** the **rain**	**4**

But then something happens:

	Stresses
She'd **nev**er **leave that** one	**3**

The three-stress line leaves us short, creating an unstable feeling—making us feel uncomfortable, like something's not quite right. The following line:

So she **can't** be **real**ly **gone**	**3**

leaves us still feeling uncomfortable. With yet a second three-stress line, a new expectation kicks in: We'd like one more three-stress line. Maybe something like:

She'll **soon** be **com**ing **home**	**3**

Which gives us:

	Stresses
Her **hat** is **hang**ing **by** the **door**	**4**
The **one** she **bought** in **Mex**ico	**4**
It **blocked** the **wind** and **stopped** the **rain**	**4**
She'd **nev**er **leave that** one	**3**
So she **can't** be **real**ly **gone**	**3**
She'll **soon** be **com**ing **home**	**3**

Read it through a few times. See how comfortable it feels?

And now see how uncomfortable this feels:

	Stresses
Her hat is hanging by the door	4
The one she bought in Mexico	4
It blocked the wind and stopped the rain	4

She'd never leave that one 3
So she can't be really gone 3

So there's a conspiracy between the number of lines and the line lengths to torpedo this guy—to expose him for the man in denial that he is. It's important to note that he isn't similarly exposed in the previous six-line structure.

There'll be a much more detailed treatment on the motion created by number of lines and line lengths in the next chapter, "Understanding Motion."

3. Rhythm of Lines

First, let's acknowledge the difference between the rhythm of words and musical rhythm. Though they should match each other on the most important levels, they can also vary in many ways. For example, when we read, we normally don't extend a syllable for four beats, nor do we speed up parts of a line and slow other parts down significantly. Music does it all the time. What should remain constant between the rhythms of words and musical rhythm is this: Stressed syllables belong with stressed notes. Unstressed syllables belong with unstressed notes. This is called "preserving the natural shape of the language."

For our purposes here, we'll concentrate on lyric rhythm and leave musical rhythm for another time.

Let's look at the rhythm of our lyric. We've already marked the stressed syllables:

Her **hat** is **hang**ing **by** the **door** **4**
The **one** she **bought** in **Mexico** **4**
It **blocked** the **wind** and **stopped** the **rain** **4**
She'd **nev**er **leave that** one **3**
So she **can't** be **real**ly **gone** **3**

This moves along in groups of two (da DUM):

Da DUM da DUM da DUM da DUM
Da DUM da DUM da DUM da DUM

Da DUM da DUM da DUM da DUM
Da DUM da DUM DUM da
Da da DUM da DUM da DUM

This is a mostly very regular lyric rhythm, with just a two variations, neither of which have much effect.

Okay, why, in a verse that feels so off balance (to support the off-balance emotion of the idea), is the rhythm so darn regular? Shouldn't it be off kilter, too?

Remember, this is a man in denial. He's trying to convince himself she's coming back. If everything in the verse were off kilter, there'd be nothing stable to rub against the unstable elements. Also, the differences in line length would become less clear and, therefore, less effective. So the regularity of the rhythm, in this case, actually highlights the elements that throw it off balance.

4. Rhyme Scheme

Songs are made for listening—we hear them rather than see them. Rhyme is a sonic event, made for listening. It provides our ear with road signs to guide us through the journey of the song. It shows us connections. It tells us when to stop and when to move forward. Look:

Her hat is hanging by the door
Her scarf is lying on the floor

This sounds finished. It stops us. It feels resolved, stable. But look at this:

Her hat is hanging by the door
She'd never leave that one
Her scarf is lying on the floor

Now we feel the push forward. Although, in this case, the line lengths also conspire to throw us off balance, leaning ahead, the rhymes can do it all by themselves:

door
one
floor

So rhyme guides our ear. Can a lack of rhyme maroon our ear without a guide? As in:

> Her hat is hanging by the door
> The one she bought in Mexico
> It blocked the wind and stopped the rain
> She'd never leave that one
> So she can't be really gone

Our ear feels a little lost. And how is our hero feeling? Yup. Lost.

Is this to say that the lack of rhyme supports the emotion of the verse? Yup. It's huge. And, with a little practice, you can do it, too. These are tools, ready for use in any situation. Just apply the right tool in the right place and watch your song take on more color and more meaning.

Listen to "The Great Balancing Act" and see how Janis Ian and Kye Fleming create prosody with their abbb rhyme scheme.

Prosody comes from many directions, and rhyme scheme can be a big player. There's much more of this to come in chapter nineteen, "Understanding Motion."

5. Rhyme Types

Remember this?

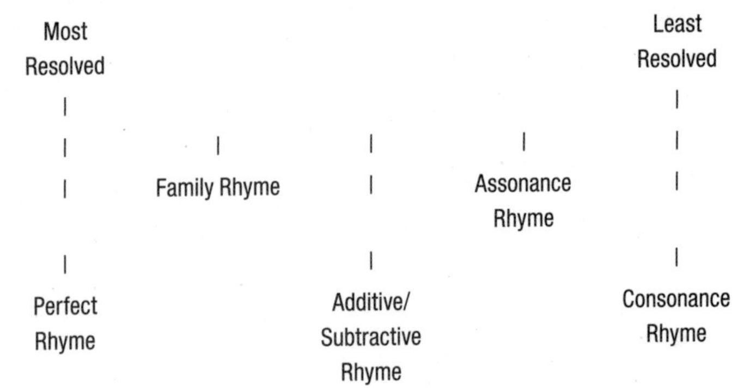

Remember, rhyme types create opportunities to add color and emotion. Use them to color your meaning, the same way a film score comments on the action on the screen.

There are no rules, only tools.

> She'd never leave that one
> So she can't be really gone

Here, the consonance rhyme, one/gone, conspires, along with the other elements of structure (number of lines, line length etc.), to help pull the rug out from under our hero, as well as to increase our feeling that something's not quite right. Good stuff.

So, did Gary Burr think about all this stuff as he wrote "Can't Be Really Gone"? Maybe, maybe not. The important issue is: You can.

The point of lyric analysis isn't to discover what a given writer intended to do. That's a fool's errand. Rather, lyric analysis digs into effective songs to discover what makes them work, to unearth tools for our own use.

Take the songs that move you and go beyond what they say and see how they're put together. You'll see how the film score of structure creates an extra dimension, adding emotion at every turn. Then use these structural tools to make your own songs dance.

Let's finish by looking at the five elements at work in Don Henley and Bruce Hornsby's "The End of the Innocence":

> Remember when the days were long
> And rolled beneath the deep blue sky
> Didn't have a care in the world
> With mommy and daddy standin'by

Stable or unstable? Right. Stable. And how stable was my childhood? Well, my childhood had an even number of equal-length lines that rhymed perfectly at the second and fourth lines.

> But happily ever after fails
> And we've been poisoned by these fairy tales
> The lawyers dwell on small details
> Since daddy had to fly

Stable or unstable? Right. Unstable. And where is it the most unstable? Right. The last line, where daddy leaves. How did daddy's leaving affect me? Well, it made me feel like my life sped up with consecutive rhymes, then dropped me over the edge with a short, unrhymed line. Darn it, daddy!

> But I know a place where we can go
> That's still untouched by men
> We'll sit and watch the clouds roll by
> And the tall grass wave in the wind

Stable or unstable? Hmm. Both? Yes. An even number of lines with matched alternating line lengths, rhyming lines two and four. That's what I'm promising you—a place where everything will feel stable again. But alas, though it might still feel better, there's not much you can do about the damage daddy's leaving did. No matter how stable the place we go feels, there's that darn men/wind consonance/additive rhyme, making everything hang. Real stability is now just an illusion. No perfect rhymes in sight.

> You can lay your head back on the ground
> And let your hair fall all around me
> Offer up your best defense
> But this is the end
> This is the end of the innocence

Stable or unstable? Yep—very unstable. We'll never get our innocence back. Our life is always destined to be an odd number of unequal-length lines topped of by another consonance rhyme, defense/innocence.

A remarkable journey, where the structure supports—indeed, helps create—the emotional intent of the song.

Structure is your film score. Learn how to use it. Learn the effects that various structures can create, and use them to support your own ideas. Sometimes, you can even use them to create emotions underneath what you're saying.

In the next chapter, we'll take a systematic look at the effects of various structures. Fasten your seatbelts.

CHAPTER NINETEEN

UNDERSTANDING MOTION

One of the best ways to give your lyric extra punch is to understand how to make your lyric move, and how to make that motion support *what* you're saying—how to create prosody.

Sometimes, you may accidentally trip onto this sort of writing, unaware of the choices you're making. But if you tune into your lyrics' motion consistently, you'll not only write and rewrite your songs more effectively, but, more important, you won't rely on lucky accidents or divine inspiration to drop those good bits into your lap.

Lots of great ideas float by every day if we're awake and pay attention to what's inside us and around us. But it's how we deal with those magical ideas that create a better song.

In this chapter, we'll look at how lyric structure creates motion, which, in turn, creates emotion to be harnessed in support of what you want to say. You'll find plenty of exercises ahead to shape your motion muscles. If you do them all, you'll finish this chapter with tools and abilities you probably don't see now. I promise.

MOTION CREATES EMOTION

We *feel* something when a song speeds up, slows down, wants to move forward to the next place, wants to come to a resolution, and then arrives at home.

All by itself, the motion we create can take listeners on an interesting journey—a journey of feelings and attitudes. Lyric structure, all by itself, can:

- move us forward to create excitement, anticipation, or an expectation of what's coming next.
- slow us down to create a sense of holding back or a sense of unresolved feelings.
- draw attention to a specific word (a spotlight), creating surprise, delight, humor, or any important emotion.
- resolve, creating a feeling of stability.
- leave us hanging and unresolved, creating a feeling of instability.

Again, motion creates *e*motion.

The primary emotion-producer in a lyric is the idea—the intent of the lyric, expressed in words and phrases. Since words "mean something," they create emotion. If we also understand certain structural principles, we can amplify and support our ideas with dramatic results.

When we look at lines like this:

> Turn down the lights, turn down the bed
> Turn down these voices inside my head
> —Mike Reid/Alan Shamblin

It makes us feel something. And I'm suggesting it's worth investigating what it makes us feel and why.

In lyrics, there are two elements that create motion and emotion:

1) the words and ideas themselves, and
2) the overall lyric structure, which consists of:
   a. groupings of lines, and
   b. line structure, a combination of three things:
      1. rhythm of the line
      2. length of the line (line length is determined by the number of stresses in a line), and
      3. rhyme scheme used in the combinations of lines.

When you control the way a lyric moves, you're able to affect your audience on two levels simultaneously, rather than just on the level of meaning.

Motion creates emotion. Or, maybe better: Motion creates and supports emotion.

Let's first look at how the motion of a lyric, using four of the five basic structural elements (we'll leave out rhyme types)—an even number of lines, matched line length, stable rhythm, and stable rhyme scheme—can create a stable feeling:

	Rhyme	Stresses
A**maz**ing **grace**, how **sweet** the **sound**	a	4
That **saved** a **wretch** like **me**	b	3
I **once** was **lost**, but **now** am **found**	a	4
Was **blind**, but **now** I **see**	b	3

It's a stable common meter; the first and third lines both have the same line length, as do the second and fourth lines.

The rhyme scheme is abab, the same configuration as the line lengths (a four-stress line followed by a three-stress line, then another four-stress line followed by a three-stress line). The rhythms move along in a regular duple pattern (da DUM).

To notate the way a structure moves, let's use capital letters (e.g., A, B, C) to stand for lines that have both the same line lengths and the same rhyme scheme. Each line labeled with the same letter will: (1) rhyme with, (2) have the same number of stressed syllables as, and (3) have the same basic rhythm as every other line in the section with the same letter, as shown here in the far right column:

	Rhyme	Stresses	Overall
Amazing grace, how sweet the sound	a	4	**A**
That saved a wretch like me	b	3	**B**
I once was lost, but now am found	a	4	**A**
Was blind, but now I see	b	3	**B**

When these features (line length, rhyme, and number of stressed syllables) line up, the section's motion becomes clearer. This will also help you understand and control the way musical phrases work with lyrical phrases and help to you organize them in stable or unstable ways.

Once you get a feel for it, you'll be able to control motion in the real world of lyric writing, where mismatches can create productive tensions, as when rhyme scheme differs from the arrangement of line lengths. (For example, you can create tension when you have four equal-length lines that rhyme abab instead of aaaa. We'll see more of that later, but for now, let's keep it simple.)

In cases where the arrangement of line lengths doesn't match the rhyme scheme, we'll simply omit the capital As and Bs.

So, the five elements of structure, our friends from chapter eighteen, make your lyric structures move:

1. the rhythms of the lines
2. the arrangement of line lengths
3. the rhyme structure
4. the number of lines
5. the rhyme types

Let's review each of these elements to see how and when they affect motion.

The Rhythms of the Lines

The rhythm of a line is the first structural thing you hear in a song. After hearing only the first line of a song, you don't yet know much about the motion of the whole section, but you might start to have a sense of what the intended emotion could be.

Rhythm is a prime mover in songwriting, and it can get complicated really fast. It has so many facets. In terms of its effect on our lyric sections, we can at least say this:

- Regular rhythms create stable motion.
- Irregular rhythms create less stable motion.
- Two lines with matched rhythms create stability.
- Two lines with unmatched rhythms create instability.

Since lyric rhythms work so intimately with musical rhythms, we'll have to leave the majority of this subject to another time. Look at chapter three of my book *Songwriting: Essential Guide to Lyric Form and Structure*, and also my online course "Writing Lyrics to Music," available through patpattison.com.

For now, we'll stay with fairly regular rhythms and concentrate our efforts on the effects of line lengths, rhyme scheme, and number of lines on the movement of a section.

Structurally, the first line, by itself, communicates motion with its rhythm, and also with its length. It sets a standard, preparing us for what's to come in the remaining lines in the section. For example:

	Rhyme	Stresses
I **hitched** to **Tul**sa **worn** and **soaked**	a	4

It's a steady duple rhythm (moving in twos—da DUM), and is four stresses long.

The Arrangement of Line Lengths

By the end of the first line, you know another basic structural piece of information: line length.

Starting at the second line, you will create structural motion, either by:

A) matching the first line, which will stop the motion, as seen here:

	Rhyme	Stresses	
I hitched to Tulsa worn and soaked	a	4	= A
A little bent, a lotta broke	a	4	= A

B) or *not* matching the first line, which pushes the motion forward, as seen here:

I hitched to Tulsa worn and soaked	a	4	= A
I couldn't find a ride	b	3	= B

Because these lines aren't matched, the structure keeps the motion moving forward, rather than slowing down or stopping it.

So, line lengths can create motion by the end of line two.

The Rhyme Structure

The earliest I can hear rhyme structure, and the motion caused by it, is at the end of the second line:

Example 1: aa rhyme structure with lines of matching length

I hitched to Tulsa worn and soaked	a	4	=A
A little bent, a lotta broke	a	4	=A

But often, we don't hear a section's rhyme structure until after line three:

Example 2: aba rhyme structure with the second line having a different length

I hitched to Tulsa worn and soaked	a	4	=A
I stopped to get a bite	b	3	
The waitress stared before she spoke	a	4	=A

And sometimes it takes until the section is over before we are able to identify the rhyme structure:

Example 3: xaxa rhyme scheme

I hitched to Tulsa tired and worn	x	4	
I stopped to get bite	a	3	=A
A little bent, a lotta broke	x	4	
A single quarter light	a	3	=A

Note the way the line structure and the rhyme structure line up in this example as compared to the previous examples.

Line length and rhyme scheme are two independent tools. When they match, they form a couplet and the motion stops (example 1). But often, rhyme structure is created later than the motion created by line lengths (examples 2 and 3).

The Number of Lines—To Balance or Not

Obviously, you don't hear the total number of lines in a section until the end of the section, so it's one of the last two determiners of motion. Strong expectations have already been created by rhythm, rhyme scheme, and line length, but we still don't know for certain how the section will end.

In a stable section, the final line delivers resolution. An even number of lines gives it a solid footing. The expectations set up by the section are fulfilled, as in "Amazing Grace." We feel like it's said its piece and really means it.

In an unstable section (like in "Can't Be Really Gone"), the final line could create a surprise or feeling of discomfort because the expectations are not completely fulfilled. An odd number of lines can certainly create a sense of discomfort. The final line could also lean forward toward the next section, in many cases moving into a contrasting section (e.g., a verse moving into a chorus).

The Rhyme Types

As we saw in the previous chapter, the kind of rhyme you choose can affect the stability of a section. More remote rhyme types will destabilize even the more stable constructions, as in lines 9–12 of "The End of the Innocence" (see page 187).

As you go through the exercises in this chapter, try using stronger and weaker rhyme types in some of the closing positions to see what differences they make. We won't put rhyme types into the mix here, since there is more than enough work to do with just line lengths, rhyme scheme, and number of lines. No need to multiply examples with different rhyme types. But you already know what a huge tool rhyme types can be, so please stop every now and then to try out other possible types in the same structure.

With the tools you're about to acquire, you'll be able to control how stable or unstable your section will be—anything from a granite boulder to a wobbly table to a capsizing ship.

STABILITY VS. INSTABILITY

Okay, it's time to get practical. You'll be looking at wheelbarrows full of different kinds of sections, organized . .cording to their numbers of lines, and listed from the most stable sections to the least stable sections.

Think of the following examples as a handy reference guide to stable and unstable structures, there for you to try in support of that idea you've got. Is the idea stable or unstable? And then you go through the examples to find something that might work for you.

We'll start by looking at two-line sections, then spend a bit of time on three-line sections. Though three-line sections are more rare as standalone sections in lyric writing, looking at them will give you a good view of what causes a section to move. Then we'll go on to four-line and five-line sections, and, finally, a few interesting six-line sections. Since larger sections are usually made up of smaller pieces, understanding how these smaller sizes move will get you ready for pretty much anything else. If you stay with it and dig into each example to see how it feels, you'll add a whole new dimension to your lyric writing.

Combinations Of Two Lines

Here are all the possible two-line sections, listed from most to least stable. Stable asks you to stop:

I hitched to Tulsa worn and soaked	a	4	=A
A little bent and really broke	a	4	=A

It stops. You can feel the resolution.

I hitched to Tulsa worn and soaked	a	4
A little bent and really tired	b	4

Even though the lines don't rhyme, their matched lengths give a feeling of balance or stability. Not as much as if they rhymed, but enough to keep you from wanting to lunge forward. It feels a little more stable than this:

I hitched to Tulsa worn and soaked	a	4
A little bent and broke	a	3

Even though these rhyme, they rhyme in different positions—most likely on different beats in the musical measure. There's a little stronger push forward here. So line length is a stronger motion creator than rhyme, huh? Yup. Unstable lines ask you to keep moving:

I hitched to Tulsa worn and soaked	a	4
I couldn't find a ride	b	3

This is the least stable. It leans forward really hard.

Here's an interesting lesson in motion: a longer line, followed by a shorter line, like this:

I hitched to Tulsa worn and soaked	a	4
I couldn't find a ride	b	3

leans ahead harder than the opposite:

I couldn't find a ride	a	3
I hitched to Tulsa worn and soaked	b	4

The longer line has matched the shorter line on its way by. Which is not the case here:

I hitched to Tulsa worn and soaked	a	4
I couldn't find a ride	b	3

You can feel the difference. Remember this, since it will also apply to larger structures: Longer followed by shorter is less stable than shorter followed by longer.

In working through these examples and the ones to follow, we'll stick to the staple four-stress, three-stress, and, later, five-stress lines that make up most lyrics. But once you absorb the principles, you'll be able to apply them to any line lengths.

Combinations Of Three Lines

The possibilities of three lines, listed from most stable to least stable, are:

AAA

She stared at me before she spoke	a	4	=A
She said the day had come to go	a	4	=A
I hitched to Tulsa worn and soaked	a	4	=A

This is the most stable of the three-line sequences. It seems almost to close down—almost to resolve. You can look at it as AA+A, and it depends on whether you see the third line leaning back or looking forward for more. The principle of sequence says it's looking to pair off, since we heard a pairing (a resolving couplet) after line two. Even if we feel the third A leaning back, the structure still feels a bit off balance. Either way, it feels less than complete.

If you think otherwise, remember that sometimes *what* you're saying can influence your structural ear. In the sequence above, line three is about what he did because of what she said. The idea feels completed. But he still doesn't feel happy about it. But look at this:

I hitched to Tulsa worn and soaked	a	4	=A
She stared at me before she spoke	a	4	=A
She said the day had come to go	a	4	=A

This feels a little less resolved, since the idea is less resolved. This is where it gets fun. Watching structure influence content, and content influence structure. Composition, in regard to songwriting, is the activity of mixing and matching these elements.

John Mayer uses the AAA effectively by simply repeating the title of his song "Your Body Is a Wonderland":

Your body is a wonderland
Your body is a wonderland
Your body is a wonderland

After the first and second verse, it feels like he wants more, leaning ahead. Only after the bridge does he finally say it four times, bringing the events to their conclusion.

★ EXERCISE 26 ★

Write an AAA structure, first using ideas that come to a conclusion, and then using ideas that feel less resolved. How much difference do you feel in the stability of the section?

ABB

It rained like hell the day I left my place	a	5	=A
She said the day had come to go	b	4	=B
I hitched to Tulsa worn and soaked	b	4	=B

The longer first line actually seems to create a bit of expectation for a matching A at line four. Though this is still unstable, it is relatively stable for a three-line sequence. Perhaps there's a difference if we begin with a shorter line:

It rained the day I left	a	3	=A
She said the day had come to go	b	4	=B
I hitched to Tulsa worn and soaked	b	4	=B

Now, it doesn't seem to lean as hard as it did with the longer first line. With the shorter first line, it feels more stable—almost like its own section. The singer feels almost resigned to leaving, like he's accepted his fate. Interesting.

★ EXERCISE 27 ★

Write an ABB structure, first with a longer first line, then with a shorter one. Keep them as much the same as possible. Do you feel a difference in attitude between them? Structure can support or even sometimes determine the attitude of the character.

XXX

I hitched to Tulsa worn and soaked	x	4
The waitress stared and smiled at me	x	4
I stopped to rest a little while	x	4

This more "floats" than leans forward. There is no rhyme sequence established here, so few expectations are raised. It sort of "suspends" him—he feels like he's just hanging out, waiting to see what happens next, but with no hurry.

AAB

I hitched to Tulsa worn and soaked	a	4	=A
She stared at me before she spoke	a	4	=A
I stopped a little while	b	3	=B

This leans pretty hard, too, though not in the same way, since our expectations are a little less clear; maybe the resolution would be AABB, or maybe AAB AAB. If we complete it either way, it becomes a stable section. But if we use it as a three-line section, it would be pretty unstable.

If it were a pre-chorus or bridge, we could maybe use the third line's vowel sound from *while* (which is asking to be rhymed) to illuminate an important vowel sound in the oncoming section—for example, in an oncoming chorus where the title of the song was something like "For One Smile in a Million." The *while* in line three, hanging there unrhymed, will emphasize *smile* in the chorus. Nifty tool, eh?

★ EXERCISE 28 ★

Make up your own title, and, using it as the first line of an oncoming chorus, write an AAB structure leading up to it, with the third line targeting a vowel sound in the title. Try not to target the end rhyme. Instead, give the words inside the title a sonic boost. Then rewrite the third line (B line) to target a different vowel sound in the title. As in the sample that follows.

I hitched to Tulsa worn and soaked	a	4	=A
She stared at me before she spoke	a	4	=A
I stopped, completely dumb	x	3	=B

For **one** smile in a million ...

Now the third line targets the short-*u* sound in the title's *one*, highlighting it and emphasizing it in the chorus.

There's also:

I hitched to Tulsa worn and soaked	a	4	=A
She stared at me before she spoke	a	4	=A
I stopped, completely still	x	3	=B

For one smile in a million ...

Now the third line targets the short-*i* and *l* sounds in *million*, highlighting it and emphasizing it in the chorus.

Now we've targeted the rhyme position. Note that the effect not only highlights it, but it also creates a bit of a sense of resolution. It feels like:

I hitched to Tulsa worn and soaked	x	4	=X
She stared at me	x	2	=X
I stopped, completely **still**	a	3	=A
For one smile in a **mill**ion	a	3	=A

Targeting the rhyme position is neither wrong nor right. It creates a different, usually more resolved feeling than if you target interior vowel sounds. It depends on the feeling you want to create. You control it.

ABA

I hitched to Tulsa worn and soaked	a	4	=A
I stopped a little while	b	3	=B
She stared at me before she spoke	a	4	=A

This is not only the most unstable of the three-line sequences, it also positively cries out for a resolving fourth line with three stresses and a rhyme with *while*. This three-line structure establishes a clear pattern, so we know what's coming next.

With this structure, we're looking at three-fourths of a common meter section, so the conclusion is more than obvious. It's interesting to see how the same principle would work with a different arrangement. Instead of longer / shorter / longer, let's try shorter / longer / shorter:

I hitched the Tulsa road	a	3	=A
I stopped a while to grab a bite	b	4	=B
She stared before she spoke	a	3	=A

You can still feel the strong lean forward, now expecting a four-stress line rhyming with *bite*. It seems to lean even harder with a five-stress line in the second position:

I hitched the Tulsa road	a	3	=A
I stopped a little while to grab a bite	b	5	=B
She stared before she spoke	a	3	=A

I'm not sure why this raises more expectations than the four-stress line. Perhaps it's because it feels like more of a departure from line one.

Of course, if you complete the sequence, you have a stable four-line structure. If you leave it as a three-line sequence, then you'll be moving pretty strongly into the next section. Perhaps this might make an interesting pre-chorus structure. Again, you could use a sound at the end of line two to target an important sound in the chorus. For example:

Pre-chorus
I hitched the Tulsa road
I stopped a little while to grab a bite
She stared, and then she spoke

Chorus
Baby I **like** what I see ...

We hear *like* with more intensity: "Baby I *like* what I see." We could try targeting *baby*:

Pre-chorus
I hit the Tulsa road
I stopped a little while to grab some shade
She stared, and then she spoke

Chorus
Baby I like what I see ...

We hear *baby* with sensual overtones. Compare this to if we don't target:

Pre-chorus
I hitched the Tulsa road
I stopped a little while to grab a drink
She stared, and then she spoke

Chorus
Baby I like what I see ...

Now we get no extra sonic action in the chorus, and line two's *drink* is still waving his arms for attention, wondering if he'll ever meet a nice noun or verb to hook up with.

★ EXERCISE 29 ★

Make up your own title, and, using it as the first line of an oncoming chorus, write an ABA structure leading up to it. Make the second line's ending vowel target a vowel sound inside your title. Then rewrite the second line's ending again to target a different vowel sound in your title.

COMBINATIONS OF FOUR LINES

Understanding basic three-line motion helps you understand how to move a section forward and how to stop it. It gives you the ability to control motion, and therefore use the way a structure moves and feels to support your ideas—for example, making the structure move haltingly when the protagonist is unsure of what to do next. Your study of three-line sequences not only helps you understand how and why lines float or raise expectations by pushing forward, it also shows you how to resolve the section, often with just one more line.

We'll now look at four-line sections from most stable to least stable; some of them pretty stable, some that fool you a little, some with little surprises, and some that are still unstable and moving forward.

AAAA

She stared at me before she spoke	a	4	=A
She said the day had come to go	a	4	=A
A little bent, a lotta broke	a	4	=A
I hitched to Tulsa worn and soaked	a	4	=A

Lots of stability here—it's basically Eenie Meenie Miney Moe. It has two balancing points: at the end of line two and at the end of line four. This is as solid as a structure can get. Relatively speaking, it doesn't move much, since it stops you in the middle, breaking into two matched two-line sections. The third A connects a bit with the first two, so, as we saw in the three-line AAA section, the lean forward toward the last line is pretty weak. So the last line isn't quite as much a "point of arrival" as it will be in other structures. The spotlights aren't as bright. If this were a chorus, it would be a good opportunity to put the title in both the first and last line:

A little bent, a lotta broke	a	4	=A
She said the day had come to go	a	4	=A
I hitched to Tulsa worn and soaked	a	4	=A
A little bent, a lotta broke	a	4	=A

It's a nice surprise to hear it repeated, but we weren't being pulled inexorably toward it. The journey was much more steady, almost matter-of-fact. The structure portrays an attitude.

★ EXERCISE 30 ★

Match the AAAA structure above using your own words and your own title at the top and bottom.

AABB

I hitched to Tulsa worn and soaked	a	4	=A
A little bent, a lotta broke	a	4	=A
I stopped a bit to get a bite	b	5	=B
Found myself a quarter light	b	5	=B

With AAB we get a stronger push forward than AAA gave. We've heard a different sound and now are looking to pair it with another B. We still get a complete stop at the end of line two, and then again creating two two-line sections. A very stable structure. When the protagonist says something using this structure, he/she's telling the truth. It's a stable fact.

ABAB

I hitched to Tulsa worn and soaked	a	4	=A
I stopped to get a bite	b	3	=B
A little bent, a lotta broke	a	4	=A
A single quarter light	b	3	=B

Boy, does this stop dead. Common meter, fully resolved but full of motion. We get a push forward by the shorter line two, then a big push when we hear line three match line one in length and rhyme. As before, ABA raises strong expectations for the repeat of B. This is called common meter for a reason. It's everywhere.

★ EXERCISE 31 ★

Find five examples of common meter in songs you know. It shouldn't take long.

XAXA

I hitched to Tulsa tired and worn	x	4	=X
I stopped to get bite	a	3	=A
A little bent, a lotta broke	x	4	=X
A single quarter light	a	3	=A

Now we're missing the big rhyme push forward at line three; the line length pushes, but without the additional momentum rhyme creates. This moves forward pretty strongly, but without the urgency we feel at line three of ABAB.

★ EXERCISE 32 ★

Modify your earlier ABAB structure to an XAXA structure. Feel the weaker push at line three?

ABAA

I hitched to Tulsa worn and soaked	a	4	=A
I stopped to get a bite	b	3	=B
A little bent, a lotta broke	a	4	=A
I bummed a meal, bummed a smoke	a	4	=A

We saw this structure in chapter fifteen, a deceptive resolution; it's a great way to call extra attention to the last line. Make sure there's something there worth looking at. ABAA is also a handy structure for putting a title on top and bottom:

A little bent, a lotta broke	a	4	=A
I stopped to get a bite	b	3	=B
I bummed a meal, bummed a smoke	a	4	=A
A little bent, a lotta broke	a	4	=A

The same targeting strategy we saw before works here, too: If a verse were ABAA, you could use a sound in the verse at the end of line two to target an important sound in the chorus. For example:

Verse

I hitched to Tulsa worn and soaked	a	4	=A
I stopped to get a **bite**	b	3	=B
A little bent, a lotta broke	a	4	=A
She smiled at me before she spoke	a	4	=A

Chorus

Baby I **like** what I see …

As before, we hear *like* with more intensity: "Baby I *like* what I see." Again, we could try targeting *baby*:

Verse

I hitched to Tulsa worn and soaked	a	4	=A
I had to get a**way**	b	3	=B
A little bent, a lotta broke	a	4	=A
She smile at be before she spoke	a	4	=A

Chorus

Baby I like what I see …

Now we hear *baby* with the same sensual overtones. Compare this to if we don't target a vowel sound in the chorus:

Verse

I hitched to Tulsa worn and soaked	a	4	=A
Stopped to get some grub	b	3	=B

A little bent, a lotta broke	a	4	=A
She smile at be before she spoke	a	4	=A

Chorus

Baby I like what I see ...

A wasted second position? Maybe not. But it's there for the picking if you want it.

★ EXERCISE 33 ★

Make up your own title, and, using it as the first line of an oncoming chorus, write an ABAA structure leading up to it, with the second line targeting a vowel sound in the title. Try not to target the end rhyme. Instead, give the words inside the title a sonic boost. Then rewrite the end sound in your second line to target a different vowel sound in the title.

XXAA

I hitched my way to Tulsa	x	3	=X
Stopped to get a bite	x	3	=X
I bummed a meal, bummed a smoke	a	4	=A
A little bent, a lotta broke	a	4	=A

This is a surprise. We had no expectations after either line two or three, so the resolution we get at line four surprises (but doesn't fool) us. It's resolved all right, but without much pushing or raising expectations to get there. Resolution coming out of chaos, as it were, which can be a useful tool to support a similar motion of ideas. It's pretty unstable for a resolved section.

Vary the rhyme, but not the line lengths, and you'd get something like:

I hitched to Tulsa worn and frayed	x	4	=X
Stopped a while to get a bite	x	4	=X
I bummed a meal, bummed a smoke	a	4	=A
A little bent, a lotta broke	a	4	=A

The lights still go on the last line, but not as brightly, given the more balanced journey through line lengths.

XAAA

I hitched to Tulsa worn and soaked	x	4	=X
I stopped to get a bite	a	3	=A
A single quarter light	a	3	=A
And such an appetite	a	3	=A

Still stable, but getting less so. Again, changing both the rhyme and line length gives us a clearer view of the motion.

With the shorter A lines above, the sequence leans a bit forward, almost as if it were asking to duplicate itself for balance. It still feels closed, but a bit unstable, certainly less stable than this:

She stared at me a while	x	3	=X
She said the day had come to go	a	4	=A
I hitched to Tulsa worn and soaked	a	4	=A
A little bent, a lotta broke	a	4	=A

As usual, longer lines following shorter lines create more stability. Think of longer lines as laying a foundation under the shorter line above them. This version of XAAA is pretty stable, as it would be if all the line lengths matched, like this:

She stared at me a little while	x	4	=X
She said the day had come to go	a	4	=A
I hitched to Tulsa worn and soaked	a	4	=A
A little bent, a lotta broke	a	4	=A

What creates the instability in all three versions is the odd number of A's. There's a mismatch between the number of lines, and the number of matched elements. The structure doesn't push forward very hard, it more "floats," because when we get our first match at line three, we have an odd number of lines preventing the rhyme and rhythm match from creating stability. We don't quite know what to expect next, making the final A create what feels like a stopping place, but without much fanfare when it arrives.

AABA

I hitched to Tulsa worn and soaked	a	4	=A
A little bent, a lotta broke	a	4	=A
I stopped to get a bite	b	3	=B
I bummed a meal, bummed a smoke	a	4	=A

This structure fools us, too, but not drastically. To the extent that we expect a match for B, we're fooled when it resolves with A.

This structure doesn't move much. It balances after line two, so there's no push forward there. The B line provides the only push, but only by being different and asking politely to be matched. We get a little spotlight on the last line.

★ EXERCISE 34 ★

Make up your own title, and, using it as the first line of an oncoming chorus, write an AABA structure leading up to it, with the third line targeting a vowel sound in your title. Then, find a different end vowel for your third line to target a different vowel sound in your title. Then see what happens when you target the end rhyme.

ABBA

I hitched to Tulsa getting worn and soaked	a	5	=A
I stopped a bit to get a bite	b	4	=B
Found myself a quarter light	b	4	=B
A little bent, a lotta really broke	a	5	=A

As you'd expect, the longer line at the end of the example above makes it feel pretty resolved. But it feels less resolved with the longer lines inside:

As thunder rolled across the sky	a	4	=A
I hitched to Tulsa getting worn and soaked	b	5	=B

A little bent, a lotta really broke	b	5	=B
Found myself a quarter light	a	4	=A

It certainly feels less stable with the shorter line on the outside. Look at it with equal-length lines:

As thunder rolled across the sky	a	4	=A
I hitched to Tulsa worn and soaked	b	4	=B
A little bent, a lotta broke	b	4	=B
Found myself a quarter light	a	4	=A

In poetry, this is called an In Memoriam Quatrain, after Alfred Lord Tennyson's lovely poem of the same title. He used an ABBA rhyme scheme and equal-length lines, creating a suspended feeling at the end of each quatrain, much as you'd do in a eulogy. The structure's feeling was so appropriate for the message of his poem (an actual eulogy), that the abba rhyme scheme has carried the poem's name ever since.

ABBA structures float. I think it's unresolved, but sometimes it's a close call. No matter, though; it's the effect of the structure that counts. It leans a bit, asking maybe for:

As thunder rolled across the sky	a	4	=A
I hitched to Tulsa getting worn and soaked	b	5	=B
A little bent, a lotta really broke	b	5	=B
Found myself a quarter light	a	4	=A
I knew I'd have to stay the night	a	4	=A

Or maybe even:

As thunder rolled across the sky	a	4	=A
I hitched to Tulsa getting worn and soaked	b	5	=B
A little bent, a lotta really broke	b	5	=B
Found myself a quarter light	a	4	=A
The waitress said she'd maybe take me home	b	5	=B
Then vanished in a lovely puff of smoke	b	5	=B

ABBA is an interesting section. Check out the verses to James Taylor's "Sweet Baby James."

AAAX

I hitched to Tulsa worn and soaked	a	4	=A
A little bent, a lotta broke	a	4	=A
I bummed a meal, bummed a smoke	a	4	=A
Bummed another ride	b	3	=X

This is an unstable section. As you've already seen, AAA doesn't push very hard, but it does lead us to expect another A, so when we don't get it, we still want it (the targeting principle). Most likely, we'll look for a whole section to match it:

I hitched to Tulsa worn and soaked	a	4	=A
A little bent, a lotta broke	a	4	=A
I bummed a meal, bummed a smoke	a	4	=A
Bummed another ride	b	3	=B
She'd closed her eyes before she spoke	a	4	=A
Said the time had come to go	a	4	=A
To vanish in a puff of smoke	a	4	=A
A phantom in the night	b	3	=B

See the verses in David Wilcox's "Eye of the Hurricane" on page 163 for an effective use of this eight-line sequence.

Another possibility for this structure is to use the X line as a title position, like this:

I hitched to Tulsa worn and soaked	a	4	=A
A little bent, a lotta broke	a	4	=A
I bummed a meal, bummed a smoke	a	4	=A
Looking for something more	x	3	=X

Okay, even though it's a dumb title, you see the point: The structure supports the content.

AXAX

I hitched to Tulsa worn and soaked	a	4	=A
I stopped to get a bite	x	3	=X

I bummed a meal, bummed a smoke	a	4	=A
Found a room	x	2	=X

This one pushes ahead pretty hard, asking for a match to line two. When the match isn't forthcoming, we fall forward. This might be a good technique for setting up a title:

I hitched to Tulsa worn and soaked	a	4	=A
I stopped to get a bite	b	3	=X
I bummed a meal, bummed a smoke	a	4	=A
Found a room	x	2	=X
Lighting the fire inside	b	3	=X

Here's a more normal version, with lines two and four matching lengths:

I hitched to Tulsa worn and soaked	a	4	=A
I stopped to get a bite	b	3	=X
I bummed a meal, bummed a smoke	a	4	=A
Found a quiet room	x	3	=X
Lighting the fire inside	b	3	=X

Each structure is what it is, but always keep an eye out for what else it could become—for what could come next.

Here's AXAX with a longer last line:

I hitched to Tulsa worn and soaked	a	4	=A
I stopped to get a bite	x	3	=X
I bummed a meal, bummed a smoke	a	4	=A
Found a place to sleep before it rained	x	5	=X

Again, the section with the longer last line feels a little more stable, since it has matched line two's length (our expectation) on its way to the end. Still, it's pretty unstable, but not as unstable as it was with the shorter line.

XAAX

I hitched a ride to Tulsa	x	3	=X
I stopped a bit to get a bite	a	4	=A

Found myself a quarter light	a	4	=A
A little bent, a lotta really broke	x	5	=X

As usual, the second A takes the wind out of the sails by throwing off any expectations of what might come next. It doesn't push forward too hard, and the section continues to float.

I hitched to Tulsa getting lost and worn	a	5	=X
I stopped a bit to get a bite	b	4	=A
Found myself a quarter light	b	4	=A
A lotta really broke	a	3	=X

This version looks forward, hoping for a stable place to land, wherever that might be.

★ EXERCISE 35 ★

Using the previous example, see if you can find our friend a landing place.

XXXX

I hitched to Tulsa getting worn and frayed	a	5	=X
I stopped to get a bite	b	3	=X
Found myself a quarter short	b	4	=X
A lotta broke	a	2	=X

Or:

A lotta broke	a	2	=X
I hitched to Tulsa getting worn and frayed	a	5	=X
I stopped to get a bite	b	3	=X
Found myself a quarter short	b	4	=X

Or:

A lotta broke	a	2	=X
I stopped to get a bite	b	3	=X
Found myself a quarter short	b	4	=X
I hitched to Tulsa getting worn and frayed	a	5	=X

Or this, unrhymed, with equal-length lines:

I hitched to Tulsa worn and frayed	x	4	=X
Stopped a while to get a bite	x	4	=X
Found myself a quarter short	x	4	=X
A lotta broke, a lotta bent	x	4	=X

Food For Thought

How does each section feel? Though all of them are unstable, which one feels most unstable? Least unstable? Why?

We've now seen some of lyric writing's most stable sections, excellent for supporting stable ideas. Of course, having four lines doesn't mean you have to stop there. Unstable four-line sequences often add more lines to stabilize or resolve themselves. But stable four-line sections can add more lines, too, and they often do, to wondrous effects.

COMBINATIONS OF FIVE LINES

Groups With Only One Matching Element

In this first group of five-line sequences, listed from most stable to least stable, any odd lines don't match anything else, including each other. This often creates a "floating" effect. The sections that feel most stable are often the ones that surprise us by feeling resolved without us expecting the resolution. Call it "unexpected closure."

These structures are probably most useful as verses, though they can also work effectively as choruses, given the proper combination of ideas.

AAAAA

It rained the day I left my home	a	4	=A
I hitched to Tulsa worn and soaked	a	4	=A
She stared at me before she spoke	a	4	=A
I told her then that I was broke	a	4	=A
I watched her turn around to go	a	4	=A

The fifth line is an unexpected closure, and though it tips a tad toward a sixth line, it just as much leans back in warm companionship with all the other A's. Line five would be an excellent place to repeat a title that's been stated at line one:

A little bent, a lotta broke	a	4	=A
I hitched to Tulsa worn and soaked	a	4	=A
She stared at me before she spoke	a	4	=A
I watched her turn around to go	a	4	=A
A little bent, a lotta broke	a	4	=A

XAAAA

It rained the day I left my home for good	x	5	=X
I hitched to Tulsa worn and soaked	a	4	=A
She stared at me before she spoke	a	4	=A
I told her then that I was broke	a	4	=A
I watched her turn around to go	a	4	=A

Expectations play leapfrog here. After line three, we want to stop with the matching As, but we can't because of the odd number of lines. When the number of lines is even, the number of As is odd, and so on. It's resolved (unexpected closure) at line four, so the fifth line is an unexpected closure, too. You can feel its instability, like it might just want to move again to balance the number of lines. It's a nice place to spotlight an important idea.

★ EXERCISE 36 ★

Write an XAAAA section that ends with a stable idea, then juggle the lines so it ends with an unstable idea. Can you feel how the content and structure interact?

XXAAA

It rained the day I left my home for good	x	5	=X
I couldn't start my car	x	3	=X
I hitched to Tulsa worn and soaked	a	4	=A
She stared at me before she spoke	a	4	=A
I told her then that I was broke	a	4	=A

As we saw above with XXAA, we have unexpected closure at line four. Line five creates another unexpected closure, but one that leans forward. We have a pretty strong push for a sixth line, since we could use both another line and another A to even things up.

Let's try it with longer As:

It rained the day I left my home	a	4	=X
I had to get away	b	3	=X
I had to find a place where I could breathe	c	5	=A
A place that had some grass and apple trees	c	5	=A
Where I could finally find a little peace	c	5	=A

Pretty stable. Does the closure at line four fool you, or simply surprise you? The answer depends on whether you have any expectations after the first three lines.

It's clear that *a place that had some grass and apple trees* stabilizes the section after four lines. If you can predict what should come next, you have expectations. Frankly, I don't have any predictions after line three—it could go anywhere. Thus, the resolution we feel is something we didn't expect—unexpected closure. It's more of the same at line five, with two lines in the spotlights here.

XAXAA

It rained the day I left	x	3	=X
I hitched to Tulsa worn and soaked	a	4	=A
My thumb my only ticket	x	3	=X
A little bent, a lotta broke	a	4	=A
She stared at me before she spoke	a	4	=A

★ EXERCISE 37 ★

Your turn to describe how this one behaves.

XXXAA

It rained the day I left my home for good	x	5	=X

I couldn't start my car	x	3	=X
I thought I'd try some thumbing	x	3+	=X
I hitched to Tulsa worn and soaked	a	4	=A
A little bent, a lotta broke	a	4	=A

This feels like it stops, too, though it's predictably off balance because of the odd number of lines. This one's a floater, though there may be a little voice asking for a 3+ line ending in *numb me*.

XXAXA

It rained the day I left my home for good	x	5	=X
I couldn't start my car	x	3	=X
I hitched to Tulsa worn and soaked	a	4	=A
Stopping at the roadside	x	2+	=X
She stared at me before she spoke	a	4	=A

This one is clearly open after line four, without much of a push forward after line three, except by our preference for stable, even numbers. It resolves, unexpectedly, at line five, but floats everywhere else. Even after line five, it feels like it might want to move. Perhaps a 2+ line ending in *low ride* would settle things down? What sort of ideas would this XXAXA structure support?

AAAAX

It rained the day I left my home	a	4	=A
I hitched to Tulsa worn and soaked	a	4	=A
She stared at me before she spoke	a	4	=A
I told her then that I was broke	a	4	=A
I watched her turn her back	x	3	=X

Five-line systems ending with an X will be the most unstable.

Groups With Two Matching Elements

In this first group with two matching elements (As and Bs), the first two lines are different, creating forward motion. They are listed from most stable to least stable.

ABABB

I hitched to Tulsa worn and soaked	a	4	=A
I had to get away	b	3	=B
She stared at me before she spoke	a	4	=A
With not a word to say	b	3	=B
Her smile began my day	b	3	=B

Closed and stable, with the additional line leaning more backward than forward. You get a nice spotlight at the end.

ABAAB

I hitched to Tulsa worn and soaked	a	4	=A
I had to get away	b	3	=B
The waitress stared before she spoke	a	4	=A
I told her then that I was broke	a	4	=A
Her smile began my day	b	3	=B

Interesting case here. Line four fools you—call it a "deceptive closure": You expected B, but got A instead. Then, at line five, you get what you originally expected but where you didn't expect it, so it's a cross between expected and unexpected closure, making it feel a bit more stable.

ABBAA

I hitched to Tulsa worn and soaked	a	4	=A
I had to get away	b	3	=B
To find another place	b	3	=B
I told the waitress I was broke	a	4	=A
I watched her turn her back to go	a	4	=A

This one is interesting. Look back at the ABB structure in "Combinations of Three Lines" on page 198 to see the effect created here. Check out the first three lines of the second verse of Gary Nicholson and John Jarvis's "Between Fathers and Sons":

Now when I look at my own sons	a	3+	=A
I know what my father went through	b	3	=B
There's only so much you can do	b	3	=B

How stable does this section feel? Do you have any expectations of where it might go? Probably not. Whatever you do, it will stay pretty unstable unless you match it with three more lines of ABB.

ABBAB

I hitched to Tulsa worn and soaked	a	4	=A
I had to get away	b	3	=B
To find another place	b	3	=B
I told the waitress I was broke	a	4	=A
Her smile began my day	b	3	=B

It looks like we've started a second ABB sequence with the addition of AB, asking for the next B, something like:

She said she'd let me stay	b	3	=B

But the push doesn't seem too strong, since the sequence, though visible, doesn't seem too audible. This five-line sequence feels a bit unstable, but only a bit.

ABAAA

I hitched to Tulsa worn and soaked	a	4	=A
Stopped to grab a bite	b	3	=B
The waitress stared before she spoke	a	4	=A
I told her then that I was broke	a	4	=A
And watched her turn her back to go	a	4	=A

There's a deceptive closure in line four, thus creating an unexpected closure in line five. As we saw in chapter fifteen "Spotlighting With Common Meter," the structure leans forward to match the B line with something like:

Have a lovely night	b	3	=B

There are four As but five lines, leaning a little for a sixth line. It stops at line five, but it's not a hard stop. It's a bit of a floater without a sixth line.

ABABA

I hitched to Tulsa worn and soaked	a	4	=A
I had to get away	b	3	=B
She stared at me before she spoke	a	4	=A
With not a word to say	b	3	=B
I told her then that I was broke	a	4	=A

This leans forward looking for another B. The alternating sequence is responsible for this feeling.

More Groups With Two Matching Elements

In this next group, the first two lines are As, creating a system that stops at the couplet before continuing.

AABBA

It rained the day I left my home	a	4	=A
I hitched to Tulsa worn and soaked	a	4	=A
I had to get away	b	3	=B
To find another place	b	3	=B
Nothing left to do but go	a	4	=A

This feels pretty stable. Though it has two couplets, the shorter third and fourth lines keep it leaning a bit, like a limerick. The final A seems to stop rather than start a new sequence, as if it's simply referring back to the opening AA.

★ EXERCISE 38 ★

Rewrite this AABBA with three-stress As and four-stress Bs. What difference does it make to the stability of the section?

AABBB

It rained the day I left my home	a	4	=A
I hitched to Tulsa worn and soaked	a	4	=A

I had to get away	b	3	=B
To find another place	b	3	=B
Where no one knew my name	b	3	=B

This also feels pretty stable. It has resolutions at each couplet. The third B feels less like it's starting a new sequence and more like it's simply joining the party. There's nice spotlights on the fifth line.

★ EXERCISE 39 ★

Rewrite this AABBB with three-stress As and four-stress Bs. What difference does it make to the stability of the section?

AAABB

It rained the day I left my home	a	4	=A
I hitched to Tulsa worn and soaked	a	4	=A
Salvation took the open road	a	4	=A
I had to find a place	b	3	=B
Where no one knew my name	b	3	=B

This feels strangely stable. It should be crying out for another B, but it doesn't seem to. It's as though the feel of the couplet interferes with the request the sequence makes for two sets of three to create an AAABBB sequence. Perhaps it's having to move to an odd-numbered B that softens the push forward.

If you kept the line lengths and only rhymed the last two lines, it would float a lot more, and you'd get something like Gary Burr's "Can't Be Really Gone":

Her hat is hanging by the door	x	4
The one she bought in Mexico	x	4
It blocked the wind and stopped the rain	x	4
She'd never leave that one	a	3
So she can't be really gone	a	3

A six-line version of AAABB would feel more balanced:

It rained the day I left my home	a	4	=A
I hitched to Tulsa worn and soaked	a	4	=A
Salvation took the open road	a	4	=A
I had to find a place	b	3	=B
Where no one knew my name	b	3	=B
To start my life again	b	3	=B

EXERCISE 40

Rewrite the AAABB example with three-stress As and four-stress Bs. What difference does it make to the stability of the section?

Groups With Three Matching Elements

Listed from most stable to least stable, these structures are groups with As, Bs, and Cs. Technically, any unmatched A, B, or C should be called an X. I think it's clearer here if we don't use Xs.

In the first group, the first two lines are different, creating forward motion.

ABCAC

It rained the day I left my home	a	4	=A
I had to get away	b	3	=B
I had to find a place where I could breathe	c	5	=C
Salvation on the open road	a	4	=A
Where I could finally find a little peace	c	5	=C

Line four suggests that a sequence is taking shape: ABCABC. Then you get the closing element immediately. To the degree that line four raises expectations that B will be matched, line five fools you, thus creating deceptive closure. You get very strong spotlights at line five.

ABCBC

It rained the day I left my home	a	4	=A
I had to get away	b	3	=B
I had to find a spot where I could breathe	c	5	=C

Where freedom rules the day	b	3	=B
Where I could finally find a little peace	c	5	=C

This is stable, and it seems to carry a little milder surprise at line five than ABCAC. You don't hear the sequence starting again at line four with an A, so it doesn't direct you forward as strongly. But once you hear B, the sequence kicks in, even though it's "out of sequence." Another deceptive closure.

★ EXERCISE 41 ★

Choose either ABCAC or ABCBC and target to a title from the unrhymed line. Construct a title that matches the unmatched line in both rhythm and rhyme. Target an inner vowel of the title line rather than the end rhyme.

ABCBB

It rained the day I left my home	a	4	=A
I had to get away	b	3	=B
I had to find a spot where I could breathe	c	5	=C
Where freedom rules the day	b	3	=B
Where peace has come to stay	b	3	=B

You can feel the effect of the longer C line on the motion if you compare it to this:

It rained the day I left my home	a	4	=A
I had to get away	b	3	=B
To find a spot to breathe in	c	3+	=C
Where freedom rules the day	b	3	=B
Where peace has come to stay	b	3	=B

The longer "C" line "sticks out," calling attention to itself, diminishing the feeling of XAXA's expected closure, and making line four float just a tad. When we shorten the "C" line, the structure really closes.

The shorter C brightens the spotlights on line five by allowing line four to resolve solidly.

ABCAA

It rained the day I left my home	a	4	=A
I had to get away	b	3	=B
I had to find a place where I could breathe	c	5	=C
Salvation on the open road	a	4	=A
Nothing left to do but go	a	4	=A

This feels unstable. It feels like it should continue forward, perhaps to something like:

Spend my hours to see what I could see	c	5	=C

Again, the arrangement of line lengths here can change how it feels. Consider:

It rained the day I left my home	a	4	=A
I had to get away	b	3	=B
To find a place to shelter	c	3+	=C
Salvation on the open road	a	4	=A
Nothing left to do but go	a	4	=A

★ EXERCISE 42 ★

Describe how the shortened line in the previous example affects the structure's motion.

ABCAB

It rained the day I left my home	a	4	=A
I had to get away	b	3	=B
I had to find a place where I could breathe	c	5	=C
Salvation on the open road	a	4	=A
Where no one knew my name	b	3	=B

Unstable. This one pushes forward pretty hard, to something like:

Spend my hours to see what I could see	c	5	=C

Even with a shortened third line:

It rained the day I left my home	a	4	=A
I had to get away	b	3	=B
To find a place to shelter	c	3+	=C
Salvation on the open road	a	4	=A
Where no one knew my name	b	3	=B

It still wants to move to:

To lose this helter skelter	c	3+	=C

That's the power of sequence.

Though, mathematically, there are more possible combinations of five lines, this should more than suffice to increase your awareness of structural motion.

COMBINATIONS OF SIX LINES

ABCABC

I hitched to Tulsa worn and soaked	a	4	=A
I had to get away	b	3	=B
Miles to go, no promises to keep	c	5	=C
She stared at me before she spoke	a	4	=A
Without a word to say	b	3	=B
She led me off to bed and off to sleep	c	5	=C

This sequence moves relentlessly forward to a satisfying and resounding resolution at line six. It's the six-line version of common meter, working according to the principle of sequence.

ABABAA

I hitched to Tulsa worn and soaked	a	4	=A
I had to get away	b	3	=B
The waitress stared before she spoke	a	4	=A
Then asked if I could stay	b	3	=B
She vanished like a puff of smoke	a	4	=A
I heard the chimes and then I woke	a	4	=A

This closes after line four (ABAB), with a final couplet finishing it off. It's very stable, especially when the couplet matches one of the elements of the quatrain.

ABABCC

I hitched to Tulsa worn and soaked	a	4	=A
I had to get away	b	3	=B
She stared at me before she spoke	a	4	=A
Without a word to say	b	3	=B
She led me off to bed and off to sleep	c	5	=C
No miles to go, no promises to keep	c	5	=C

This also stops after line four (ABAB), with a final couplet closing it down. Very stable. The final couplet decelerates a bit with the longer lines, but makes up for it with the immediate (and thus accelerating) rhyme.

AABAAB

I hitched to Tulsa worn and soaked	a	4	=A
A little bent, a lotta broke	a	4	=A
Miles to go, no promises to keep	b	5	=B
She stared at me before she spoke	a	4	=A
And presto in a puff of smoke	a	4	=A
She led me off to bed and off to sleep	b	5	=B

Another solid citizen. It's a favorite structure of Leonard Cohen's. It doesn't push forward as hard as ABCABC, since the opening couplet stops the section. It's also harder for sequence to kick in, though it's in full force at the end of line five.

★ EXERCISE 43 ★

Rewrite AABAAB with B=3 stresses. Is there a difference in how the section feels?

ABABAB

I hitched to Tulsa worn and soaked	a	4	=A
Stopped to grab a bite	b	3	=B
A little bent, a lotta broke	a	4	=A

A half a dollar light	b	3	=B
She stared at me before she spoke	a	4	=A
And offered me a ride	b	3	=B

Another solid citizen, though the final AB might clear its throat a bit, wondering whether the larger ABAB sequence will be matched again to make ABABABAB. So, just a touch of instability—looking forward to another AB.

ABBABB

With miles to go and promises to keep	a	5	=A
I hitched to Tulsa worn and soaked	b	4	=B
A little bent, a lotta broke	b	4	=B
Without a bed without a place to sleep	a	5	=A
She stared at me and when she spoke	b	4	=B
My past became a puff of smoke	b	4	=B

This feels stable, though we might add another line, something like:

I felt my spirit finally breaking free	a	3	=A

With this added A, it still feels stable, perhaps more stable than the six-line section. Interesting, those line lengths.

But look what happens if we shorten the As:

With promises to keep	a	3	=A
I hitched to Tulsa worn and soaked	b	4	=B
A little bent, a lotta broke	b	4	=B
Without a place to sleep	a	3	=A
She stared at me and when she spoke	b	4	=B
My past became a puff of smoke	b	4	=B

It feels a bit more solid. Again, it shows the power of line lengths. The challenge with this structure is that it doesn't establish sequence, and thus doesn't raise much expectation, giving it a tendency to float.

ABABBA

I hitched to Tulsa worn and soaked	a	4	=A
Stopped to grab a bite	b	3	=B

A little bent, a lotta broke	a	4	=A
A half a dollar light	b	3	=B
She offered me a ride	b	3	=B
And vanished in a puff of smoke	a	4	=A

I like how this one plays tricks. Two unexpected closures, but in reverse order, creating a nifty surprise to support her vanishing act. Neat.

At this point, because you've done the exercises and understand the principles of motion, you should be able to construct all sorts of sections, both stable and unstable, using whatever number of lines you need to say what you have to say.

You're an expert at assessing and controlling motion. Now use that skill to create motion supporting your lyric's message. Have fun.

CHAPTER TWENTY

FORM FOLLOWS FUNCTION
BUILDING THE PERFECT BEAST

OhMyGod, Artie, stop!" yells Herbie. Artie's '69 VW microbus wobbles over to the side of the road, next to a cream-and-baby-blue Maserati convertible parked in the lot. "Boy, I'd like to drive that beauty. Looks like it really flies." "Whew," whistles Artie, "look at it—low, wide wheelbase, scooped front, rear foil. Definitely built for speed." A physicist or aeronautical engineer could give a more precise description, but Artie and Herbie have it nailed anyway. As much as they love Artie's microbus, they know it won't win any races, because it isn't built for speed. But that Maserati sure could. Intuitively, they apply the principle *form follows function*. If you asked them the right questions, they'd be able to describe the two ways this principle works:

1. When you look at an individual car, you can figure out what it's built to do (function) by its design (form). Conversely, when you build a car, you figure out its design by what you want it to do. If you want a racecar, build it heavy, wide, and lower in front than in back so the wind will press it to the track. If you want an economy car, build it light and shape it to cut wind resistance. You already know this as the principle of prosody.
2. When you look at two cars, you see whether they're different or the same. When they're the same design, they should have the same function. When they have different designs, they should have different functions. This is the principle of contrast.

It doesn't matter whether we're talking about cars, rhyme schemes, architecture, or lyrics.

As a writer, you'll usually look from a car designer's perspective—from function to form. You know what you want to say, so you have to design form to support your ideas.

As we've seen, your tools for designing your lyric's shapes are phrase lengths, rhythms, and rhyme schemes. For example, say there's a place in your verse where emotion gets pretty active or intense. You might try putting rhymes (both phrase-end and internal rhyme) close together, and try using short phrases. Like this:

You can't play Ping-Pong with my heart	a
You dominate the table	b
My nerves are shot, you've won the set	c
Your curves have got me in a sweat	c
My vision's blurred, can't see the net	c
I'm feeling most unstable	b

Built for speed. The consecutive rhymes, "set/sweat/net," slam the ideas home. The internal rhymes, "nerves/curves/blurred" and "shot/got," put us in overdrive. The acceleration creates prosody, the mutual support of structure and meaning—form follows function.

You can think of rhyme as a car's accelerator: The closer the pedal is to the floor, the faster the car moves. The closer the rhymes are to each other, the faster the structure moves. The farther away the pedal is from the floor, the slower the car moves.

Let's see what the ride would feel like if we toned down the rhyme action in the previous example:

You can't play Ping-Pong with my heart	a
You dominate the table	b
My nerves are shot, I've come apart	a
You wink and smile, still feeling playful	b
Weak and numb, I miss the mark	a
Feeling most unstable	b

Out pops the rear parachute. Prosody evaporates, or at least diminishes, when the rhymes are spread out into a regular pattern. But the short phrases in lines three, four, and five still press on the accelerator. If we lengthen some of the shorter phrases, we let off the gas even more:

You can't play Ping-Pong with my heart	a
You dominate the table	b
My nerves are shot, I've really come apart	a
You wink and smile, still feeling pretty playful	b
Weak and numb, I really miss the mark	a
Feeling most unstable	b

Look at what happens if we ease off on the rhymes, too, pushing them further apart:

You can't play Ping-Pong with my heart	x
You dominate the table	b
My nerves are shot, at last you've won the point	x
Your slams have put me in an awful sweat	x
My vision's weak, can't even see the ball	x
I'm feeling most unstable	b

Now the structure acts more like a slow-moving '68 VW microbus, while the meaning still dreams of checkered flags on the Grand Prix Circuit. Bad combination.

EXERCISE 44

We might as well destroy prosody completely while we're at it. This time, you do it. Rewrite the example below so lines three and five contain one long phrase each, instead of two shorter ones. Be careful not to rhyme.

You can't play Ping-Pong with my heart	x
You dominate the table	b
...	x
Your slams have put me in an awful sweat	x
...	x
I'm feeling most unstable	b

Compare your result to the original and you will see what an important role structure can play in support of meaning. If you're careful how you build your form, you can make it work for you. Tend to the prosody of form and function, and your structure will become a powerful and expressive ally rather than an obstacle standing between you and what you really meant to say.

THE PRINCIPLE OF CONTRAST

Herbie and Artie know the difference between their microbus and the cream-and-baby-blue Maserati. No big mystery—they're built different. This is another way to look at "form follows function." Simple logic: Things that look the same should do the same thing. Things that look different should do different things. A microbus is not a Maserati.

Verses in a song should all have the same function—they develop the plot, characters, or situations of the song. That's why they're all called verses. Because the verses all have the same function, they should all have the same form. Easy, huh?

Or this: When you move from a verse to another function—for example, to a chorus function (commentary, summary)—the form should change: the rhyme scheme, phrase lengths, number of phrases, or rhythms of phrases. Maybe all four.

"Form follows function" is the real rationale behind what often look like silly rules:

- All verses should have the same rhyme scheme!
- Change the rhyme scheme when you get to the chorus.

Look at this verse and its chorus:

Southern Comfort

Verse 1

Spanish moss hanging low
Swaying from the trees
Honeysuckle, sweet magnolia
Riding on the breeze

Southern evenings, Southern stars
Used to bring me peace
But now they only make me cry
They only make me realize

Chorus

There's no Southern Comfort
Unless you're in my arms
You're the only cure
For this aching in my heart
I've searched everywhere
Tried the bedrooms, tried the bars
But there's no Southern Comfort
Unless you're in my arms

Each section contains, roughly, the same number of phrases. No contrast there.

The verse rhymes its alternate lines, except at the end, where it accelerates with a couplet. The chorus rhymes every other line, too, without the couplet acceleration at the end:

Verse	**Chorus**		
low	x	comfort	x
trees	a	arms	a
magnolia	x	cure	x
breeze	a	heart	a
stars	x	where	x
peace	a	bars	a
cry	b	comfort	x
realize	b	arms	a

Still not much contrast between the sections. The verse contains two complete sections of common meter rhythm. The only variation is the extra stressed syllable in the last line:

	Stresses
Spánish móss hánging lów	4
Swáying fróm the treés	3

Hóneysúckle, sweét magnólia	4
Ríding ón the breéze	3
Soúthern évenings, soúthern stárs	4
úsed to bríng me peáce	3
But nów they ónly máke me cry	4
They ónly máke me réalizé	4

That's a lot of common meter, but there's more. Look at the chorus:

	Stresses
There's nó Sóuthern Cómfort	3+
Unléss you're ín my árms	3
Yoú're the ónly cúre	3
For this áching ín my heárt	3
I've seárched éverywhére	3
Triéd the bédrooms, triéd the bárs	4
But there's nó Sóuthern Cómfort	3+
Unléss you're ín my árms	3

Although most of the phrases have three stresses, the section still leans toward common meter:

1. The balancing phrases are three stresses, the signature length of common meter.
2. The opening phrase is longer than three stresses, three plus—a normal variation of common meter's four-stress line. When you want two sections to contrast, the opening phrase of the new section must make a difference immediately. If you don't make a difference there, don't bother.
3. The two three-stress phrases with extra weak syllables are in the same positions as four-stress phrases in common meter, leaving only two contrasting phrases in the entire chorus. And they're the same length as half the lines in the verse.

Essentially, by the time we finish the chorus, we have been through four common meter systems. That's a lot. Imagine the boredom by the time you finish four more:

Verse 2

I've tried my best to ease the hurt
Leave the pain behind
But evenings sitting on the porch
You're always on my mind
Southern Comfort after dark
Helps me face the night
But there's nothing to look forward to
'Cept looking back to loving you

Chorus

There's no Southern Comfort
Unless you're in my arms
You're the only cure
For this aching in my heart
I've searched everywhere
Tried the bedrooms, tried the bars
But there's no Southern Comfort
Unless you're in my arms

Ho-hum structure. If the lyric's meaning were more interesting, there might be some hope, but it's not that interesting. Even if the meaning shone in eleven shades of microbus DayGlo, the structure still should help the meaning, not hurt it.

The bridge finally delivers a contrast:

Bar to bar
Face to face
Someone new takes your place
No one's ever new
I always turn them into you

But by the time we get to the bridge, it's too late; everyone has wandered off for a hot dog. Then there are two more lumps of common meter for the tombstone:

Chorus

There's no Southern Comfort

Unless you're in my arms
You're the only cure
For this aching in my heart
I've searched everywhere
Tried the bedrooms, tried the bars
But there's no Southern Comfort
Unless you're in my arms

★ EXERCISE 45 ★

As an exercise, try to design a verse that contrasts with the chorus. You might look at Jim Rushing's "Slow Healing Heart" or Janis Ian's "Some People's Lives" for how to handle eight-line structures. Alternately, you might try unbalancing the structure by shortening it. Try it before you read further.

The rewrite below balances six lines against two, rather than dividing the verse into two four-line sections of common meter:

	Rhyme	**Stresses**
Spánish móss hánging lów	x	4
Bówing fróm the trees	a	3
Hóneysúckle ríding ón the breéze	a	5
Sóuthern évenings, sóuthern stars	x	4
Swéet magnólia níghts	x	3
Uséd to bring me hármony and péace	a	5
Látely théy just máke me cry	b	4
They ónly máke me réalize	b	4

Chorus

There's no Southern comfort
Unless you're in my arms
You're the only cure
For this aching in my heart
I've searched everywhere
Tried the bedrooms, tried the bars
But there's no Southern comfort
Unless you're in my arms

Now the verse and chorus look different. Even Artie would notice. Though this lyric could still use major rewriting, at least its structure isn't stuck in the mud.

Prosody and Contrast

Of course, contrast between sections can also add prosody:

Verse

If I went into analysis	a
And took myself apart	b
And laid me out for both of us to see	c
You'd go into paralysis	a
Right there in my arms	b
Finding out you're not a bit like me	c

Chorus

Ready or not	d
We've got what we've got	d
Let's give it a shot	d
Ready or not	d

The chorus really zips along by changing to short phrases and consecutive rhymes. The speed is really a result of contrast; it seems so fast only because the verse has been so leisurely. Paul Simon's "50 Ways to Leave Your Lover" and Beth Nielsen Chapman's "Years" both work on this same principle. Here's the first verse and chorus from "Years":

	Stresses (with musical setting)
I went home for Christmas to the house that I grew up in	6
Going back was something after all these years	5
I drove down Monterey Street and I felt a little sadness	6
When I turned left on Laurel and the house appeared	5
And I snuck up to that rocking chair	
where the winter sunlight slanted on the screened-in porch	9
And I looked out past the shade tree	
that my laughing daddy planted on the day that I was born	9

Chorus

And I let time go by so slow	3
And I make every moment last	3
And I thought about years	2
How they take so long	2
And they go so fast	2

The verse lines are lingering and relaxed, just like the daughter. The chorus shows how fast years go by, accelerating the pace with shorter phrases. Not only is there contrast, but the contrast supports the meaning. Even within the chorus, the longer phrases slow time down, while shorter phrases step on the accelerator.

Chapman sets the first two lines into four bars of music. The last three also fit into four bars, but the last line, *and they go so fast*, is only one bar, supporting the lyric prosody perfectly. Nice stuff.

Become a designer; fit form to function. When you run with the LA fast-track set, step out with the Maserati. But when you want to join Artie and Herbie for the next Grateful Dead concert, go in style in the DayGlo microbus. Stop to consider what you need, and then build it. Have an effective, interesting structure ready for any occasion.

CHAPTER TWENTY-ONE

THE GREAT BALANCING ACT

COURTING DANGER ON THE HIGH WIRE

★ ★ ★ ★ ★ ★ ★ ★ ★ ★ ★ ★ ★ ★ ★

Imagine a high-wire artist at the circus. There she is, arms extended, stepping ever so carefully along the thin wire. Step. Wobble ...(Gasps from the crowd!) Steadies herself. (Audible relief.) Step. Ooops. Step ... No doubt she could move smoothly and quickly across, but she is making (or barely making) her aerial journey for our pleasure and excitement. She plays with our emotions, knowing we will remember her trip long after the lights and noise fade to nothing.

Writing lyrics is a high-wire act: The way you keep or lose your balance makes all the difference to your audience. Sometimes a little aerial drama may be just what you need to get and keep your listeners' undivided attention.

Here's a very simple balancing (or unbalancing) technique: Control the number of phrases in your sections, and you can learn to keep or lose your balance in just the right places.

In general, assuming that phrase lengths are more or less equal, and the rhyme scheme moves more or less evenly, an even number of phrases creates a balanced section; an odd number, an unbalanced section. The simplest case is repetition. An even number of phrases creates a stable section:

> Your body is a wonderland
> Your body is a wonderland

While an odd number creates an unstable section:

Your body is a wonderland
Your body is a wonderland
Your body is a wonderland

Not a hard concept, but a very useful one. You can get the same effect without repetition, like this three-phrase section:

How am I to reach you
When am I to touch you
How am I to hold you

Common meter pairs off its longer second and fourth phrases and its shorter first and third:

Mary had a little lamb
Its fleece was white as snow
Everywhere that Mary went
The lamb was sure to go

In this example, the two short phrases of the third line add up to equal the first phrase, giving us another balanced piece of common meter:

Yes I'm the Great Pretender
Pretending that I'm doing well
My need is such, I pretend too much
I'm lonely but no one can tell

But if we trim it to three phrases, it unbalances:

Oh yes I'm the Great Pretender
Pretending that I'm doing well
I'm lonely but no one can tell

How do we *use* balancing and unbalancing? Stated simply, unbalanced sections make you want to move to find a stable spot. Balanced sections stop motion; they pause for a rest. Balancing and unbalancing a lyric in the right places gives you at least four audience-grabbing strategies: (1) spotlighting important ideas; (2) pushing one section forward into another section; (3) contrasting one section with another one; and (4) setting up a need for a balancing section or phrase.

Watch the high-wire work of Janis Ian and Kye Fleming in this lovely lyric, "Some People's Lives":

	Rhyme
Verse 1	
Some people's lives	a
Run down like clocks	b
One day they stop	b
That's all they've got	b
Verse 2	
Some lives wear out	a
Like old tennis shoes	b
No one can use	b
It's sad but it's true	b
Chorus 1	
Didn't anybody tell them	x
Didn't anybody see	a
Didn't anybody love them	x
Like you love me?	a
Verse 3	
Some people's eyes	a
Fade like their dreams	b
Too tired to rise	a
Too tired to sleep	b
Verse 4	
Some people laugh	a
When they need to cry	b
And they never know why	b
Chorus 2	
Doesn't anybody tell them	x
Doesn't anybody see	a
Doesn't anybody love them	x
Like you love me?	a

Bridge

Some people ask, a
If tears have to fall b
Then why take your chances? a
Why bother at all? b

Verse 5

And some people's lives a
Are as cold as their lips b
They just need to be kissed b

Chorus 3

Didn't anybody tell them x
Didn't anybody see a
Didn't anybody love them x
Like you love me? a
'Cause that's all they need a

1. SPOTLIGHTING IMPORTANT DETAILS

This is the easiest and most practical use of balancing. When a section has an even number of phrases, the sections stops for a rest along the high wire. The pause allows the spotlight to shine on the last phrase. The first verse of "Some People's Lives" uses the position well:

Some people's lives a
Run down like clocks b
One day they stop b
That's all they've got b

That's all they've got is the climax of the section. The balancing position allows us to savor it by letting it rest in the spotlight a few seconds. Note, however, that the rhyme scheme, abbb, is a little unstable. Though the line lengths and rhythms match, we have the same effect at the end of line three that we saw earlier in the second verse of "Fathers and Sons"—the abb rhyme pattern raises no expectations:

Some people's lives a
Run down like clocks b
One day they stop b

Adding the fourth line provides a balancing position, but we still have an odd number of rhymes:

Some people's lives	a
Run down like clocks	b
One day they stop	b
That's all they've got	b

Compare how it feels to this:

Some people's lives	x
Run down like clocks	a
One day they cease	x
That's all they've got	a

Now it feels really stable. The stability actually adds an emotion (motion creates emotion).

Whereas the real version's rhyme scheme, because it's unstable, adds a different emotion:

Some people's lives	a
Run down like clocks	b
One day they stop	b
That's all they've got	b

Isn't it sad? It makes me feel like something's missing. It's especially noticeable when you look at the first three sections together:

	Rhyme
Verse 1	
Some people's lives	a
Run down like clocks	b
One day they stop	b
That's all they've got	b
Verse 2	
Some lives wear out	a
Like old tennis shoes	b
No one can use	b
It's sad but it's true	b

Chorus 1

Didn't anybody tell them	x
Didn't anybody see	a
Didn't anybody love them	x
Like you love me?	a

Both verses have the unstable rhyme scheme abbb. The chorus is very stable. So we have two unstable sections (sad lives), moving into a stable section— "our love makes me stable. I wish everyone had this kind of love in their lives." If the rhyme scheme in the verses were stable, the arrival at a stable section in the chorus wouldn't have the same power:

	Rhyme
Verse 1	
Some people's lives	x
Run down like clocks	a
One day they cease	x
That's all they've got	a
Verse 2	
Some lives wear out	x
Like old tennis shoes	a
No one would want	x
It's sad but it's true	a
Chorus 1	
Didn't anybody tell them	x
Didn't anybody see	a
Didn't anybody love them	x
Like you love me?	a

Now we feel stable for the whole trip. The chorus, and therefore the singer's gratitude for the love she receives, is diminished by the stable rhyme scheme. The chorus is less of a landing place than it is in the original version.

2. PUSHING ONE SECTION FORWARD INTO ANOTHER SECTION

Rhyme scheme can create instability, but you can get even more dramatic results with an odd number of lines. It can work wonders when you want the audience to hold their breath. Ian and Fleming teeter on the wire in verse four, then pause (gasp), then they step forward into a balanced chorus:

Verse 4

Some people laugh	a
When they need to cry	b
And they never know why	b

Chorus 1

Didn't anybody tell them	x
Didn't anybody see	a
Didn't anybody love them	x
Like you love me?	a

The chorus settles us down, but some tension still remains. Three phrases plus four phrases still leaves us a little uneasy. The last phrase of the chorus is a question; the problem of loneliness still looms for some people.

3. CONTRASTING ONE SECTION WITH ANOTHER ONE

The number of lines in the first three verses of "Some People's Lives" are even and balanced:

Verse 1

Some people's lives	a
Run down like clocks	b
One day they stop	b
That's all they've got	b

Verse 2

Some lives wear out	a
Like old tennis shoes	b

No one can use	b
It's sad but it's true	b

Verse 3

Some people's eyes	a
Fade like their dreams	b
Too tired to rise	a
Too tired to sleep	b

The contrast with these balanced sections gives verse four its power. We expect stability. Instead, it totters on the brink for a moment:

Verse 4

Some people laugh	a
When they need to cry	b
And they never know why	b

The crowd tenses up and begins to sweat. Will she fall?

Another way to unbalance a section is to add a phrase. Look again at "The Great Pretender." Verses one and two are balanced, so we expect verse three to be balanced as well:

Verse 1

Yes I'm the Great Pretender
Pretending that I'm doing well
My need is such, I pretend too much
I'm lonely but no one can tell

Verse 2

Yes I'm the Great Pretender
Adrift in a world of my own
I play the game but to my real shame
You've left me to dream all alone

Verse 3

Yes I'm the Great Pretender
Just laughing and gay like a clown
I seem to be what I'm not, you see
I'm wearing my heart like a crown
Pretending that you're still around

The extra phrase in verse three is a surprise. Line four, the balancing position, is still a spotlighted power position, but the extra phrase stumbles forward on the wire to turn additional spotlights onto the most important phrase in the song.

Ian and Fleming pull the Great Pretender trick at the end of "Some People's Lives." The balanced first and second choruses set up the surprise of the third chorus:

Chorus 3

Didn't anybody tell them	x
Didn't anybody see	a
Didn't anybody love them	x
Like you love me?	a
'Cause that's all they need	a

The crucial idea gets bathed in spotlights.

4. CREATING A NEED FOR A BALANCING SECTION OR PHRASE

The real beauty of "Some People's Lives" is that the two short sections, verses four and five, each prepare us for a headlong pitch to the sawdust. Chorus two left us queasy, since we were still struggling to balance an odd number of phrases (seven):

Verse 4

Some people laugh	a
When they need to cry	b
(unbalancing) And they never know why	b

Chorus 2

Doesn't anybody tell them	x
Doesn't anybody see	a
Doesn't anybody love them	x
Like you love me?	a

The bridge balances again with an even number of phrases:

Bridge

Some people ask,	a
If tears have to fall	b
Then why take your chances?	a
Why bother at all?	b

But again, verse five loses its balance (the crowd holds their breath ...):

Verse 5

And some people's lives	a
Are as cold as their lips	b
(unbalancing) They just need to be kissed	b

The last chorus tries to get home, but seems to end short of the platform:

Chorus 3

Didn't anybody tell them	x
Didn't anybody see	a
Didn't anybody love them	x
Like you love me?	a

The crowd remains restless. Things still wobble on the high wire. The bridge / verse / chorus last system certainly did need something more, a need set up by the unbalanced three-phrase verses. Something more finally arrives, in spades: *'cause that's all they need.*

Spotlights blaze onto the extra phrase as it balances the entire last system with an even number of phrases (twelve), and steps onto the platform at the other side of the high-wire journey. We breathe a sigh of satisfaction and relief, not only because we have arrived, but because the trip has been fraught with danger and the result has been so satisfying. The last phrase stands firm and strong in the carefully prepared balancing position and delivers its message forcefully: Love is all you need. The crowd goes wild.

You can try this stuff yourself. First try some simple balancing and unbalancing of a single section. Take something like:

Eenie meenie minee moe
Catch a tiger by the toe

If he hollers let him go
Eenie meenie minee moe

Add a phrase:

Eenie meenie minee moe
Catch a tiger by the toe
Take him to a picture show
If he hollers let him go
Eenie meenie minee moe

Take one away:

Eenie meenie minee moe
Catch a tiger by the toe
If he hollers let him go

Or maybe:

Eenie meenie minee moe
Catch a tiger by the toe
Eenie meenie minee moe

★ EXERCISE 46 ★

Pick a couple of your own lyrics and try it. Then take the next step and surprise us by unbalancing a section we expected to be balanced. Set up the surprise by starting with a balanced section, like:

Eenie meenie minee moe
Catch a tiger by the toe
Take him to a picture show
Eenie meenie minee moe

Eenie meenie minee may
If he hollers make him pay
Fifty dollars every day

The technique works best in lyrics with at least three verses. Try it, taking small steps at first, and advancing further until you can work without a net.

CHAPTER TWENTY-TWO

SONG FORMS:
(IM)POTENT PACKAGES

Song form should be your friend, helping you deliver your message with power. But too often, an inefficient or inappropriate form weakens your message, weights it down, and drags it helpless and sagging into the dust. Beware, oh beware, of song form. Consider it carefully before you choose.

Verse / verse / chorus / verse / verse / chorus is a common but relatively impotent song form. We've all used it, but, if your experience is anything like mine, too often you've gotten mixed results. This song form probably attracts more of the dreaded "seems too long" comments from friends, co-writers, publishers, producers, and even mothers than any other song form does.

There have been some great songs written in this form, so why pick on such a successful form? What makes it inefficient?

Simple; v / v / ch / v / v / ch repeats the same melody, chords, phrase lengths, and rhyme schemes four times. Four times is a lot. You risk boring your listeners when you make four trips through the same structure. Your verses, especially the crucial fourth verse, had better be *very* interesting to risk all that repetition. At best, if your message is powerful and compelling, the v / v / ch / v / v / ch song form won't get in the way, but at worst, you risk it working against effective delivery of your message.

Look at this version of Jim Rushing's "Slow Healing Heart," arranged as a v / v / ch / v / v / ch lyric:

Verse 1

When I left I left walking wounded
I made my escape from the rain
Still a prisoner of hurt
I had months worth of work
Freeing my mind of the pain

Verse 2

I had hours of sitting so lonely
Singing sad songs in the dark
Feeling my days
Slipping away
Woe is a slow healing heart

Chorus

A slow healing heart
Is dying to mend
Longing for love
Lonely again
When a spirit is broken
And the memories start
Nothing moves slower
Than a slow healing heart

Using two verses before the chorus runs a small risk. Sometimes publishers (bless their hearts) might say "it takes too long to get to the chorus." But here, the problem comes more from "commercial considerations" than boredom.

After the chorus, verse three starts the second system:

Verse 3

How I prayed for blind faith to lead me
To places where I'm not afraid
Now I'm doing fine
Both in body and mind
But some hurts take longer to fade

Now the crucial fourth verse. Here's where you run the risk of making the song seem too long:

Verse 4

There's a part of me still on the lookout
Alert for those cutting remarks
Looks that are sweet
Soon will cause you to bleed
Woe is a slow healing heart

Chorus

A slow healing heart
Is dying to mend
Longing for love
Lonely again
When a spirit is broken
And the memories start
Nothing moves slower
Than a slow healing heart

Now, go back and read the entire "Slow Healing Heart" lyric without the interruptions. Does it seem too long? Maybe, maybe not. The answer can vary for individual listeners. All I know is that it's a risk—even if verse four is killer, it's still a risk. If you can avoid the risk effectively, you should. There are three risk-avoidance techniques outlined in this chapter. Get familiar with all of them.

First Risk-Avoidance Technique

Try dumping a verse. This is not as easy as it sounds, because unless you've written a real dead dog for one of your verses, you probably need at least some of the material in each one. So try to select the most important stuff, on a sort of "best of" principle, and distill one verse from two. Let's try it with verses three and four. How about this as a distilled verse:

Verse 3

There's a part of me still on the lookout
Alert for cutting remarks
But the sweetest of words

Only sharpen this hurt
Woe is a slow healing heart

Or how about this:

Verse 3

How I prayed for blind faith to lead me
Away from those cutting remarks
Now I'm doing fine
Both in body and mind
But woe is a slow healing heart

Now, go back and substitute each one into the lyric. Read the whole thing together. Why did you keep reading? Go back and read the lyric with each distilled verse.

This resulting verse / verse / chorus / verse / chorus song form is more streamlined. It gives the second chorus a boost by seeming to get to it early—a distinct advantage. And the distilled verse is often stronger than the two separate verses it came from.

★ EXERCISE 47 ★

What do you think of my distilled verses? Did I lose too much, or did I keep the necessary stuff? You try it. Distill the original third and fourth verses into one verse of the same structure. Remember to end the verse with the refrain: *Weak is a slow healing heart.*

Second Risk-Avoidance Technique

Turn one of the verses into a bridge, making the overall form fit the following structure:

v / v / ch / v / ch / br / ch.

Be careful with this option. A bridge is a contrasting element, both in structure and in content. You'll have to change both the structure and the kind of information you give.

Maybe this will work:

Verse 3

There's a part of me still on the lookout
Alert for those cutting remarks
Looks that are sweet
Soon will cause you to bleed
Woe is a slow healing heart

Chorus

A slow healing heart
Is dying to mend
Longing for love
Lonely again
When a spirit is broken
And the memories start
Nothing moves slower
Than a slow healing heart

Bridge

I pray that someday
I won't be afraid
But some hurts take longer to fade

Chorus

A slow healing heart
Is dying to mend
Longing for love
Lonely again
When a spirit is broken
And the memories start
Nothing moves slower
Than a slow healing heart

The move to future tense in the bridge helps shift away from the verse material. Shorter lines and a three-line unbalanced section (rhyming AAA) change the structure.

Now, take a minute to go back and read the whole song in the new form. Whad'ya think?

★ EXERCISE 48 ★

Now come up with your own bridge to fit "Slow Healing Heart."

Third Risk-Avoidance Technique

Keep all the lines, but restructure both verses into a single unit. Of course, this means more than not skipping a space between verses on your lyric sheet. It means changing the form of the verses so they don't repeat each other. Here's the actual full lyric by Jim Rushing:

Verse 1

When I left I left walking wounded
I made my escape from the rain
Still a prisoner of hurt
I had months worth of work
Freeing my mind of the pain
I had hours of sitting alone in the dark
Listening to sad songs and coming apart
Lord knows I made crying an art
Woe is a slow healing heart

Chorus

A slow healing heart
Is dying to mend
Longing for love
Lonely again
When a spirit is broken
And the memories start
Nothing moves slower
Than a slow healing heart

Verse 2

How I prayed for blind faith to lead me
To places where I'm not afraid
Now I'm doing fine
Both in body and mind
But some hurts take longer to fade
There's a part of my feelings ever on guard

Against looks that are tender and words that are hard
I still remember those cutting remarks
Woe is a slow healing heart

Chorus

A slow healing heart
Is dying to mend
Longing for love
Lonely again
When a spirit is broken
And the memories start
Nothing moves slower
Than a slow healing heart

Look how the verse structure works:

	Rhyme	Stresses
When I left I left walking wounded	x	3+
I made my escape from the rain	a	3
Still a prisoner of hurt	b	2
I had months worth of work	b	2
Freeing my mind of the pain	a	3
I had hours of sitting alone in the dark	c	4
Listening to sad songs and coming apart	c	4
Lord knows I made crying an art	c	4
Woe is a slow healing heart	c	3

The first half is basic common meter, in three-quarter time, with a rhyme acceleration in the third line. The second half moves two by two in four-stress couplets, creating a whole different feel (which will force a musical change). Rushing creates two interesting, unified verses rather than four helpings of the same structure. Big difference.

Any of these three risk-avoidance techniques solve the problem created by the verse / verse / chorus / verse / verse / chorus form. They will help structure work for you, rather than risking songs that seem too long. Even if every line of all four verses is to die for, you can reorganize them into a form that delivers power rather than sags. All it takes is time, energy, and—most importantly—focus on the importance of potent song form. It's worth the work.

CHAPTER TWENTY-THREE

SONG FORMS:
(IM)POTENT PACKAGES II

Bored? Try a little variety. That was the principle behind chapter twenty-two, where we looked at the verse / verse / chorus / verse / verse / chorus form.

Here, I want to look at another common form—one that also risks boredom: verse / chorus / verse / chorus / verse / chorus. Here's a sample that we'll title "Love Her or Leave Her to Me":

> You're living with a woman you ain't true to
> Playin' round but keep her hanging on
> If you don't want her, let me have her
> You won't believe how fast I'll grab her
> You'll hardly even notice that she's gone
>
> Love her or leave her to me
> Keep her or let her go free
> Don't go two-timing her
> 'Less you're resigning her
> Love her or leave her to me
>
> You're out all night while she's alone without you
> Just for fun she calls me on the phone
> She comes to me, I play the friend
> I know she'll love me in the end
> As long as you keep leaving her alone
>
> Love her or leave her to me

Keep her or let her go free
Don't go two-timing her
'Less you're resigning her
Love her or leave her to me

Well I guess some men got no appreciation
They never see the finer things in life
When they leave the best behind 'em
Someone else is bound to find 'em
Won't be long she's someone else's wife

Love her or leave her to me
Keep her or let her go free
Don't go two-timing her
'Less you're resigning her
Love her or leave her to me

Not a bad lyric. It chugs along nicely for two verse / chorus systems, developing its ideas with light, cute structure. The third system, however, seems to fall a little flat, not so much for what it says, but because we've seen its structure twice before. There's nothing wrong with the form—the form just doesn't help add interest. Let's look at some options to use instead of this third verse / chorus system.

Option 1

The most obvious boredom quencher is to insert a contrasting section—a bridge—between the second and third system. As usual, the contrast should be significant. The structure of the bridge should be different from the verse and chorus structures, including a different rhyme scheme, a different number of lines, and different line lengths. It should also say something different.

When you're writing a bridge, start by looking at what you've already said, then look for a missing piece. In this case, we know the speaker wants the wife, and that the husband is fooling around. We know the wife calls the speaker and that the speaker has plans. But we don't know what makes her so desirable. This might be an interesting angle, especially since the third verse starts:

Well, I guess some men got no appreciation
They never see the finer things in life ...

★ EXERCISE 49 ★

A bridge focusing on her qualities would lead smoothly into the third verse. Start by making a list of her qualities—things she is, things she does. Draw the list from your own experiences. Do a little object writing. For example:

Kicking through the fallen leaves, gold-brown and red. Cheeks flushed and soft, glowing with the afternoon sunlight. You don't speak, I don't dare speak; our shoulders touching, lingering a little, skin electric, breath coming a little faster. You step slowly, patiently, listening to the leaves swirling and dancing in colors as we move together.

Your object writing will create a mood and character for you to respond to. Then try a few bridges. Be sure your bridge is a contrasting section. Keep it short and effective.

Simply inserting a bridge is always an option when you need a boredom breaker. The risk here, though, is that the lyric may get (or seem) a little long because it returns to a verse again before the chorus.

Option 2

Another option is to create a verse / chorus form that stops with two verse / chorus systems, creates a bridge as a contrasting system, then moves to a chorus: verse / chorus / verse / chorus / bridge / chorus.

Again, be careful. A bridge isn't a verse—it doesn't do the same job or use the same structure. It is a contrasting section. Verses usually develop plot. A chorus usually steps away from, comments on, or summarizes the verses. In our lyric, the verses develop the situation, the chorus gives a warning. A bridge will have to take a different angle.

You're living with a woman you ain't true to
Playin' round but keep her hanging on
If you don't want her, let me have her

You won't believe how fast I'll grab her
You'll hardly even notice that she's gone

Love her or leave her to me
Keep her or let her go free
Don't go two-timing her
'Less you're resigning her
Love her or leave her to me

You're out all night while she's alone without you
Just for fun she calls me on the phone
She comes to me, I play the friend
I know she'll love me in the end
As long as you keep leaving her alone

Love her or leave her to me
Keep her or let her go free
Don't go two-timing her
'Less you're resigning her
Love her or leave her to me

Leave the finest things behind, an'
Someone else is bound to find 'em

Love her or leave her to me
Keep her or let her go free
Don't go two-timing her
'Less you're resigning her
Love her or leave her to me

★ EXERCISE 50 ★

Try substituting the bridge you wrote for the one I wrote. Do you like how it works?

Option 3

If you can't translate your third verse into a bridge—say that you really need that third idea as a verse—try a verse form that thrives on three-idea development: the AABA verse / refrain form.

This song form has been around a long time, mostly because it works so well. Let's try it for our three-verse lyric, using the title as a refrain:

You're living with a woman you ain't true to
You play around, she sits home faithfully
If you don't want her let me have her
Wait and see how fast I grab her
Love her or leave her to me

While you're out she gets a little lonesome
What to do, she's got her evenings free
She calls me up, I play the friend
I know she'll love me in the end
Love her or leave her to me
Boy just keep your blinders on
You'll never notice when she's gone

I'm glad some men got no appreciation
The finest things are just too hard to see
You just keep two-timing her
Soon you'll be resigning her
Love her or leave her to me

An AABA song form is effective because it creates a strong sense of resolution when it moves back to the third verse. The first two verses define "home base," then the bridge takes you away from home—away from the familiar structure. When you come back to the third verse, you come back home to familiar territory. It's a real homecoming, seeing the old neighborhood again after a long trip. The tension created by moving away has been resolved.

An AABA's last system is actually bridge / verse, providing a nice contrast to the opening verses, as well as sponsoring the homecoming parade.

The temptation to write verse / chorus / verse / chorus / verse / chorus is sometimes strong. Resist it. Look instead for forms that present your ideas in more potent packages.

CHAPTER TWENTY-FOUR

PROCESS

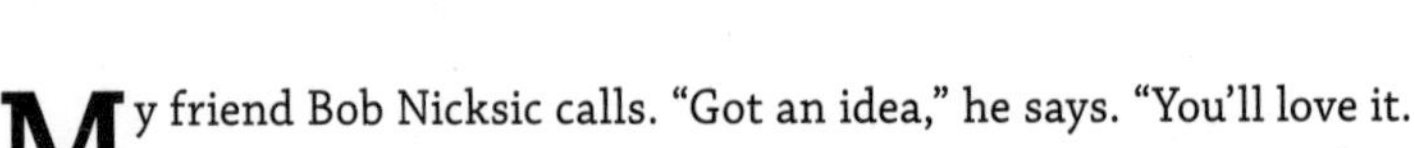

My friend Bob Nicksic calls. "Got an idea," he says. "You'll love it. It's about a girl whose parents fight all the time. Whenever they do, she goes into this fantasy world and sings a little song." Pause.

Right. Like I'm going to guess. "*We will, we will rock you*?" I offer.

"Nope."

"Was I close?"

"*She sells seashells*! Neat, huh?"

It was weird, not that that ever stops me. But *she sells seashells*? "Hmm," I say.

"No. Think about it. I've got some ideas for verses. Listen."

I press record on my machine. Here's what he gives me:

Planted in the hallway
Hands over her ears
Shaken by the shouting
Growing wise beyond her years

Daddy's voice is thunder
Mommy's voice is rain
She's too scared not to watch
The hurricane

And then she sells seashells
'Cause her mind can't handle any more

So she sells seashells
On the shore

She knows daddy's leaving
But this time he says good-bye
Mommy's chest is heaving
This time she doesn't cry

Daddy bends to kiss her
Sea spray on his face
..............................?
..............................?

Yup, pretty weird. But there was something about it—the sort of spooky that slips in when you're not looking. It was slipping in. Besides, picture a singer in the studio getting to the chorus and stiffening for the tongue twister. Better yet, picture people trying to sing along. Irresistible. It appealed to the sadist in me.

I need to get the lay of the land. Time for a little object writing. I think the most productive place to look is at the title, since that's the centerpiece of the song.

Seashells

Buried, scooping sand with little mouths like front loaders; Rrrrr of the ocean their motors as they excavate tunnels, trenches, digging to China. Bodies heaped on broken bodies, clattering as waves break and wash over them, polishing and shining, smooth and tumbling. Pick one up, glistening in the sun, rings etched in spirals circling deeper and deeper, little whirlpools sucking, letting me float and spin dizzy like rolling down a grassy hill, the trees in green blurs appearing and disappearing humming in my ears, ringing like waves, like listening to the ocean in a shell. Hold it up, can you hear the ocean. No, the sounds of infinite space tucked in spirals, lost planets bobbing and sinking, the chill and emptiness. Wrap your arms around yourself. There is no warmth or comfort here, winds churning, waves tumbling, tides rolling like huge voices back and forth between continents, sea foam spilling in spirals circling and crashing over shells, crushing them to sand and dust, building into dunes, shifting, disappearing, piling up again.

Not that I'll use it all, or even any of it, but the process of object writing helps me find out what I have to offer that originates from my own unique sense experiences. The closer I stay to my senses, the more real and effective my writing will be. The front loaders are out of my childhood and may not be helpful in the scene Bob gave me. I like the shells digging to China. The carnage on the beaches and the trenches could well lead to a World War I scene. The spirals etched in the shells may be useful, since the song seems concerned with the consequences for the girl of the parents' breakup. Listening to the shell is a means of escape, though in this world the escape isn't a prosperous one. I like the tides as a metaphor for the parents' voices. The dunes are nice.

CREATE A WORKSHEET

Before I look at the lyric, I'll make an abbreviated worksheet for additional stimulation. I want to find the sonic lay of the land for the keywords so far: *sea, shells, shore, sand, tide.*

Sea has no final consonant, so we'll look at perfect rhymes, then additive rhymes.

Debris has wonderful possibilities. Think about a beach scene and let it echo through your own senses and imagination.

I'll pass on three-syllable adverbs like *breathlessly.* First, I'm not a real fan of adverbs in lyrics; second, rhyming the secondary stress with a primary stress sounds awkward. Ditto for three-syllable nouns like *memory* and *rhapsody.* I'll stick to words ending on a primary accent.

Disagree isn't bad in this context, but probably not very evocative. I think it's already shown in the verse about thunder and rain. *Free* is overused. No thanks. You've never used *plea* in your life unless you've been in court. Why use it in a lyric just to get a rhyme? *Referee* is tempting, but it takes me somewhere I don't want to be in this song. *Refugee* is terrific. So, I found two stimulating perfect rhymes: *debris* and *refugee.* On to additive rhymes.

Remember, the less sound you add, the closer the rhyme is. The least possible sound comes from the voices plosives, *b, d,* and *g.* Nothing under *eb. Recede* is nice. *Seaweed* is possible. Maybe *bleed.* Nothing helpful under *eg.*

On to the unvoiced plosives, *p*, *k*, and *t*. *Deep* and *sleep*. Where do they take you? *Streak* gives me a beach sky at sunset. Perhaps *streaked*. I'm a sucker for *bittersweet*, though I don't see what's sweet in this circumstance. Maybe *retreat* for the waves' ebb and flow.

So here are our rhymes for *sea*: *debris, refugee, recede, weeds, bleed, deep, sleep, streaked, retreat.*

We'll look up perfect and additive rhymes for *shell*. Additives are particularly effective because *l*, together with the vowel, make all the sonic connection you'll ever need.

Swell, as in ocean swell. If I could get swelling around the eyes, too, so much the better. *Hell* is too dramatic—it's one of those words that seems to mean so much more than it conveys. Like *soul*. Avoid those clunkers. *Carousel* has the circles and childhood. Maybe, though it seems a little off-center for our beach scene.

That's it for perfect rhyme.

Now browse in the rhyming dictionary through short-*e* + *l* + anything else. All I can find is *withheld* and *help*.

Okay. Try consonance rhymes, since we're dealing with *l*. (Change the vowel and keep the final consonants—remember?) Stay with closely related vowel sounds, either short-*a* or short-*i*. Nothing under short-*a* + *l*. Short-*i* looks better: *chill, spilled.*

Here's our rhyme column for *shell*: *swell, carousel, withheld, help, chill, spilled.*

Shore ends in another strong consonant. We'll look at perfect rhyme, additive rhyme, and consonance rhyme. This time, you let each word carry you into its possibilities: *roar, pour, storm, outworn, torn, blur, search, submerged, curled.*

For *sand*, we'll look at perfect rhyme, family rhyme (since the consonants after the vowel belong to phonetic families), and subtractive rhyme (dropping either consonant after the vowel).

I find nothing interesting under perfect rhyme except the tired old *hand/understand/command* nonsense.

Let's subtract *d*, since it's the least noticeable sound. Nothing good. Maybe *ran*.

Let's substitute for *d* from the plosive family (*b*, *d*, *g*, *p*, *t*, *k*): *chant*.

Substitute for *n* from the nasal family (*m*, *n*, *ng*): *slammed*, *stamped*.

Continue through the rest of the short-*a* + *n* columns: *inheritance*.

Our results for *sand*: *ran*, *chant*, *slammed*, *stamped*, *inheritance*.

Not bad. Our last word, *tide*, ends with a plosive. If it were plural, *tides*, it would also contain members of the fricative family (*f*, *th*, *s*, *sh*, *ch*, *v*, *z*, *zh*, *j*) after the vowel. Lots of places to look. Perfect rhymes: *glide*, *slide*.

Into the plosive family: *inscribed* (patterns etched), *flight*, *harbor light*.

Go to the plural, *tides*, and subtract *d*: *sacrifice*.

Look at the *s* family: *still life*, *revived*, *rise*, *arise*.

Our final results for *tide* are: *glide*, *slide*, *inscribed*, *flight*, *harbor light*, *sacrifice*, *still life*, *revived*, *rise*, *arise*.

So here's our abbreviated worksheet:

1. sea
2. shells
3. shore
4. sand
5. tide

1. sea	2. shells	3. shore	4. sand	5. tide
debris	swell	roars	ran	glide
refugee	carousel	pour	chants	slide
recede	help	storm	slammed	inscribed
weeds	chill	outworn	stamped	flight
bleed	spilled	torn	inheritance	harbor light
deep		blur		sacrifice
sleep		search		still life
streaked		submerged		revived
retreat		curled		rise, arise

Use the worksheet for reference. Remember, its main purpose is to get additional ideas and pictures. It is a brainstorming device, not a rhyme-finding device. It's a nice reference, though. Ask Stephen Sondheim: He uses worksheets all the time. Back to Bob's original ideas.

Planted in the hallway
Hands over her ears
Shaken by the shouting
Growing wise beyond her years

Daddy's voice is thunder
Mommy's voice is rain
She's too scared not to watch
The hurricane

And then she sells seashells
'Cause her mind can't handle any more
So she sells seashells
On the shore

She knows daddy's leaving
But this time he says good-bye
Mommy's chest is heaving
This time she doesn't cry

Daddy bends to kiss her
Sea spray on his face ... ?

Look at the chorus. I don't really know what the verses will end up doing, especially since even the rough verses are incomplete. So I don't want to make too early a commitment to a lot of ideas in the chorus. It's best to keep it streamlined and simple at first. My first job is to make sure the verses set up the title. Additional lines can come along later when I'm sure the title works with the verses. So:

And then she sells seashells
'Cause her mind can't handle any more
So she sells seashells
On the shore
becomes:

She sells seashells, she sells seashells
She sells seashells by the shore

The first two verses seem backwards. The reaction is before the action. Try this instead:

Daddy's voice is thunder
Mommy's voice is rain
She's too scared not to watch
The hurricane

Planted in the hallway
Hands over her ears
Shaken by the shouting
Growing wise beyond her years

She sells seashells, she sells seashells
She sells seashells by the shore

Better opening. Now look at the line before the chorus (I call it the trigger line because it releases its meaning into the chorus; whatever the trigger line says will determine how we see the chorus):

Shaken by the shouting
Growing wise beyond her years

She sells seashells, she sells seashells
She sells seashells by the shore

I don't get the connection. And I want the first chorus to be the clearest of all. So we need a stronger trigger line. How about:

She hums a tiny melody
Hands over her ears

She sells seashells, she sells seashells
She sells seashells by the shore

Better, but I still don't quite get the connection. How about:

She hums this tiny melody
Hands over her ears

She sells seashells, she sells seashells
She sells seashells by the shore

Now the chorus *becomes* her tiny melody. It's important to take time to work on your trigger lines. They are power positions, but more important, they are the last thing you hear before you enter your chorus. Always take time to check them, the earlier the better.

The chorus seems pretty locked in just the way it is—something the little girl can sing, at least in the first system. A commentary line like *'cause her mind can't handle any more* seems inappropriate.

Let's finish the verse. For now, how about:

Shaken by their shouting
Wise beyond her years
She hums this tiny melody
Hands over her ears

Our whole first song system is:

Daddy's voice is thunder
Mommy's voice is rain
She's too scared not to watch
The hurricane

Shaken by their shouting
Wise beyond her years
She hums this tiny melody
Hands over her ears

She sells seashells, she sells seashells
She sells seashells by the shore

It seems to work okay. It sets up the scene, and it sets up the chorus pretty clearly. We'll work out the kinks later.

Bob's third verse has the fight turning into a separation. Something unusual is happening:

She knows daddy's leaving
But this time he says good-bye
Mommy's chest is heaving
This time she doesn't cry

Not bad development. Daddy's leaving should increase her isolation; in fact, it will change her life. So what can we do with daddy's good-bye?

Daddy bends to kiss her
Sea spray on his face ...

I was tempted to start looking for ideas with a rhyme search for *face* (avoiding some of the ugly possibilities like *that time will not erase* or *gone without a trace*). I would have gone for family rhymes like *safe* or *rage*, or additive or subtractive rhymes like *waste* or *stray*. Even assonance rhymes like *ache* or *rain* would work, since they would provide a sense of a closed section, yet leave it hanging a little bit, which is perfectly fine in this context.

But wait a minute: *sea spray on his face*?

Where the hell did the *spray* come from? In my mental picture, they're inside. Sure, spray could be a way of saying *tears*, but if there is no place for the spray to come from, it's confusing. A metaphor has to be grounded in something real. If they were on the beach, *sea spray on his face* would be just fine. It could be both what it actually is, plus more. Remember to ground your metaphors in reality. They must have a legitimate place in the context. So I've got to decide. Are they in the house or at the ocean? I can't just assume that my mental picture is everybody's mental picture. I've got to *make* it everybody's mental picture.

It also seems like this verse has got to be the little girl's verse. It seems like a waste of space to let daddy linger. He said good-bye three lines ago—get him out. We have to set up the little girl's isolation. How about this for verse four:

Shuts the door behind her
Escaping to her room
Days stretch out before her
Like sand and shifting dunes

She's isolated inside her room. Let's look at the trigger:

Days stretch out before her
Like sand and shifting dunes

She sells seashells, she sells seashells
She sells seashells by the shore

Now the little girl becomes *she* in the chorus. She's in her room (in my head) with the sands of time (it's suggested rather than stated, which is actually pretty neat) stretching out before her. Plus, we get the overlay of the little song she sings in the first chorus. Not bad.

So here's box two so far:

She knows daddy's leaving
But this time he says good-bye
Mommy's chest is heaving
This time she doesn't cry

Shuts the door behind her
Escaping to her room
Days stretch out before her
Like sand and shifting dunes

She sells seashells, she sells seashells
She sells seashells by the shore

The whole thing:

She Sells Sea Shells (Version 1)

Daddy's voice is thunder
Mama's voice is rain
She's too scared not to watch
The hurricane

Shaken by their shouting
Wise beyond her years
She hums this tiny melody
Hands over her ears

She sells seashells, she sells seashells
She sells seashells by the shore

She knows daddy's leaving
But this time he says good-bye

Mommy's chest is heaving
This time she doesn't cry

Shuts the door behind her
Escaping to her room
Days stretch out before her
Like sand and shifting dunes

She sells seashells, she sells seashells
She sells seashells by the shore

I like common meter for the verses. Sort of nursery rhyme-ish with a lot of musical flexibility. I thought Bob would be impressed. I call back. "What d'ya think?"

"Words okay. But who's 'she' in the first verse? Sounds like the mother is the one that's scared, not the daughter. And who isn't crying in the third verse?"

Right. "Call you back."

Round Two

She Sells Sea Shells (Version 2)
Daddy's voice is thunder
Mama's voice is rain
Baby's too scared not to watch
The hurricane

Shaken by their shouting
Wise beyond her years
She *sings* this tiny melody (rather than *hums*, since the chorus has words)
Hands *cupped* over ears

She sells seashells, she sells seashells
She sells seashells, *seashells* by the shore (I was tapping in threes, and the repetition felt right and sounded good)

Daddy says he's leaving (more direct)
This time it's good-bye (better rhythm match; more direct)
Mama's chest is heaving
Too upset to cry (clearer reference to mama; more elegantly stated)

Baby shuts the door behind her
Escaping to her room
Days stretch out before her
Like sand and shifting dunes

She sells seashells, she sells seashells
She sells seashells, seashells by the shore

I really liked her hands cupped over her ears, like she was listening to the ocean rather than the fight. I think *sings* sets up the first chorus even better. And it's clear who the daughter is and who the mother is. I call back. "What d'ya think?"

"Not a bad sketch."

Sketch? "Thanks," I mumble. "What else do you think it needs?"

"Some of the lines are a little weird. Could be more elegantly stated," he says, tossing one of my favorite critiquing phrases back in my face. I hate being on the receiving end of those little grenades.

Back to it. I thought maybe, in addition to looking for better lines, I'd take a shot at a bridge that looked ahead to her later life—sort of the consequences of her childhood isolation.

Round Three

Here's attempt number three. (Instead of looking only at the rewritten lines, read it all the way through each time to immerse yourself in it. Otherwise, the changes won't make much sense or difference.)

She Sells Sea Shells (Version 3)
Daddy's voice is thunder
Mama's voice is rain
Baby's scared to watch (the double negative was too complicated)
The hurricane

Shaken by their shouting
Choking back her tears (wise beyond her years was a cliché, plus it led to a dead end)
She sings this tiny melody
Hands cupped over ears

She sells seashells, she sells seashells
She sells seashells, seashells by the shore

Daddy says he's leaving
This time it's good-bye
Mama's chest is heaving
Too upset to cry

Baby stumbles down the hall (it wasn't clear what door she shut; better rhythmic match)
Escaping to her room
Years stretch out before her (Takes us deeper and further into her life)
Like sand and shifting dunes

She sells seashells, she sells seashells
She sells seashells, seashells by the shore

Patterns etched those years before (like patterns on seashells)
Circle through her life
She wanders down the beach alone
Watching tides

She sells seashells, she sells seashells
She sells seashells, seashells by the shore

The bridge sort of fell out like that. It seemed like the right idea, but something bothered me about it. Structurally, it was the bridge from Paul Simon's "Still Crazy After All These Years," with the telltale short last line. But how bad could that be? I love that bridge.

Maybe the last line could be longer to slow everything down, like the bridge in Paul Simon's "Train in the Distance." How bad could that be? I love that bridge, too. No one would know, unless I told them. Plus, it would give me more room to "state it more elegantly." Let's try it:

Patterns etched those years before
Circle through her life
She wanders down the beach alone
Searching through the leavings of the tides (this came from *debris* in the worksheet)

After trying this, it hits me. This bridge can't be in common meter—the verses already are. I'd fallen into the same old trap of locking into a pattern mentally and writing it automatically. C'mon, stupid, a bridge is supposed to contrast, and you've got to make a difference right away, at the first line. I liked the five-stress last line, so I tried it in the first line, and decided on a three-line bridge for a little asymmetry:

Years have etched their patterns in her life
She walks the beach alone
Searching through the leavings of the tides

Better. I hope Bob likes it. Sometimes my preference for asymmetry drives him nuts. Go back and read version three with the new bridge.

Before I call, one more thing. I've written at least three articles insisting that you check every lyric you write from all points of view. This one was a third-person narrative. I have to check out first-person narrative, with the little girl as the speaker:

She Sells Sea Shells (Version 4)

Daddy's voice is thunder
Mama's voice is rain
I'm too scared to watch
The hurricane

Shaken by their shouting
Choking back *my* tears
I sing this tiny melody
Hands cupped over ears

She sells seashells, she sells seashells
She sells seashells, seashells by the shore

Daddy says he's leaving
This time it's good-bye
Mama's chest is heaving
Too upset to cry

Stumbl*ing* down the hall*way*
Escaping to *my* room

Years stretch out before *me*
Like sand and shifting dunes

She sells seashells, she sells seashells
She sells seashells, seashells by the shore

Years have etched their patterns in *my* life
I walk the beach alone
Searching through the leavings of the tides

She sells seashells, she sells seashells
She sells seashells, *seashells* by the shore

Hmm. It doesn't work very well, does it? There's got to be a tense change for it to make sense. The little girl has to be looking back from adulthood:

She Sells Sea Shells (Version 5)
Daddy's voice *was* thunder
Mama's voice *was* rain
I *was* scared to watch
The hurricane

Shaken by their shouting
Choking back my tears
I'd sing this tiny melody
Hands cupped over ears

She sells seashells, she sells seashells
She sells seashells, *seashells* by the shore

Daddy *said* he's leaving
This time it's good-bye
Mama's chest *was* heaving
Too upset to cry

Stumbling down the hallway
Escaping to my room
Years *stretched* out before me
Like sand and shifting dunes

She sells seashells, she sells seashells
She sells seashells, *seashells* by the shore

Years have etched their patterns in my life
I walk the beach alone
Searching through the leavings of the tides

She sells seashells, she sells seashells
She sells seashells, *seashells* by the shore

The move from past-tense verses to a present-tense bridge works. And each chorus has her cupping her hands over her ears and singing her little song, even as an adult. Kind of a spooky effect.

Now let's try it as a second-person narrative, on the model of Bob Seger's "The Fire Inside" (see page 132):

She Sells Sea Shells (Version 6)
Daddy's voice is thunder
Mama's voice is rain
You're too scared to watch
The hurricane

Shaken by their shouting
Choking back *your* tears
You sing this tiny melody
Hands cupped over ears

She sells seashells, she sells seashells
She sells seashells, *seashells* by the shore

Daddy says he's leaving
This time it's good-bye
Mama's chest is heaving
Too upset to cry

You stumble down the hallway
Escaping to *your* room
Years stretch out before *you*
Like sand and shifting dunes

She sells seashells, she sells seashells
She sells seashells, *seashells* by the shore

Years have etched their patterns in *your* life
You walk the beach alone
Searching through the leavings of the tides

She sells seashells, she sells seashells
She sells seashells, *seashells* by the shore

Oops. The chorus has to stay in third person. That's the attraction of the song. But the third-person chorus doesn't work very well with *you*, especially the second and third times. Goodbye to second-person narrative.

So it's between third- and first-person narrative. Close call. Look at versions three and version five side by side:

Version 5	**Version 3**
Daddy's voice was thunder	Daddy's voice is thunder
Mama's voice was rain	Mama's voice is rain
I was scared to watch	Baby's scared to watch
The hurricane	The hurricane
Shaken by their shouting	Shaken by their shouting
Choking back my tears	Choking back her tears
I'd sing this tiny melody	She sings this tiny melody
Hands cupped over ears	Hands cupped over ears
She sells seashells, she sells seashells	
She sells seashells, *seashells* by the shore	
Daddy said he's leaving	Daddy says he's leaving
This time it's good-bye	This time it's good-bye
Mama's chest was heaving	Mama's chest is heaving
Too upset to cry	Too upset to cry
Stumbling down the hallway	Baby stumbles down the hall
Escaping to my room	Escaping to her room
Years stretched out before me	Years stretch out before her
Like sand and shifting dunes	Like sand and shifting dunes

She sells seashells, she sells seashells
She sells seashells, *seashells* by the shore

Years have etched their	Years have etched their
patterns in my life	patterns in her life
I walk the beach alone	She walks the beach alone
Searching through the	Searching through the
leavings of the tides	leavings of the tides

She sells seashells, she sells seashells
She sells seashells, *seashells* by the shore

Make your own list of pros and cons for each version. I like the intimacy of first person. Here, however, we lose some immediacy in past tense. The distancing of third person can be effective, but we really don't feel that much distance because the present tense verses are so immediate.

What locks in my decision is the way the third-person bridge flows into the chorus. *She* in the bridge becomes *she* in the chorus!

Now, stop to think: Is there any reason to try a version of third person with the verses in past tense? Yup. Process. Go back to version three and do it.

I don't like it. It loses our treasured immediacy. So the verses stay in present tense.

One more thing. How about keeping the narrator focused on the little girl the whole song? We could put the bridge in future tense (never forget future tense—sometimes it can work miracles):

Years *will* etch their patterns in her life
She'*ll* walk the beach alone
Searching through the leavings of the tides

She sells seashells, she sells seashells ...

A big difference in focus. I really like the future tense. It moves into the present-tense chorus just as effectively, and it keeps the speaker looking at the little girl in her room. So here's what we've got:

She Sells Sea Shells (Version 7)

Daddy's voice is thunder
Mama's voice is rain
Baby's scared to watch
The hurricane

Shaken by their shouting
Choking back her tears
She sings this tiny melody
Hands cupped over ears

She sells seashells, she sells seashells
She sells seashells, seashells by the shore

Daddy says he's leaving
This time it's good-bye
Mama's chest is heaving
Too upset to cry

Baby stumbles down the hall
Escaping to her room
Years stretch out before her
Like sand and shifting dunes

She sells seashells, she sells seashells
She sells seashells, seashells by the shore

Years have etched their patterns in her life
She walks the beach alone
Searching through the leavings of the tides

She sells seashells, she sells seashells
She sells seashells, seashells by the shore

There. Point of view and tense check out. Finally, let's look to see how effective the form is. Right now, it's verse / verse / chorus / verse / verse / chorus / bridge / chorus.

When we get to verse four, we've seen the same structure three times, threatening to make the song feel too long. So what are our options?

Option 1

Dump verse four (or three). That would give us the more streamlined and effective form of: verse / verse / chorus / verse / chorus / bridge / chorus. Look at verses three and four again. Can we dump one?

Daddy says he's leaving
This time it's good-bye
Mama's chest is heaving
Too upset to cry

Baby stumbles down the hall
Escaping to her room
Years stretch out before her
Like sand and shifting dunes

Try reading from the top, leaving out verse three. She doesn't seem to have a reason to stumble down the hall, nor is there a basis for the dramatic lines *years stretch out before her / like sand and shifting dunes*.

We need to know daddy's leaving.

We can't do without verse four, either. We couldn't get into the chorus effectively.

Option 2

Combine verses three and four into one effective verse:

Daddy says he's leaving
This time it's good-bye
Mama's chest is heaving
Too upset to cry

Baby stumbles down the hall
Escaping to her room
Years stretch out before her
Like sand and shifting dunes

Four ideas, each one two lines long. Maybe the bridge can cover the final two lines.

Years stretch out before her

Like sand and shifting dunes

Years will etch their patterns in her life
She'll walk the beach alone
Searching through the leavings of the tides

They're not the same, but let's suppose that the bridge will at least suggest the last two lines' idea. We're left with:

Daddy says he's leaving
This time it's good-bye
Mama's chest is heaving
Too upset to cry

Baby stumbles down the hall
Escaping to her room

Let's get rid of mama's reaction and adjust the rhymes:

She Sells Sea Shells (Version 8)

Daddy's voice is thunder
Mama's voice is rain
Baby's scared to watch
The hurricane

Shaken by their shouting
Choking back her tears
She sings this tiny melody
Hands cupped over ears

She sells seashells, she sells seashells
She sells seashells, seashells by the shore

Daddy says he's leaving
This time it's good-bye
Baby stumbles to her room
They won't hear her cry

She sells seashells, she sells seashells
She sells seashells, seashells by the shore

Years will etch their patterns in her life
She'll walk the beach alone
Searching through the leavings of the tides

She sells seashells, she sells seashells
She sells seashells, seashells by the shore

What do you think? Certainly the form is more effective. I miss the picture of mama, and its drama. I like the way the bridge fills in for the last two lines of the old verse four, though. Let's see what else we can do.

Option 3

Rather than identical verse structures, change the structure of verses two and four so the same structure doesn't repeat four times. The structure of verses two and four still match each other. Let's work with the first song system:

Daddy's voice is thunder	x
Mama's voice is rain	a
Baby's scared to watch	x
The hurricane	a
Shaken by their shouting	x
Choking back her tears	b
Hands cupped over ears	b
She sings this tiny song so she won't hear	b

Changing the rhyme scheme and extending the last line in verse two gives us a nice contrast with verse one. The two structures are related, but verse two develops and will force musical development as well.

Let's see if we can we play the same trick in the second song system:

Daddy says he's leaving	x
This time it's good-bye	a
Mama's chest is heaving	x
Too upset to cry	a
Baby stumbles down the hall	x
Escaping to her room	b

Lost inside her childish tune b
Years stretch out like sand and shifting dunes b

Not bad. This is the result:

She Sells Sea Shells (Version 9)

Daddy's voice is thunder
Mama's voice is rain
Baby's scared to watch
The hurricane

Shaken by their shouting
Choking back her tears
Hands cupped over ears
She sings this tiny melody so she can't hear

She sells seashells, she sells seashells
She sells seashells, seashells by the shore

Daddy says he's leaving
This time it's good-bye
Mama's chest is heaving
Too upset to cry

Baby stumbles down the hall
Escaping to her room
Lost inside her childish tune
Years stretch out like sand and shifting dunes

She sells seashells, she sells seashells
She sells seashells, seashells by the shore

Years will etch their patterns in her life
She'll walk the beach alone
Searching through the leavings of the tides

She sells seashells, she sells seashells
She sells seashells, seashells by the shore

Option 4

Change verses two and four into transitional "pre-choruses" to go between verse and chorus. Extend verse two into two five-stress lines:

Daddy's voice is thunder
Mama's voice is rain
Baby's scared to watch
The hurricane

Cold and shaken, choking back her tears
She sings this song, hands cupped over ears

She sells seashells, she sells seashells
She sells seashells, seashells by the shore

Not bad. Let's see about the second song system:

Daddy says he's leaving
This time it's good-bye
Mama's chest is heaving
Too upset to cry

Baby disappears inside her room
Years stretch out like sand and shifting dunes

She sells seashells, she sells seashells
She sells seashells, seashells by the shore

The transitional sections have the virtue of forcing a strong musical development. Each song system becomes an integrated unit. Here's our result:

She Sells Sea Shells (Version 10)

Daddy's voice is thunder
Mama's voice is rain
Baby's scared to watch
The hurricane

Cold and shaken, choking back her tears
She sings this song, hands cupped over ears

She sells seashells, she sells seashells

She sells seashells, seashells by the shore

Daddy says he's leaving
This time it's good-bye
Mama's chest is heaving
Too upset to cry

Baby disappears inside her room
Years stretch out like sand and shifting dunes

She sells seashells, she sells seashells
She sells seashells, seashells by the shore

Years will etch their patterns in her life
She'll walk the beach alone
Searching through the leavings of the tides

She sells seashells, she sells seashells
She sells seashells, seashells by the shore

Version 7

Daddy's voice is thunder
Mama's voice is rain
Baby's scared to watch
The hurricane

Shaken by their shouting
Choking back her tears
She sings this tiny melody
Hands cupped over ears

She sells seashells, she sells seashells
She sells seashells, seashells by the shore

Daddy says he's leaving
This time it's good-bye
Mama's chest is heaving
Too upset to cry

Baby stumbles down the hall
Escaping to her room

Version 8

Daddy's voice is thunder
Mama's voice is rain
Baby's scared to watch
The hurricane

Shaken by their shouting
Choking back her tears
She sings this tiny melody
Hands cupped over ears

Daddy says he's leaving
This time it's good-bye
Baby stumbles to her room
They won't hear her cry

Years stretch out before her
Like sand and shifting dunes

She sells seashells, she sells seashells
She sells seashells, seashells by the shore

Years will etch their patterns in her life
She'll walk the beach alone
Searching through the leavings of the tides

She sells seashells, she sells seashells
She sells seashells, seashells by the shore

Version 9

Daddy's voice is thunder
Mama's voice is rain
Baby's scared to watch
The hurricane

Shaken by their shouting

Choking back her tears

Hands cupped over ears
She sings this tiny song so she can't hear

She sells seashells, she sells seashells
She sells seashells, seashells by the shore

Daddy says he's leaving
This time it's good-bye
Mama's chest is heaving
Too upset to cry

Baby stumbles down the hall

Escaping to her room

Lost inside her childish tune

Version 10

Daddy's voice is thunder
Mama's voice is rain
Baby's scared to watch
The hurricane

Cold and shaken, choking back her tears
She sings this song, hands cupped over ears

Daddy says he's leaving
This time it's good-bye
Mama's chest is heaving
Too upset to cry

Baby disappears inside her room
Years stretch out like sand and shifting dune

Years stretch out like sand and
shifting dunes

She sells seashells, she sells seashells
She sells seashells, seashells by the shore

Years will etch their patterns in her life
She'll walk the beach alone
Searching through the leavings of the tides

She sells seashells, she sells seashells
She sells seashells, seashells by the shore

Perhaps the final choice is a matter of taste, but the important part is the process—developing alternatives is what makes the decisions based on taste possible.

Maybe I could have written lines in option three and option four that would have made me like them better, but my choice is number two. I like the way the second verse sets up the chorus both as her little song (with *cry* in the sense of *call*) and as a commentary ("they won't hear her weeping while she sells sea shells"). No, I don't expect everyone to get it, but it's still there resonating and making the emotions richer. Plus, given the last line, *they won't hear her cry, their patterns* in the bridge now refers both to the parents' patterns and the patterns etched by the years.

My next step: Fax Bob. Then call. Confidently, already salivating at the prospect of watching the blood drain from the demo singer's face when the first chorus comes around, I say, "What d'ya think?"

Minutes pass. He clears his throat. Is he trying to torture me? I suddenly understand my students' suffering as I sit in silence looking over and over their lyrics. Finally he says, "A three-line bridge?"

I knew it.

Of course, we're not done. Now the setting process begins, and things may change radically. But I'm ready for anything, since I've gone through the process thoroughly.

"Wait till you hear the music I've started for it," he says.

Oh goody. My turn.

APPENDIX

CO-WRITING:
THE "NO"-FREE ZONE

The best advice I ever got on co-writing was from Stan Webb, my first professional co-writer. When Tom Casey, a VP at SESAC in Nashville, set up the appointment for me, he asked Stan to talk to me a bit about the Nashville co-writing process, a process that dominates the songwriting culture there.

I was waiting in the SESAC writers' room with my notes and titles, some complete lyrics, some song ideas, but I was feeling pretty nervous. I am, after all, a big-time professor at the biggest-time music school in the world—Berklee, where I teach lyric writing, and, like most writers, I'm a bundle of insecurities. What if I can't come up with anything? What if he thinks all my ideas are dumb? (They don't look too good to me right now.) What if he thinks I'm a fraud? Not only would that humiliate me, but it would put my students' credibility in question, too, and it'd be all my fault. Why am I here? Maybe I should leave while there's still time. Couldn't I say I got food poisoning?

Too late. The door opened and there stood Stan Webb, my co-writer for the day, a guy with hits. Stan is a burly guy. He looked a bit shaggy, wearing bib overalls, a tattered T-shirt, and work boots, looking like he'd just come off the farm (which, in fact, he had—he owns one, bought with songwriting royalties). He came in, and then he did something curious: He shut the door, re-opened it, shut it again, and then pushed hard to make sure it was closed. Hmm. Was he worried about folks listening in and stealing our good ideas? I was deeply concerned just with *having* a good idea. I'd be so relieved if I managed to just have one that, as far as I was concerned, the secret listener would be welcome to it.

He sat down opposite me on a couch and seemed to size me up. He grinned and said, "Is that door closed?" Yikes. "Yes, it is," I answered carefully, not knowing where he was going with this. Was it a secret initiation? "Good, I'm glad it's closed," he said, "because you can probably tell by looking at me that I'm gonna say some of the dumbest things you've ever heard." I stayed quiet. I was more worried about what he thought of me. He went on, "And if you do your job right today, you're gonna say some of the dumbest thing I ever heard, professor or not." *No doubt there*, I thought. He grinned again and said, "But, as long as that door is closed, nobody needs to know how dumb we are. I won't tell if you won't."

He told me that he hoped I didn't mind, but Tom had asked him to talk to me about the co-writing process in Nashville, so he wanted to tell me just a couple things before we got going on a song. I told him to take his time.

He said, "Say everything that comes into your head. Say it out loud, no matter how dumb it is. Don't censor anything. If you say something really dumb, you might give me an idea that's not quite as dumb. And then I might have a decent one that gives you a better one that gives me a great one. If you'd never said the dumb one, we would never get to the great one.

"So that means that we'll never say 'no' to each other. A co-writing room is a 'no'-free zone. If you suggest a line and I don't like it, I just won't say anything. Silence is a request for more, more, more. It says 'just keep throwing stuff out there.' When either one of us likes something, we'll say 'yes.' Otherwise, just keep going."

We had a great writing session. I lost my fear of looking like a fool. I came up with a lot of dumb ideas, and my dumbest idea of all led us to the best part of the song. We really did say everything. And the silences were golden—what a great way to ensure that we always get the best out of each other. Nobody has to defend anything, and the only ideas in the song are automatically ones we both love. The "no"-free zone gets the best out of both writers. There are no arguments, and there never needs to be compromise.

I've always been grateful to Stan for his wise advice that day. It helps me every time I co-write, but also every time I write. My inner critic (my most frequent co-writer) has also learned to abide by the "no"-free zone. And Stan's words still echo in the songwriting classrooms at Berklee College of Music, where hundreds of students have worked in the "no"-free zone, and have had great co-writing experiences because of it.

Thanks, buddy.

I'll add some advice of my own to Stan's, because, in Berklee writing classes, we talk about writing a lot. Lots of process, lots of techniques. And it really helps their writing—learning what goes into it, what tools are available. My students learn to talk about writing very well. They are good technicians, as well as good writers.

Thus, my advice: Never talk *about* writing in a co-writing room, especially about technique. Telling what you know about writing isn't writing. You're supposed to be writing, not talking about it. Stay inside the song, inside the characters. Don't run away to the intellectual level. Most people are tempted to talk about those wonderful technical effects in their lines—assonance, rhythm, deep thoughts, metaphors—out of fear to cover their bases and try to dress up what they're afraid might be a dumb idea in academic robes. A dumb idea is still dumb, even with professorial robes on. Don't worry about dumb. Just write. And write fearlessly.

Don't be afraid to write crap—it makes the best fertilizer. The more of it you write, the better your chances are of growing something wonderful.

PERMISSIONS

"Between Fathers and Sons" by John Jarvis and Gary Nicholson. © Copyright 1986 Tree Publishing Co., Inc., and Cross Keys Publishing Co., Inc. All rights administered by Sony/ATV Music Publishing. All rights reserved. Used by permission.

"Can't Really Be Gone" by Gary Burr. © Copyright 1995 Gary Burr Music, MCA Music Publishing. All rights reserved. Used by Permission.

"Child Again" by Beth Nielsen Chapman © Copyright 1990 BGM Songs Inc. (ASCAP). All rights reserved. Used by permission.

"Closing Time" © Copyright 1992 Sony/ATV Music Publishing. All rights reserved. Used by permission.

"Dress Rehearsal Rag" © Copyright 1967 Leonard Cohen Stranger Music, Inc. All rights administered by Sony/ATV Music Publishing. All rights reserved. Used by permission.

"The End of the Innocence" by Don Henley, Bruce Hornsby. © Copyright 1989 Woody Creek Music and Zappo Music. All rights administered by WB Music Corp. All rights reserved. Used by permission.

"The Eye of the Hurricane" by David Wilcox. © Copyright 1989 by Irving Music Inc. and Midnight Ocean Bonfire Music (BMI). All Rights Reserved. International rights secured. Used by permission.

"The Fire Inside" by Bob Seger. © Copyright 1988, 1991 Gear Publishing Co. All rights reserved. Used by permission.

"Give Me Wings" by Don Schlitz and Rhonda Fleming © Copyright 1986 by MCA Music Publishing. All rights reserved. Used by permission.

"The Great Pretender" by Buck Ram. © Copyright 1955 Panther Music Corp. Copyright renewed. International rights secured. All rights reserved. Used by permission.

"Hasten Down the Wind" by Warren Zevon. © Copyright 1973 Warner-Tamerlane Publishing Corp. & Darkroom Music. All rights administered by Warner-Tamerlane Publishing Corp. All rights reserved. Used by permission.

"Kid Charlemagne" by Walter Becker and Donald Fagen. © Copyright 1976. Used by permission of the Publisher.

"One More Dollar" by Gillian Welch. © Copyright 1996. Used by permission of the Publisher.

"Slow Healing Heart" by Jim Rushing. © Copyright 1984 Sony/ATV Music Publishing. All rights reserved. Used by permission.

"Some People's Lives" by Janis Ian and Kye Flemming. ©1986 Irving Music Inc. and Eaglewood Music (BMI) and MCA Music Publishing. All rights administered by Almo-Irving Music Inc. All rights reserved. Used by permission.

"Still Crazy After All These Years" by Paul Simon. © Copyright 1974. Used by permission of the Publisher.

"Strawberry Wine" by Matraca Ber and Gary Harrison. © Copyright 1996 EMI Music Publishing. All rights reserved. Used by permission.

"Top of the Roller Coaster" by David Wilcox. © Copyright 191991 Irving Music Inc. and Ocean Bonfire Music (BMI). All rights administered by Irving Music, Inc. (BMI). All rights reserved. Used by permission.

"Train in the Distance" by Paul Simon. © Copyright 1981. Used by permission of the Publisher.

"Unanswered Prayers" by Pat Alger, Larry Bastian, Garth Brooks © 1990 Major Bob Music, Inc. (ASCAP) / Mid-Summer Music, Inc. (ASCAP). All rights reserved. Used by permission.

"The Wreck of the Edmund Fitzgerald" by Gordon Lightfoot. © 1976 Moose Music Ltd. All rights reserved. Used by permission.

"Where've You Been" by Don Henry, Jon Vezner. © Copyright 1988 Cross Keys Publishing Co., Inc. All rights administered by Sony/ATV Music Publishing. All rights reserved. Used by permission.

"Years" by Beth Nielsen Chapman. © Copyright 1990 WB Music Corp. (ASCAP) and Macy Place Music (ASCAP). All rights administered by WB Music Corp. All rights reserved. Used by permission.

All original examples contained herein, unless where otherwise attributed are by Pat Pattison, © 1979-94 by Featherrain Music. All rights reserved. Used by permission.

INDEX